AF579992

Development and Maintenance of Large Software Systems

Development and Maintenance of Large Software Systems

Antonio Pizzarello

Lifetime Learning Publications
Belmont, California
a Division of Wadsworth, Inc.
London, Singapore, Sydney, Tokyo, Toronto, Mexico City

Production Service: Bernie Scheier
Designer: Joe di Chiarro
Copy Editor: Carol Beal
Illustrator: Georg Klatt
Compositor: Graphic Typesetting Service

Printed in the United States of America

1 2 3 4 5 6 7 8 9 10 88 87 86 85 84

Library of Congress Cataloging in Publication Data

Pizzarello, Antonio, 1931–
Development and maintenance of large software systems.

Bibliography:
Includes index.
1. Computer programming management. 2. Electronic digital computers—Programming. 3. Software maintenance.
I. Title.
QA76.6.P59 1984 001.64'2 84-10010
ISBN 0-534-02785-7

To Elsa, Rocco, Francesco, Annalisa, and, of course, Sandra.

CONTENTS

Chapter 13 Hierarchy Of Abstract Machines, Part 2 169

Chapter 14 An Example Of Hierarchical Development 181

Chapter 15 Experiences with Hierarchical Design 199

Chapter 16 Analysis of Implementation And Maintenance 213

PREFACE

PURPOSE OF THIS BOOK

The best means of gaining a competitive advantage in industry is to create products which apply the results of pertinent scientific research before the competition does so. In order to do this successfully research findings must be understood not only in an academic sense, but also in terms of their relevance to product development. This is particularly the case with the development and maintenance of large software systems.

Such systems are associations of several separate individual programs which are expected to cooperate in order to obtain some required global goals. These systems deal usually with complex problems, are of considerable size, and require the labor of several people for their development and/or modification.

The production of such systems is universally recognized as expensive, risky and very difficult to manage. These difficulties have a much higher impact than could have been expected, from the experience of preparing individual programs. Also, some aspects of their behavior defy common intuition. The intrinsic rigidity of the process of their development and modification is a cause of considerable frustration for both developers and managers.

The most evident aspect of these difficulties is the existence of numerous errors, that is, a deviation from desired behavior. The work needed to remove these errors represents a large percentage of the total work invested in the production process. Furthermore, the difficulty in predicting error occurrence and the amount of effort needed for error removal are the prime causes in the rigidity of the production process for large systems.

Over the past decade the computer science community has produced a number of theoretical results which shed light on the nature of these difficulties and indicate possible effective cures. Consistent with the above views and reflecting these recent developments, this work has a twofold purpose:

a. to inform the reader about the latest research results in the design and verification of software systems, and

b. to interpret the special characteristics of large software systems in light of recent research

These purposes converge towards the book's principal goal, which is to provide the reader with guidelines, suggestions and tools for implementing in *everyday practice* the most significant findings from recent research.

AUDIENCE

Development and Maintenance of Large Software Systems should be of interest to systems architects and designers and to technical managers involved in either new development or modification of systems of substantial size.

APPROACH

In its presentation this book goes from the general to the specific—from scientific principle to its application. Applications are introduced in such a manner as to allow the reader to visualize the relevance of the examples presented. Numerous specific techniques and experimental evidence gained in practical applications are included and the author strongly emphasizes their respective advantages, disadvantages or difficulties.

Because not all practitioners can be expected to have a background in the broad range of concepts pertinent to software development, this book also presents a discussion of program language semantics, program specification, program derivation from specifications, and data abstraction. These and related subjects are treated in detail because they are essential to understanding the characteristics and peculiarities of large software systems.

Antonio Pizzarello

ACKNOWLEDGMENTS

The ideas expounded in this book were created over a long period of time by both the study of the technical literature and the observation of real-world events. I have attempted to recognize the source of information used and apologize for the inevitable omissions.

Discussions with colleagues and friends were of great benefit for the clarification of my ideas. Thanks are due to Ira Foreman, Jane King, Frank Little, Dan Schoffelman, Bill Wood, and John Wertz for many illuminating discussions. The view of the development process presented in Chapter 1 owes much to discussions with Jack Ring.

I cooperated with Don Boyd for the research work that produced the technique of data abstraction presented in this text. Don's contributions to that research were most significant.

I wish to thank the management of Honeywell Information Systems for permitting the publication of this book and for allowing the use of the company's word processing services. In particular, I am grateful to Pete Dressen, director of software development in Phoenix, for his personal encouragement. Special thanks are due to Rita Huard and the personnel of the word processing service in Phoenix for the patient and accurate typing of the manuscript.

Finally, Steve Keeble of Lifetime Learning Publications suggested the idea of writing this book and helped the inexperienced author to avoid a large number of stylistic and organizational pitfalls.

All blame for errors and omissions obviously should be addressed only to the author.

Everything must be made as simple as possible, not simpler.

Attributed to Albert Einstein

CHAPTER ONE

Software Systems and Their Problems

INTRODUCTION

In this chapter the characteristics of software systems, which are the subject of the studies presented in this book, are defined. In particular, the problems presented by the development process used currently for the production of software are identified.

It is not unusual for a solitary programmer, possibly working with a personal computer, to create a program and be rewarded by years of completely satisfactory operation. Also, the same programmer, when required to modify the program to cope with some unpredictable change in the requirements, will not find its modification particularly demanding.

In contrast, the same person, when required to produce a program that interacts with programs written by other programmers, usually faces many problems when his or her program is put together with the others to form a software system. In addition, the modification of one of the programs integrated in a system is not a simple, straightforward task, even when these modifications are performed by the author of the program. This book addresses these problems of system design, integration, and modification.

A collection of several programs written by different persons is usually larger than a single program written by a single person. So it is customary to refer to a collection as a *large program* or as a *software system*. A single program is called a *small program* or, since it is produced by a single individual, an *individual program*.

It follows that a software system may be defined as a development involving several individuals who may work separately on the construction of the various parts of the system. The difference between individual programming and system development is very similar to the difference between the individual crafting of a product and the corporate development of a modern engineering product, which involves separate organizations and individuals of specialized expertise working together in an industrial organization.

THE IMPORTANCE OF A CONCEPTUAL BASIS FOR SOFTWARE DEVELOPMENT

In the past few decades many large software projects were initiated and completed. Consequently, software system creation has itself created a large industry. The problems experienced by this industry attracted considerable attention from the academic communities, who have conducted a good deal of research on the fundamental issues of software development. Surprisingly, some of the most interesting results of this large body of research are not yet known to practitioners in software development, and therefore the potential advantages of their application are not being realized in the world of practical developments.

This book presents some of the results of this research work relevant to the design, implementation, and maintenance of large software systems. The emphasis is on the presentation of the concepts behind the research work rather than on an explanation of particular techniques. This emphasis was chosen because software development practice appears to be lacking solid scientific foundations that can guide the developer's intellectual activity. And many software practitioners feel that the introduction of a scientific basis will give software development an engineering discipline, which will greatly improve the effectiveness and controllability of the development and maintenance of software systems.

Software development lacks solid scientific foundations

In contrast, other practitioners feel that software problems are so complex that they defy any attempt at rigorous treatment. It is true that the complexity involved in the task of rigorously defining software is of a very discouraging order of magnitude. However, many of the difficulties have been created by that very lack of rigorous definition and understanding of basic principles underlying software development. Therefore the software developer who becomes aware of the advances of computer science research may be able to avoid unnecessary complexity in the future development of large systems.

Another reason for focusing on concepts is that in cases when the scientific results were applied to practical system developments, quite impressive results were obtained. We will analyze these results in detail later in this book. And while it is true that these applications have also demonstrated considerable difficulties, these difficulties, when analyzed in light of the concepts expressed in this book, supply additional insight about the complexity of the software development process.

A point usually made by practitioners who received a superficial exposure to computer science methods is that they are more difficult to use than traditional, informal methods. That point may be superficially true. But in reality, the development of software, even for programs judged easy to develop, is of tremendous logical complexity. This complexity, however, is not apparent from the informal approach. Rather, the informal approach hides the complexity, with the result that many programmers receive some sobering experiences in the form of discovering unpredicted difficulties. Thus an important result of learning computer science methods is an understanding of both the nature and the extent of the hidden difficulties of software development. With this understanding many misjudgments about software project costs, duration, and objectives will be avoided.

THE SOFTWARE CRISIS

The traditional, overly optimistic view of software development created what was called the *software crisis* in the late sixties and early seventies. During the initial use of computers relatively small problems were successfully solved. These successes encouraged the computer community to enlarge its objectives by attempting to solve problems of much larger size and difficulty. The results were so disappointing that the phrase software crisis was created.

In his celebrated book about the philosophy of the scientific method, Kuhn (1962) introduces the view that all regular science is a series of observations and deductions, performed within a set of ideas, concepts, theories, and beliefs accepted by the scientific community as a common paradigm. The activity of regular science in Kuhn's view is to plan and to interpret the observations and deductions in terms of the currently accepted paradigm. At certain times a crisis arises when the theories and beliefs of the current paradigm cannot plausibly explain some observations. The crisis is resolved by the revolutionary introduction of a new paradigm, which supplies plausible justification to the crisis-generating observation and which can be used for continuing the progress of regular science.

The computer science community responded to the software crisis in a truly revolutionary manner: by introducing a completely different outlook to the software problem. This new outlook, which includes a much more mathematical approach to computer science, can be considered the currently accepted paradigm for the academic community. However, the industrial software development world appears to be lagging, since little use has been made of these scientific achievements (Zelkowitz et al., 1983).

ANALYSIS OF THE SOFTWARE DEVELOPMENT PROCESS

Software systems are currently produced in considerable quantity to respond to user's needs. However, a widespread feeling is that both the development process and the quality of the resulting product should be improved. To illustrate why this concern has arisen, we now present an analysis of the currently used development process in comparison with the engineering development process. The purpose of this analysis is to identify any aspects of the current development practice that are peculiar to software products.

Concerns with Software Developments

Two concerns: the development process and product quality

The concerns about large software systems focus on two major areas. The first is the *development process* itself, which is considered difficult to manage, unnecessarily expensive, and nonproductive, using too much specialized labor. The second area of concern is the *quality of the product,* which is often regarded as unreliable and expensive to modify.

These concerns are based on observed facts. Software managers are quite often frustrated by slipping schedules and budget overruns. Although a high level of system reliability is obtained in many cases, existing systems still contain many errors, which may manifest themselves at any time with unpredictable consequences.

All these concerns would become amenable to scientific analysis if they could be quantified by measurements of significant parameters, for the evaluation of both the effectiveness of the currently used development process and the product quality.

Paucity of experimental measurements

But the first problem we encounter in an analysis of software systems is the difficulty in obtaining significant measurements. Nevertheless, it is imperative to collect whatever quantitative measurements are available. Of course, if we want to measure, we must be able to define the object of the measure. Since we are concerned about the development process and its product quality, we have to define significant parameters that can be (or currently are) measured for both these areas.

The Elements Of A Development Process

Three elements: architecture, tools, and methods and disciplines

There are three essential elements in any product development. The first is the design of the product *architecture,* i.e., the determination of an arrangement of functions and features that maximizes (or minimizes) the product characteristics with respect to some objectives. The second is the set of *tools* used to support the activities of conceiving, constructing, testing, and evaluating the product (or a prototype). The third element is the set of *methods* and *disciplines* that form the intellectual paradigm accepted and used by the development personnel.

Software systems and any other engineering product development show these elements. In the development of a bridge, for example, the architecture is the layout that will minimize the cost for that particular span and perhaps also maximize the aesthetic appeal. The tools are the pencils and paper for drawing, scaled-down models, surveying equipment, etc. The methods and disciplines are the principles and results of Euclidean geometry and strength of materials that form an accepted (and effectively working) paradigm for the community of civil engineers.

Engineering design is an act of creativity tempered by the ironclad discipline of some scientific theory that cannot be violated (Horikoshi, 1981). In all modern engineering communities both the architectural element and the tools are consequent to the methods and disciplines. For instance, the architectural layout of a bridge cannot be in conflict with the results of strength of materials. In fact, the process of choosing a particular architecture is driven by the results of geometry and strength of materials. Tools are created to support activities suggested by the accepted development methods and disciplines. In other words, methods and disciplines play a dominant role in the process of developing an engineering product.

Predictive power of modern engineering

The reason for this dominance is that in modern engineering these elements work. That is, considerable practical advantages are obtained by using them, advantages such as the ability to predict relevant characteristics of the product before its construction is completed. Thus bridge engineers can determine the size of various elements of the bridge on paper, without going through expensive construction and destruction of prototypes. And if these paper prototypes cannot give a sufficiently reliable response, then the engineer experiments with scale models. In summary, the methods and disciplines used by modern engineers are the dominant force of the development process, because their prediction power allows engineers to experiment economically with many paper or scaled-down prototypes.

Verification of Software Design Ideas

Software system developers do not construct models that reliably predict the behavior of the product before its construction. Most verification of design ideas occurs during the construction, testing, and modification of the final product. Tools are introduced only to support the construction and testing activities. This last-minute verification may be a consequence of the perceived facility of software production. However, in practice, the final behavior of the product is often very different from the required behavior. Yet software developers have no way of reliably predicting how their final product will perform.

This lack of predictability shows up in various aspects of the product. For example, performance below expectation or even (very rarely) above expectation is noticed only at product-testing time. Consequently, disappointments can be frequent. Particularly annoying is the inability to predict correct functioning. A system performing below expectations can be shipped with apologies to the user, but a system that is unable to perform cannot be shipped at all.

The lack of power of prediction for software development may be traced to the element of methods and discipline. We have seen that the prediction power of the various engineering fields stems from the use of scientific disciplines to support all activities of the development process. By contrast, in the software world the absence of effective methods and discipline is the cause of unsuitable architectural arrangements of the design. And since the unsuitability can be detected only when the product is finished, it is usual to "patch it up" and to pay the price.

Lack of predictive power of software design produces unsuitable architectures

When we examine the software development process with respect to methods and disciplines, we find the predominant paradigm that software can be conceived only by some informal reasoning, possibly supported by discussions with peers, then coded and tested in the machine. This paradigm's major flaw is in the assumption that the actual test of code is a reliable discipline for the verification of design ideas. But it is not. Therefore any potentially effective technique for the development of software must improve the practitioner's ability of verifying design ideas at the lowest possible cost.

It is interesting to point out that preindustrial engineers did not use any scientific basis for their methods and disciplines to create paper prototypes. Design ideas were tested by the construction of the product. While some exceptional achievements were made, those engineering developments show difficulties disturbingly similar to those resulting from the current approach to development of software systems.

For example, a gothic cathedral is an impressive achievement, but it is a fact that schedules and budgets for the construction of such a cathedral did not exist. Also, the number of engineering accomplishments during the history of all preindustrial society is much less than the number of products created by modern engineering in a few decades. It was impossible for the intelligent and creative engineers of the past to produce anything like the bewildering variety of gadgets available today, because they did not have the predictive power supplied by mathematics applied to physical sciences. Because of this predictive power,modern engineering processes are centered on design.

CHARACTERISTICS OF THE SOFTWARE LIFE CYCLE

Like any complex and expensive engineering product large software systems are not produced, put in service, and forgotten. Continual changes in the user's requirements make it impossible to produce systems that are not subject to modification and extension once they are put in use. A frequently used schematization of the software development process divides a software product's life cycle in the following phases:

- Requirement analysis
- Design
- Coding
- Unit tests
- Integration and system tests
- Deployment and maintenance

Note that this categorization is no different from one identified for any engineering product development. In fact, if coding and unit tests are interpreted as the construction of the parts and if system tests and integration are interpreted as assembly of the final product, then no characteristic specific to software development is visible in the above schematization.

The requirement analysis phase defines the mission of the product. On the basis of this description the next phase divides the creation of the system into modules, each representing some function of the system.

It is in this phase that the architecture of the system is chosen. The modules are coded during the coding phase, and they are verified in the unit test phase. During the unit tests a module is executed in some simulated environment that reproduces the interactions of the entire system. All these modules are then put together during the integration phase, and their ability to cooperate as a system satisfying the user's requirements is verified by system tests.

At this verification stage a major difference between software and other engineering product development becomes apparent. Software systems, because of the poor prediction power of the design phase, must be subjected to extensive changes to make the system work according to the requirements. Nothing of this order of magnitude is observable in the development of any other complex engineering product.

We do not mean to imply that design flaws do not exist in a modern engineering product when it is built. But the magnitude and the nature of these flaws are quite different from the flaws in a software product. For example, an aircraft carrier is a large system. Undoubtedly, many functional problems are discovered at test time after launching. However, the propeller axis will not be discovered to be several degrees off the correct direction as a result of the observation, during acceptance tests, that the ship cannot navigate straight.

In software systems, in contrast, major inconsistencies are often discovered when the system is put together and tested. As a consequence, a considerable amount of design work is done during the unit test phase and the integration and system test phase. There is no method or discipline available to verify design ideas with any degree of acceptable precision before the code of the module is executed in a simulated environment. So it is during these phases that some of the design assumptions are first demonstrated to be erroneous, thus forcing a new design. It may also be inferred that the simulated environment used for the unit tests does not faithfully represent the real environment because of the many module design changes required during the integration and system test phase.

During the deployment phase two types of misfits may be detected. One is that the original requirements may not be satisfied by the software under certain circumstances. Some of these errors may be so critical that they must be corrected before system operation can continue. Others may produce only limitations in system operation that can be circumvented until the problem is corrected. The second type of misfit is that the mission of the software system may be partially changed, thus changing the overall requirements.

In both cases of misfits the existing software must be changed. Usually, software is changed by reading the code of the affected modules in order to understand their functions and the way they interact with other modules. On the basis of this understanding the code itself is modified and/or new modules are added to the system.

Finally, so that the continuous request for changes can be accommodated, the life cycle of a software product is usually organized in a sequence of releases. A *release* is a new version of the software system that incorporates changes both for fixing known (not critical) errors and for adding new capabilities. The development of a software system is thus realized by the cyclic repetition of development phases, each cycle culminating in a new release.

PRODUCTIVITY OF THE DEVELOPMENT PROCESS

The effectiveness of a development process is measured by its ability to reach its goals at the lowest possible cost. In this sense it is possible to talk about process productivity as an attribute whose increase would reduce the cost of obtaining the process goals. Increasing productivity is always a desirable goal. Our problem is to define productivity in such a way that it can be quantitatively evaluated.

Programmer Productivity

Economists have a direct way to identify the productivity of an economic process: the amount of dollars of output per person per month (or any similar measure of applied resource). However, this measure does not apply very well to a software system or to any engineering activity. The pricing process, because of its dependence on the market demand, will unavoidably introduce distortions in this form of productivity measurement (dollar earned). A better way to define productivity is to use the number of essential elements of the product per unit of applied resource. For example, the productivity of a farmer is better measured by tons of grain produced per person per month than by dollars generated per person per month, because the first figure is not affected by the fluctuation of the price of grains.

But what is the essential product of a software developer? The only visible outputs are computer code and documentation for the software produced. It seems reasonable, therefore, to define the productivity of programming personnel by the lines of code generated per person per month. This definition is, in fact, widely used in the industry today, although it is somewhat controversial. The definition of a line of code, of course, is by no means unequivocal. However, a reasonable and useful definition is the one presented by Nelson (1978), which is often used by the U.S. Department of Defense.

According to this definition, *programmer productivity* is the number of delivered source lines of code (DSLOC) per person per month. A *line of code* is, in turn, defined as one 80-character record of source code (the code written by the programmer, not the code resulting from an automatic compilation or code generation), including blanks, comments, data declarations, JCL statements, linker/loader commands, or anything needed for the installation of the piece of software in its practical use. It does not include throwaway code, test drivers, or anything that was necessary for the software development process but is not needed for software use. Also, since a large amount of work in the real world of software is in modifying existing code to add new features or to change functionalities, the line count includes all those lines in which at least one character was changed (even if it is in a comment) and, of course, all the added lines.

The above metric applies fairly well to the productivity measure of newly developed software systems. It is often considered as satisfactory as more sophisticated metrics (Boehm, 1978, 1981). However, this productivity measure does not please several software experts, who consider it very criticizable. Some of their criticisms and a refutation are listed next:

1. *Programming language dependence:* It seems reasonable to assume that writing a certain logical function in one language instead of another will produce a different number for the DSLOC. This criticism, however, is based on evidence relative to certain types of problems written in some language appropriate to that problem. A typical example is the coding of numerical calculations in FORTRAN. But barring any extreme misuse of programming languages, DSLOC count is more or less constant for the same problem using different languages. Furthermore, by including in the DSLOC count the linker/loader directives, JCL commands, etc., which are not affected by the use of any language used for coding the modules, the percentage of the DSLOC count due to the use of a particular language is further reduced. Note that if we were to use the number of object code lines as a metric, we would be in a much more uncertain situation because of the variability of compiler efficiency in code generation. Also, the argument about the differences between languages applies to the differences between machine architectures as well.

   This author conducted some experiments for programs of a few hundred lines of code implementing typical system functions, written both in assembly and in other languages; the results showed variation on the DSLOC count (measured as defined above) within 20%. There is no claim, however, that this result is any definitive proof of language independence. More work on this subject is needed, and the subject will be examined further in Chapter 10, where the causes of large size in systems are studied.

2. *Varying degrees of difficulties*: It is common experience that some code is much more difficult to conceive and write than others. However, this criticism is likely to be of little relevance. It appears reasonable to assume that a large piece of software is a blend of easy and difficult code. Also, as we will see in detail in the following chapters, most problems with large software are problems relative to module interaction, not to the specific module-coding difficulty.

3. *Difficulty of application*: Because of the intrinsic difficulty of tracing lines of code that are modified, since modification both adds lines of code and modifies (replaces) existing lines, the measure of productivity of software modification work is not easy to determine. A solution here is to use automatic source code control systems that can track both the modified lines and the added lines. Also, added lines can be estimated by sampling (Zaharchuck, 1979).

   In conclusion, there may be some inadequacy in the measure of productivity based on DSLOC count. But for lack of a better metric and because of the relatively large number of existing data measured in this way, we will use this productivity measure.

Use of Automation

Productivity in DSLOC eventually must be translated to dollar values, which implies considerations of the cost of the development process itself. This cost is measurable in dollars per line of code (DSLOC.) A large percentage of these dollars is consumed by the personnel producing the DSLOC. But a nonnegligible part is also related to the investment in automatic tools, an investment made in the hope of increasing the productivity of the programmers and therefore reducing the total dollar cost.

Operating systems and language compilers are effective automatic tools for software development

There are few industrial activities that use automation to the extent that the programming community of today uses it. This extensive use of automatic tools to support the development of software is actually the reason for the existence of a large part of the software industry. In fact, operating systems are created (among other reasons) for the purpose of supporting the development of other software systems. Compilers for high-order languages are another very common example of software tools created for the purpose of making development of other software easier. It may be asserted that except for the development of the most basic parts of the operating system itself, all software systems produced today are developed by using other usually very complex software systems, which must be considered as part of the automatic tools available to reduce the cost of software development.

It appears, however, that the cost of software development is not substantially affected by the use of automatic tools. In fact, the pace of the introduction of these automatic tools has accelerated in recent years, but there is no clear evidence of a corresponding reduction in development cost. It should be noted, however, that these tools are mostly addressing the problem of machine use. Very few are designed to support the mental process of problem solving.

Understanding the nature of software systems, as can be gained by the study of the recent progress of computer science, may be of fundamental importance in creating more effective tools. Since a large amount of the development cost is spent in assembling the various modules in such a way that they form a working system, greater emphasis on overall system design should result in major productivity gains.

QUALITY OF SOFTWARE PRODUCTS: RELIABILITY, AVAILABILITY, MAINTAINABILITY

Let us now examine the quality of large software products. The most widespread concern about quality is reliability. An example of the seriousness of this concern is the reluctance to use large software products to control vital applications such as life-support systems and artificial stability of civil aircraft. However, these applications are needed by society, so software systems are beginning to be used in critical systems. Thus reliability of software products is of extreme importance.

Reliability means uninterrupted service

In the context of a computer system *reliability* can be defined as the ability of the system to supply, uninterruptedly, the services desired by the users. It follows that reliability can be measured by the expected mean time of the system's satisfactory service between interruptions or externally manifested errors. Note that internally detected errors successfully recovered by the system itself have no effect on reliability. Similarly, *availability* can be defined as the percentage of the total time a system is working reliably.

Because no system is currently able to supply, with absolute certainty, uninterrupted service after its shipment, systems must be maintained; i.e., they must be subjected to repair and change. A system's ability to accept changes directed toward the goal of ensuring acceptable levels of reliability and availability is called *maintainability*. Thus maintainability is a measure of the time (and cost) needed to ensure system reliability and availability.

The above discussion applies to both hardware and software systems. However, some properties become intrinsically different when we refer to software instead of hardware systems. The reason for this difference is that the predominant cause of hardware failures is the alteration of the physical properties of components that otherwise would have worked properly. In the case of software, failures are the detection of a design or implementation error. In other words, the operation executed during a hardware failure would have been satisfactorily completed if the physical properties of the system were not altered, and therefore simply restoring these physical properties to their original levels will put the system back in reliable operation. In the case of software, however, the operation being performed when the failure occurred was never performed before; otherwise, the failure would have occurred earlier. There is no possibility of restoring system properties to original levels specified in the design, because this specification (implicitly or explicitly expressed) is the cause of the failure. Maintenance thus becomes the operation of *redesign* of the failing part.

Software maintenance may be redesign of one or several modules

Some of the failures of a software system arise from the identification of the correct realization of the wrong (misinterpreted) requirements. Also, the environment in which the system operates may change, thus making system operation unsatisfactory. Although these faults cannot be strictly called failures, modification work will be required. It is this aspect of software maintenance that differs most from hardware maintenance. Even though this work does not fit exactly with the above definition of maintainability (applicable to both hardware and software), it is common to classify it as maintenance.

PRODUCT DOCUMENTATION AND EXTENSIBILITY

A hardware system exists in two different forms. One is the physical object itself (usually in many copies), and the second is the documentation of its design represented by blueprints, schematics, logic diagrams, etc., which supply not only a faithful representation of the layout of the physical components but also the acceptable ranges of the parameters stating the correct functioning of the machines (voltage, current, temperature, size, etc.). From this detailed design documentation one can model any addition or removal of functionalities on paper before making these changes on the physical object. In the case of a hardware system this modeling is mandatory because of the high cost of changes in the manufacturing process.

In contrast, for software systems the cost of changes in the manufacturing process is negligible. Software exists mostly in the form of final product, i.e., executable (perhaps source) code, and design documents. However, these documents are informal descriptions of the design rationale and do not present the same level of confidence as hardware blueprints. So changes to software systems very often require an understanding of the original design rationale through direct examination of the final product (code).

Executable code is *not* a convenient documentation of the system functions

It may be argued that the code is the most accurate and complete documentation of the product. However, the code (including in this term all the commands needed to execute the system functions, such as the module code, linker/binder directives, and JCL commands) is a perfect documentation only of the sequence of commands a machine must execute; it can give no justification for why these commands should be executed to satisfy the system's mission. Thus the system's mission must be described separately from the code. If it is not, it is hard for someone to decide whether the implementation realizes this (undescribed) mission. And even in those cases where some documentation of design exists, correcting an error and/or adding a new functionality requires a difficult and uncertain reconstruction of the thought process of the original designer.

Very often new functionalities are to be added to an existing system to satisfy new user's demands. The system's ability of accepting work for the extension of its functionalities is called *extensibility*.

ERRORS AND TESTING

Software Errors

The cause of unreliability—and consequently of reduced availability and increased maintenance costs—is software error. Even though this assertion may appear to be obvious, it is not necessarily a straightforward conclusion. Some may feel that most software errors have only marginal effect on system reliability; i.e., interruption or major disruption of service may occur only in very few cases because of software errors. Also, the system's recovery process may provide an effective way to hide disruptions of service caused by software errors.

To resolve any doubts, we will examine experimental data. These data were collected by J. Musa (1975), who described a software reliability model based on several assumptions. The assumption of interest here is that the rate of system crashes (a quantity proportional to the inverse of reliability) is in direct proportion to the quantity of residual errors. This hypothesis has been confirmed by experiments (with a very strong correlation), specifically on data relative to four large-scale systems that extended over the entire system life cycles. We will not go into the details of the experiments but simply note that this particular assumption of the Musa model appears to be the least doubtful of all the model's assumptions. Also, the Musa model has shown excellent overall correlation with experimental data relative to forty real-time systems and six operating systems. The data include a total sample of 2831 documented system failures. Considering that most of the real-time systems were for military use (and presumably were developed with great attention to reliability and probably included refined system recovery features), this sample is a satisfactory demonstration that software errors are a significant cause of events (such as system crashes) that negatively affect reliability.

Experimental data show software errors are causes of system failures

As indicated above, software errors are manifestations of discrepancies between the developer's intention and the actual realization of the system as well as the omission of functions due to misstated requirements. Some of these errors cause overtly undesirable events, such as system crashes, deadlocks, and infinite loops. However, for other events the use of the term *error* is not so clear-cut. In fact, unless an unequivocal description of the system's functionalities exists, some may argue that any system that does not end up in a state where no further work can be performed is actually doing correct work for some specification of behavior. Obviously, the last statement is an exaggeration. The point here is that a software error, whenever it does not cause an interruption of service (which also includes the case of infinite loops), is judged as an error only in terms of some (often unwritten) specification.

Note that for a hardware system this statement is not necessarily true. Hardware system errors can be judged and detected by comparing the erroneous behavior of a particular system operation with the behavior the same operation showed at any previous time or with the behavior of another identical system under exactly the same circumstances. Software errors, however, are detected only by weird behavior of an operation that was never performed before.

To make the above statement clearer and more precise, we should clarify the meaning of the word *operation*. An operation that can cause an error is *not* a specific instruction or a module (a procedure), nor even any intermediate sequence of instructions. An individual instruction may be correctly performed several billions of times, producing successful results. Also, pieces of code (i.e., carefully thought-out sequences of instructions) may be executed repeatedly, producing the desired results. An error occurs through the execution of a piece of code performing changes on some data configuration that was never presented to this piece of code before. Note that exactly the same sequence of instructions that produced correct results millions of times will manifest an error when this particular data configuration appears.

The Role of Testing

Software correctness is checked exclusively by testing

Testing is used almost universally to verify that an individual program or a complete system is working as desired. Concerns about software reliability are, indirectly, concerns about the effectiveness of testing as a way to reduce errors to an acceptable level.

An error is a consequence of a wrong decision made by the system's designer, by the programmer of an individual module, or even by the agency that expressed the external requirements of the system. Decisions are based on some knowledge acquired by observation and analysis of the elements contributing to the decision process (Sowell, 1979). Most practitioners feel that observation of a physical phenomenon, such as the execution of a program, is the safest way to show the correctness of a decision. Unfortunately, observation of phenomena without theory to support their interpretation conveys incomplete information, which may be interpreted as having universal value, thus contributing to the creation of erroneous knowledge and, in turn, causing erroneous decisions.

Because software systems show an undesirable level of residual errors after testing, it is reasonable to assume that the knowledge about correctness gained through the testing process is not adequate. This inadequacy stems from the lack of an underlying theory within which design decisions can be articulated in some precise way. Undoubtedly, the programmer and the system designer have some intuition about the effects of their decisions, but they may be unable to articulate it in all its aspects. Verification by testing the software thus becomes an unreliable activity.

Recent research on testing (limited to individual program testing only) has shown that the determination of a set of test cases that ensure correctness of a program requires a very deep analysis of the programming problem. No methods currently exists for performing this analysis with a reasonable level of assurance of results. Therefore, this problem cannot be considered satisfactorily solved. In fact, it may be that this problem is not solvable at all, at least not in its full generality (Pizzarello, 1984; Weyuker and Ostrand, 1980).

A different attack to the testing problem has been proposed by J. Duran and J. Wiorkowsky (1980). Instead of the attempt to derive test cases from knowledge of the programming or the system problems, these authors suggest the creation of test cases at random. Once this random approach is tied in with rigorous development methods and discipline for designing and coding the program or the system, it appears to be considerably effective. The assumption is that correct programs

Test cases selected at random is effective approach

are defined by using an appropriate development discipline that produces nearly correct programs and systems. Any discrepancy would be the result of a human oversight or some problem feature that cannot be handled at design time. These oversights are of very diverse origins, so they could be considered random events and thus would be likely to be detected by random test cases. We will discuss this subject in more detail in Chapter 8.

PROBLEMS WITH SOFTWARE DEVELOPMENT

The problems we have described in the preceding sections may be surprising in the sense that they are unique to the software development process. And they appear in most large software systems. We have so far only *described* the problems, however, not *identified* them. To identify them as problems, we must supply some other criteria, such as the following:

Software problems

- Predictability of schedule and cost both in the predeployment phases and in the maintenance phase.
- Reliability of the final product.
- Predictability of the working characteristics of the product (such as performance, size, user acceptance).
- Flexibility of the development process in the sense of accepting changing management demands.
- Modifiability of the product design so that it may be adapted to changing user requirements.

It is in these criteria that the development process of large software systems shows problems on a scale unknown to other engineering developments. We will discuss each criterion in turn.

Most software projects show schedule and cost overruns. These problems are by no means limited to software development; they are observed in the development of various complex products. What is peculiar in the software case is that these problems are much more frequent and of a larger magnitude than similar problems in other engineering fields. Of particular concern is the size of the cost and the personnel for the maintenance phase, i.e., to repair erroneous design decisions and omissions.

Software systems can be very reliable; it is not unusual for a software system to work with no interruption of service for several thousand hours. On the other hand, all deployed software systems contain residual errors that can manifest themselves at any time under unusual circumstances with highly unpredictable consequences. Because of the unpredictability of software errors, large software systems are not as reliable as other modern technological products.

Another common characteristic of software systems is the difficulty of predicting performance and other working characteristics. Usually, performance of software systems is measured at the system tests phase, and if it is found unsatisfactory, changes in the code are made at that time to improve execution speed and/or the size of the code.

The software development process is also rather inflexible. Management frequently complains about how little it can do to accelerate a schedule (additional personnel may be completely ineffective), to reduce development costs, or to respond rapidly to some drastic change in requirements.

Finally, modification of software systems is an expensive enterprise. One reason for this expense may be the lack of suitable documentation of design decisions similar to the documentation created and used by modern engineering.

In summary, the development process for large software systems appears to be unusually difficult to control when compared with the development processes for other high-technology products. Also, the quality of the products is negatively affected by the presence of residual errors in the deployed systems. Both characteristics appear to be a consequence of the lack of predictive power in the design phase.

HIGHLIGHTS

In this chapter we compared the software development process with the engineering development process. We found a considerable philosophical difference in spite of superficial similarities between the two processes, namely, software development is implementation-driven while modern engineering is design-driven. We also identified process and product quality parameters, which are susceptible to quantitative evaluation and may indicate the extent of these problems.

We can conclude that software systems developed by using the current process present the following peculiar characteristics:

- There is no clear distinction between a design and a fabrication phase. It may be said that the design of a software system is never completed in the sense that many design decisions are made during phases of development well beyond the design phase. This incompleteness appears to be a consequence of the absence of any practical way to verify the correctness of the design except by actual use (testing) of the final product. However, this continuous design does not usually involve major architectural changes but, rather, definition of details within the architecture.

- The amount of redesign work needed during the system integration phase makes the cost of the integration and system tests phase a substantial percentage of the cost of the whole development process before the deployment and maintenance phase. This author's experience with the development of other engineering products suggests that such a high cost is peculiar to software development. In fact, in engineering product development most (but by no means all) design errors are discovered by analysis performed during the design phase, well before the actual product is constructed.

- The verification of design decisions is done almost exclusively by testing the final product or its parts. These tests are based on the developer's intuition, since no rigorous theory exists to support the selection of an adequate set of test cases. This point may be interpreted as a cause (or as *the* cause) of the peculiar behavior of software listed above.

We have indicated in our brief discussion of the engineering development process that all phases are effectively controlled by the documented decisions produced during the design phase. We saw that this control does not exist for software development. It appears that the actual construction of the modules and their assembly into the system at the integration phase are the driving forces for software. Thus as we stated earlier, traditional engineering development is design-driven; software development is implementation-driven.

REFERENCES

Boehm, B. W. 1978. Personal communication.

———. 1981. *Software engineering economics*. Englewood Cliffs, N.J.: Prentice-Hall.

Duran, J. W., and Wiorkowsky, J. J. 1980. Quantifying software validity by sampling. *IEEE Transactions on Reliability* R–29 (no. 2): 142–144.

Horikoshi, J. 1981. *Eagle of Mitsubishi*. Seattle: University of Washington Press.

Kuhn, T. S. 1962. *The structure of the scientific revolution.* Chicago: University of Chicago Press.

Musa, J. D. 1975. A theory of software reliability and its application. *IEEE Transactions of Software Engineering* SE–1 (no. 3):312–327.

Nelson, R. 1978. Software data collection and analysis. Draft of a partial report, Rome Air Development Center, Air Force Systems Command, Griffiss Air Force Base, N.Y.

Pizzarello, A. 1984. A view of program and system tests. In *Proceedings of the 3rd Phoenix Computer and Communication Conference*, pp. 168–173.

Sowell, T. 1979. *Knowledge and decisions*. New York: Basic Books.

Weyuker, E. J., and Ostrand, T. J. 1980. Theories of program testing and the application of revealing subdomains. *IEEE Transactions on Software Engineering* SE–6 (no. 3): 236–246.

Zaharchuck, A. 1979. Software Development Data Report, Honeywell internal note, Phoenix. Ariz.

Zelkowitz, M. V.; Yeh, R.; Hamlet, R. G.; Gannon, J. D.; and Basili, V. R. 1983. Software productivity survey of industry. University of Maryland report, College Park, Md.

CHAPTER TWO

Experiments Relating to the Development of Large Systems

INTRODUCTION

In this chapter we examine some experimental evidence relative to the salient points made in the preceding chapter. We will examine productivity and error data from several software projects. Then we will discuss experimental studies of the behavior of large software systems during their life cycle, i.e., throughout the history of their various releases.

As we have pointed out before, the interpretation of disjointed experimental results without a theory of the underlying process is dubious and difficult. The purpose of the presentation of experiments in this chapter is to indicate and to comment about observations that need explanation. In the rest of the book, as we proceed to examine the foundations of software, we will indicate plausible explanations for these observations.

MEASUREMENT OF PRODUCTIVITY

Some experimental results about productivity come from the collection of data related to software system developments made by the Rome Air Development Center (RADC) of the U.S. Air Force Systems Command. RADC has collected and analyzed data in 407 projects for a total DSLOC of more than 21 million (Nelson, 1978). The average size of the projects was about 52K DSLOC, and 28 different programming languages were used for their development. The projects covered a vast range of problems, such as avionics, numerical calculation problems, commercial data processing, command and control systems, ground-based missile control systems, and space-borne control systems. Also, the developers were very different groups from various Department of Defense vendors throughout the United States, with the systems developed mostly in recent years (mid to late seventies).

The data were analyzed and, whenever possible, productivity and error rate results were grouped by language used and by the development technique used. The mean productivity value, calculated over 379 projects for which productivity data were available, is 388 delivered source lines of code per man-month (DSLOC/MM). Also, the error rate for the same projects was measured, and the results are examined in a later section of this chapter.

Productivity and Program Size

Productivity does not depend on project size

An attempt to correlate the productivity with the project size presented in Nelson (1978) shows that no correlation exists between productivity and size. In fact, a least squares best fit shows an almost flat line with a correlation factor of .0334, which is too low to give any confidence in this correlation. The only result that can be inferred from the statistical analysis presented in Nelson is that the larger the project, the more people are used and for a longer time.

Productivity and Programming Language

The effect of some programming languages on productivity, as indicated by Nelson's (1978) data, is shown in Table 1. The interesting point in the data presented here is that no sharp conclusion can be reasonably drawn. It seems that use of COBOL increases productivity, but use of FORTRAN and PL/I shows a decline with respect to assembly languages (ASSY). It is highly possible that the type of problem attacked by the projects in the various language groups had a definite effect. Thus assembly language and PL/I might have been used for system development of a much higher level of difficulty than the data processing problems solved in COBOL. Also, as we pointed out in Chapter 1, it is not easy to evaluate whether the number of DSLOC using a high-order language (HOL) to realize a specific functionality is much lower than the number of DSLOC used in assembly. Another element that may be a source of uncertainty is that the term *assembly language* actually refers to a multitude of different languages presenting quite significant differences because of both the different hardware architecture and the presence of more or less extensive macro capabilities. In spite of all these uncertainties, the differences do not indicate that any language is much better than another from the point of view of development process productivity.

No conclusion can be drawn for productivity and language

A similar result about the relative independence of the development of software from the language used is presented in Boehm (1980), where the results of an experimental realization of the same project by two teams using different languages are presented.

Productivity and Development Techniques

The effect of development technique on productivity is shown in Figure 1. The numbers in parentheses are the number of projects examined in each of several categories. Term TP refers to traditional programming and indicates projects developed without any significant use of what are called modern programming (MP) disciplines, such as HIPO charts, control constructs, top-down development, and code reviews and

TABLE 1 MEAN PRODUCTIVITY PER PROGRAMMING LANGUAGE

Language	Number of Projects	Mean Project Size (DSLOC)	Mean Productivity (DSLOC/MM)	Total Sample Size (DSLOC)
ASSY	244	30.7K	420	7500K
FORTRAN	25	10.7K	321	270K
COBOL	33	27.1K	566	890K
PL/I	22	40.7K	391	890K

Source: Data from Nelson (1978).

inspections. Of the total of 379 projects, 210 are classified as TP.

Results for MP indicate that at least 90% of project development was performed by using modern programming disciplines. Figure 1 indicates that 58 projects out of 379 are classified as MP. Term SPECS indicates the use of a formal language for program design description. Figure 1 shows that 17 of 58 MP projects used a program design language.

Note that all modern programming discipline emphasizes the design phase and attempts to guide the programming process by results derived from contemporary computer science research. Moreover, the use of a formal (or semiformal) language to express design decisions can only be interpreted as an attempt to increase the weight of the design decisions throughout the whole development process. In other words, MP is an attempt to introduce methods and disciplines akin to the ones used

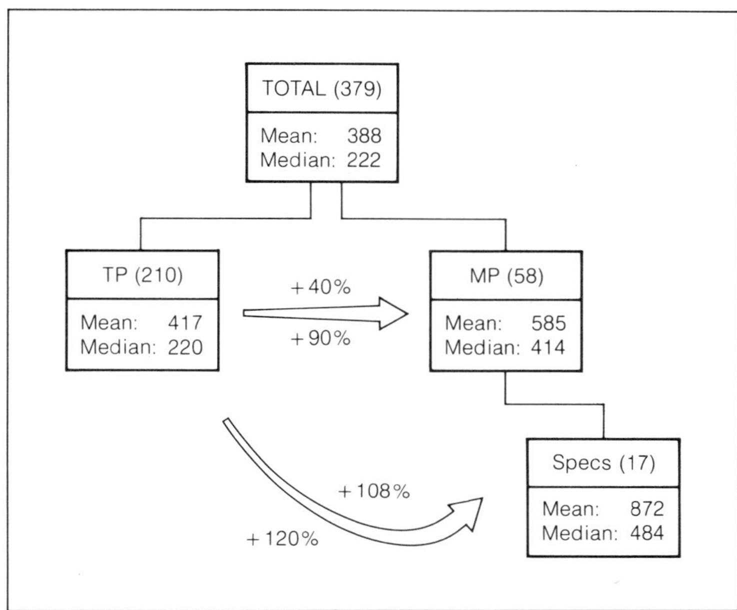

FIGURE 1 EFFECT OF DEVELOPMENT TECHNIQUES

Source: Data from Nelson (1978).

in modern engineering, which emphasizes the design phase of development.

Programming techniques may improve productivity

Figure 1 gives both the mean and the median of the analyzed data. Since the data distributions are rather skewed, the median may be a better measure than the mean. Also, tests on the mean show that the null hypothesis must be rejected at a significance level of .05, and the test for a type II error shows that the probability of making an error in accepting the claims of the improvement shown by MP and SPECS is 18% and 26%, respectively, at a significance level of .05.

The comparison of TP with MP shows an improvement of 90% on the median value and of 40% on the mean value. More impressive is the improvement shown by SPECS over TP: 108% and 120% for mean and median values, respectively.

Conclusions

In summary, the examined data show the following features:

1. For the type of projects whose data are analyzed in Nelson (1978) (i.e., relatively large-scale development), it is impossible to correlate the project size with productivity.
2. Use of different languages does not show any consistent effect on productivity in the development of large systems.
3. Modern programming techniques and disciplines are likely to be a factor in improving productivity.
4. Among the various MP techniques the description of program design by the use of some program design language (SPECS) appears to be the most effective technique for productivity improvement.

Point 1 is rather counterintuitive. It seems to suggest that productivity is a characteristic of the development organization rather than of the product. Points 2 and 3 could have been hinted at by someone with experience in the development of large-scale software. Point 4 is quite surprising; i.e., superficially, the formal description of design may appear to require more work, not less. Yet the result is a doubled productivity rate.

The only possible conclusion that can be drawn for these results is that unequivocal documentation of design issues during the early phases of development has a positive impact on productivity. The use of an appropriate programming language will certainly help to implement the system, but since language does not play a major role during the design stage, it will have limited effect on overall productivity.

EXPERIMENTS ON ERROR RATE

The collection of experimental data by RADC (Nelson, 1978) also presents data relative to errors. Errors are defined as officially reported defects before shipment (of a release).

Error Rate and Project Size

Project size does not affect error rate

RADC data about error rate, measured as the number of errors per thousand DSLOC, show the same absence of correlation with project size as productivity did. Again, the least squares best fit is an almost flat (slightly declining with increasing project size) curve, with a correlation coefficient so low as to discourage any conclusion. Of course, the total number of errors is an increasing function of project size. This nonresult again may suggest a dependency of error rate on the development organization (or the development process) rather than on any characteristic of the product. It seems as if the process can handle a fixed rate of errors (as well as productivity), and therefore longer development times would be needed to handle the larger total number of errors manifested by larger projects.

Error Rate and Programming Language

Table 2 lists error rate data by language. However, these data may be deceptive. In fact, mean values are exactly what their name indicates: Averages valid on the average only. Large variances may be present, and the mean value does not supply any information about them. Nevertheless, these data do not show any sharp effect on error rate for the use of any particular language. Some languages, such as FORTRAN and COBOL, show better error rates than assembly. But PL/I and JOVIAL J3 go the other way.

TABLE 2 ERROR RATES PER LANGUAGE USED

Language	Error Rate (Mean)	Size of the Sample (No. of Jobs)
ASSY	26.6	244
FORTRAN	15.1	25
COBOL	12.9	33
PL/I	33.3	22
JOVIAL J4	16.4	2
JOVIAL J3	50.3	4
JOVIAL J3B	17.0	1
CENTRAN	19.4	11

Source: Data from Nelson (1978).

If the available numbers for all HOLs are put together, the mean value of error rate is 23.5 per thousand lines of code for an average job size of 37.9K lines. This average shows a little improvement over the one for assembly coding (26.6 errors per thousand lines, with an average job size of 30K). From these data it is not possible to conclude that HOLs are a major factor in reducing error rates.

It is common belief, however, that HOL reduces error rates. In fact, there is no doubt that the use of HOL does reduce the number of errors produced during individual program development. What these data may indicate, again, is that programming for large-scale software is affected by factors that are not substantially influenced by the coding technique but are characteristic of the development process, a task that includes considerable work in integrating individual modules in a system. It is common experience that many errors are discovered at this late stage of development.

In fact, Hamilton and Zelding (1976), in another experiment about error rates, measured the proportion of errors found during the integration and system tests phase. They found that 73% of the problems for the Apollo software were integration-related. A similar conclusion about a large-scale operating system is presented in Richter (1979).

These experimental results do not mean that HOLs are of no use in large-scale software development. But they do indicate that the development of large systems with low error rates requires something more than the currently available HOLs. Also, no conclusion can be drawn about the possibility of conceiving some new HOL that is effective in reducing error rates.

Error Rate and Development Techniques

The RADC data do not show the effect of programming techniques and/or the use of a program design language on error rates. And in Vessey and Weber's (1983) study—limited, however, to a group of COBOL programs written by three different organizations—the effect of modern programming on the error repair rate after deployment appears to be irrelevant. No data are available for the use of a program design language.

Another series of experimental observations about error rates sheds additional light on the software development process, though. Jones (1979) presents a set of observations that help in pinpointing the problems of development of large software systems. Let us examine the chart of Figure 2. This chart, viewed in terms of represented trend rather than numerical values, points out that while several causes contribute to the number of errors, the rate of growth of errors with system size caused by logic design specifications is clearly much more significant than all other causes. Jones relates this result to another observed phenomenon: The percentage of a system's internal functionalities—i.e., design decisions—documented *in any form* decreases with the size of system. Note also that the increase in error rates is sharper for system sizes of 1K to 50K lines, which may be the dividing line between small and large software products.

ERROR-PRONE MODULES

Other experimental data are related to the error-proneness of a rather limited number of modules in a software system. Both Jones (1983) and Zaharchuck (1980)—Jones observing a large number of software systems

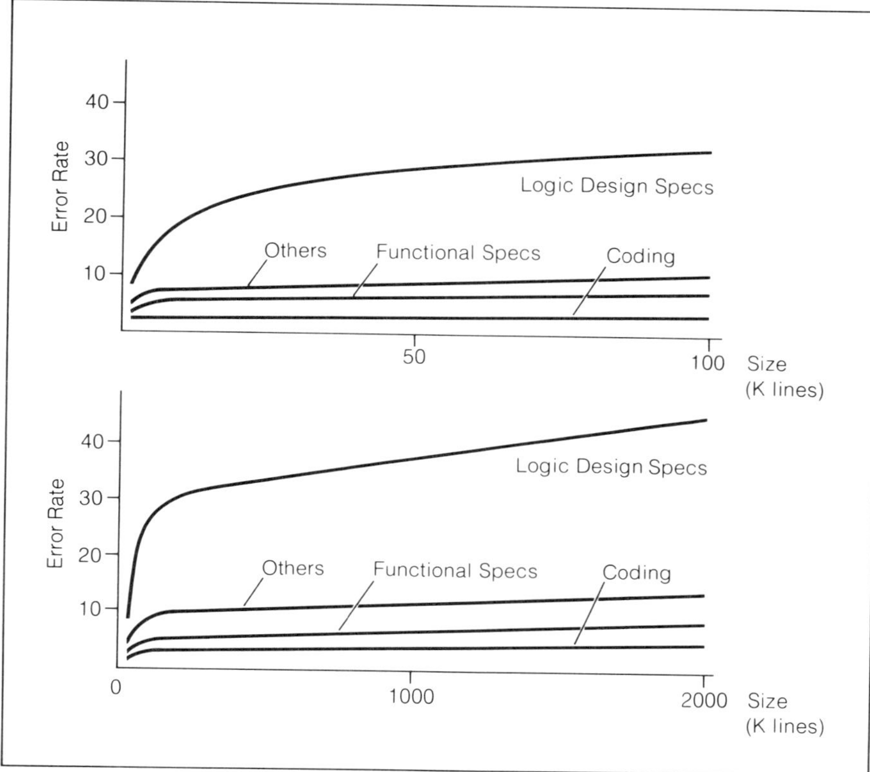

FIGURE 2 ERROR RATES VERSUS JOB SIZE

Source: C. Jones, A survey of programming, design and specification techniques, *Proceedings for the Specifications of Reliable Software, Cambridge, Mass., 1979.*

of different natures and Zaharchuck observing several releases of an operating system—remarked that most of the modules present zero or near zero error rates during the system tests phase. Jones stated that it is very likely that 60% of all modules in a large software system are error-free. He also gave the rule of thumb that 50% of all system errors are found in 5% of the system modules. Zaharchuck's data also point out that the error-prone modules are essentially the same in different releases, even when the functionalities added to these releases are rather different.

Error-proneness of some modules is a characteristic of the system

No particular development technique (or lack of one) or programming language can be associated with these error-prone modules. In fact, these modules are coded in different languages within the same system. Also, their size is not much different from the average size of other system modules. Their error-proneness appears to be a specific characteristic of the role of these modules in the system. We will discuss this point in more detail in Chapter 16 after we have presented the necessary background to justify a plausible explanation of this phenomenon.

COMMUNICATION OF DESIGN DECISIONS

Correct behavior of software systems must be isomorphic to existing (or conjectured) real-world behavior. In that sense all the code of a software system can be judged correct only by comparison with some (often unexpressed) desirable behavior. Any code, per se, is correct for *some* (possibly senseless) specifications.

The specification of what a software system is supposed to do is of great importance for the design phase. During this phase the specifications of the software system are supposed to be defined and "written." Unfortunately, even if the specifications are written [and for the most part, in a large system they are not, according to Jones (1979)], they would not necessarily be readable by human beings. The reason is the sheer size of such a document, which, even if properly organized, would require a lifetime of reading to get a complete view of the system design. And the effectiveness of written design specifications to support communication among developers is limited to the extent that this documentation can be organized—an impossible task. Consequently, verbal transmission of information is the most widespread tool for communicating design decisions.

The problem with verbal communication is the inherent imprecision of human languages. It is quite likely that misunderstandings arising from verbal communication about module interactions cause the creation of erroneous code.

A widely publicized solution to the communicaiton problem is the chief programmer team (Baker, 1972). The essential idea is to stretch one programmer's mind by freeing it from all tasks that are not essential to the creation of the system. Thus code is written by other programmers, and the overall task is stored in the chief programmer's mind. So that catastrophic events, such as a chief programmer's desertion to another company or an influenza epidemic, are avoided, a backup programmer is supposed to record the same information. Therefore the backup could take charge of the development if the chief programmer is not available.

The chief programmer may be a limited solution to the communication problem

Experience has shown that the scheme is both clever and workable—with a catch. The cleverness stems from the fact that a proven technology, i.e., the ability of a solitary programmer to realize effectively correct and efficient products, is extended to a larger area of application by the simple means of work efficiency improvement. The catch is that the scheme is only as good as the chief programmer's mind (and his or her ability to lead, communicate with, and control other developers). Also, if the system is larger than any chief programmer's brain capacity, the idea becomes unworkable. A proposed team of teams—a hierarchy of chief programmers—is simply not applicable (and its application has not yet been recorded in the literature) because it presents formidable problems of communication among chief programmers.

The discussion above could be interpreted to mean that the use of a formal language to express design decisions suffices to supply the necessary conciseness and precision. In fact, the data about the increase of productivity for developments using a formal program design language tend to support this conjecture. However, it would be helpful if any formal language used to describe design decisions could also be used to support effective predictions of the correctness of the design.

Some of the results of computer science research are addressing this problem of verification of the correctness of software without reading and executing the actual code. These techniques are thus interesting candidates for introduction into the software development process to increase the predictive power of the design phase, and they will be discussed in detail later in this book.

EXPERIMENTS CONCERNING THE SOFTWARE SYSTEM LIFE CYCLE

The most illuminating experimental study of large software systems during their life cycle has been done by Lehman and Belady (1979). This study demonstrated that a large software system, when in use, is invariably subject to modifications because of continuous changes in its context (user's requirements, hardware and/or other software modifications, etc.). Also, the amount of development (modification) work executed on the system per unit of time *is essentially constant* when averaged over a long period of time. The study found strong experimental evidence for the existence of a linear relationship between the total amount of modification and enhancement work done for a system and its age. The study also showed that anytime the constant slope of the cumulative work was forced (presumably by management action) to increase for some period of time, this increase was followed by a decrease, thus keeping the average amount of work per unit of time constant in the long run.

Modification work is constant over the system's life cycle

Note that this constant amount of work per unit of time is largely unaffected by variations in the quantity of used resources, development techniques, languages used for coding, etc. A large system actually shows intrinsic dynamics that are affected by external factors (such as applied personnel) only in the short term and in a limited measure. Consequently, it is very frustrating for software managers to cope with requirements of accelerated schedules or work load increases.

The evidence for a constant amount of modification work can be interpreted as supporting a contention expressed earlier in this chapter. Namely, the lack of correlation of productivity and error rate with the size of the project indicates that those two parameters depend on development process characteristics rather than on some characteristic of the product, such as size or coding technique. However, we point out that the development process for modification depends on characteristic of the product itself, such as understandability of code and system organization.

The study of Lehman and Belady pointed out another characteristic of large systems. The process of continuous modification of a system causes a deterioration in the system's intellectual structure, thus making

Modifications cause deterioration of the system structure

all work in the system increasingly more difficult. So there is a growing difficulty in anyone's understanding the meaning of existing code, and additional errors are introduced as a consequence of code changes and other error corrections. Therefore process productivity becomes lower with time.

To counteract this structural deterioration, one must reconstitute the system's intellectual structure (therefore productivity may rise again). However, restructuring work adds to the cost of the system during its life cycle. Also, it cannot be done at a rate much faster than the system's intrinsic dynamics permit, thus delaying the introduction of changes for modified requirements.

The concepts introduced above may be better understood by examining Figure 3. Figure 3A shows the typical diagram of the total work done on the system vs. the system's age. The linear relation implies that the work per unit of time executable on the system is constant. Figure 3B shows a second-order effect (neglected in Figure 3A). During periods 1 and 3, possibly because of management decision, an effort was made to output more work per unit of time (the slope of the curve, i.e., the work per unit of time, during these periods is higher than the one naturally accepted by the system). Invariably, periods such as 1 and 3 are followed by periods such as 2 and 4, where the slope of the work curve is lower (less work per unit of time is done) to compensate for the preceding periods of higher work output. During these periods, presumably, restructuring work is done to restore the system's capacity to accept modification and enhancement. But in some cases management may decide against using personnel for restructuring work. The consequence is a drop in productivity for the workers in the system so that very few new functionalities can be added to the system.

If restructuring work is done, productivity declines

To perform system modifications, because of the absence of complete and formal documentation of design, software developers are forced to read the actual code in order to determine the design rationale with any precision. Consequently, it is reasonable to suppose that maintenance

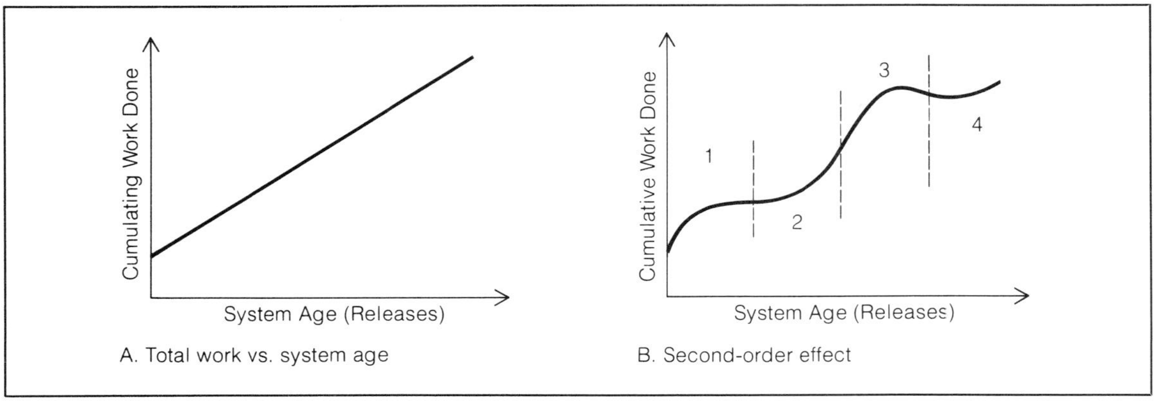

FIGURE 3 DYNAMICS OF LARGE SYSTEMS

work is in some measure affected by programming language. However, some studies (Boehm, 1981; Lientz and Swanson, 1981) show that the amount of *source* instructions modified per man-month is independent of the programming language used. The difficulty of maintenance of a large software system is primarily a function of the system's organization. Different systems developed in the same programming language (even for the same hardware) show considerable differences in their maintenance cost. So in terms of the Lehman-Belady observations this result amounts to saying that the slope of the curve in Figure 3A is largely unaffected by the programming language or the hardware used to develop the system.

The above statement, however, applies only to programming languages currently in use. We have no way of establishing at this time whether it is possible to conceive a programming language that affects the slope of the maintenance curve of Figure 3A.

These experimental results show another counterintuitive behavior in the development of large software systems: These systems behave as though they were channels of fixed capacity. When this fixed capacity is reached, no more flow can pass through it. Furthermore, this capacity may be reduced over time unless specific work is done to maintain it at the original level.

Different systems, however, show *different values* for this fixed capacity. Some accept more work per unit of time than others. So it appears that the architectural arrangement of the system is responsible for the fixed capacity to accept modification and enhancement. It is thus important to find which features of system architecture are more suitable for the execution of future modification work. We will deal with this topic in Chapter 16.

HIGHLIGHTS

Experimental data shows that productivity is not significantly affected by project size or by implementation tools such as HOL. Modern programming techniques that emphasize the design phase do appear to be effective in increasing productivity, however. The same indifference to project size and language is also shown by experimental data about error rate. This invariance of productivity and error rate may be interpreted as an intrinsic rigidity of the development process of software systems. The observation of difficulties in communication of design decisions among developers may be a cause of this rigidity.

Another important experimental observation is the existence of a small number of system modules accounting for most of the system errors. This result is an indication of some characteristic of these modules' role in the system that has great impact on the overall system reliability.

The behavior of software systems during their entire life cycle has also been the object of experimental study. These studies shed light on some additional characteristics of process rigidity, namely, the constant amount of modification work accepted by a system and the deterioration of the system's intellectual structure as a consequence of modifications.

REFERENCES

Baker, F. T. 1972. Chief programmer team management of production programming. *IBM System Journal*, Vol. 11, no. 1: 56–73.

Belady, L. A., and Lehman, M. M. 1979. The characteristics of large systems. In *Research directions in software technology*, edited by P. Wegner. Cambridge, Mass.: MIT Press.

Boehm, B. W. 1980. Developing small-scale application software products. In *Proceedings of the 1980 IFIP Congress,* edited by S. H. Lavington, pp. 321–326. North-Holland Publishing.

________. 1981. *Software engineering economics*. Englewood Cliffs, N.J.: Prentice-Hall.

Hamilton, M., and Zelding, S. 1976. Higher order software—a methodology for defining software. *IEEE Transactions on Software Engineering* SE–2 (no. 1): 9–32.

Jones, C. 1979. A survey of programming and specification techniques. In *Proceedings of the Conference on Specification of Reliable Software, Cambridge, Mass.*, pp. 91–103.

________. 1983. An ITT internal presentation as reported by E. Kirby at an RAS–ASU meeting, Phoenix, Ariz.

Lientz, B. P., and Swanson, E. B. 1981. Problems in application software maintenance. *Communications of ACM* 24 (no. 11): 763–769.

Nelson, R. 1978. Software data collection and analysis. Draft of a partial report, Rome Air Development Center, Air Force Systems Command, Griffiss Air Force Base, N.Y.

Richter, J. C. 1979. Note on testing effectiveness. Honeywell Informations Systems internal note.

Vessey, G., and Weber, R. 1983. Some factors affecting program repair maintenance: An empirical study. *Communications of ACM* 26 (no. 2): 128–134.

Zaharchuck, A. 1980. Error-prone modules. Honeywell Informations Systems internal memo.

CHAPTER THREE

Mathematics and Computer Software

INTRODUCTION

The new outlook to software introduced by the computer science community considers programs and systems as intellectual objects subject to mathematical analysis. Thus in the development of software we can introduce techniques that permit the prediction of correctness of design, which should improve process productivity and increase product reliability.

Most engineering disciplines use mathematics, but in software we have to use the mathematical method itself. This procedure is unusual for most engineers, who are trained to use mathematical procedures to solve their problems but not to create mathematical results.

In this chapter we briefly introduce the essential philosophy of the mathematical method, and we discuss its relevance for software system design. Keep in mind, however, that mathematics is only the scientific basis for the introduction of more effective methods and disciplines in the software development. Its role is analogous to the role of physical sciences in engineering methods and disciplines. In other words, the software specialist should not be envisioned as a mathematician but as an engineer who uses methods and disciplines based on the philosophy of the mathematical methods.

MATHEMATICAL THINKING

There is hardly any field of pure or applied science today not affected by mathematics. The tremendous predictive power of the engineering design process that permitted us to send human beings to the moon, with a reasonable assurance about their safety, is for the most part due to the use of mathematical thinking.

Mathematical theories find applications in applied sciences

Mathematics, of course, has an independent existence. Even if the origin of mathematics is rooted in the experience of the real world, most of its results relate to abstract entities. But many of its esoteric theories often find application in the real world of applied science. Einstein's theory of relativity, for example, would never have become a scientific theory without a mathematical theory to give it rigorous form and predictive power.

Generally speaking, mathematical theories are created first, independently from their possible application (a lot of these theories go unapplied forever); then some practical scientist—a physicist, an engineer, or an economist—will use these theories to give order to some observation and intuition. The practical scientist uses mathematics not only because its precise language permits an unequivocal expression of scientific ideas but also because once the real-world phenomenon is expressed in mathematical terms, the tools of mathematics can be used to predict the behavior of the physical objects.

We are interested here in the prediction of the behavior of large software systems, particularly their correctness. For example, we may wish to predict whether a particular arrangement of data and procedures will behave in some prescribed way. Or we may wish to predict quantitatively a particular system's performance. We limit ourselves in this book to the use of mathematics for predicting the behavior of software systems in the sense that they satisfy certain requirements. For this purpose we will examine an aspect of mathematics usually neglected in the education of the traditional engineer: mathematical thinking. By applying the fundamental principles used by mathematicians in creating abstract theories, we may be able to repeat their successes when we create the abstract entities called software systems.

MATHEMATICS AND LANGUAGE

The common characteristics of abstract objects, both mathematical and software entities, is their need to be unequivocally defined. From this point of view it is unfortunate that we are accustomed to using human languages, because they are highly inadequate for precise definitions. So whenever we want to deal with abstract objects to a fine degree of precision, we must be retrained to use more precise language. Hence the first step in the presentation of the mathematical method (and of the desired software systems theory) is a discussion of language.

Uses of Language

Let us begin by examining a few uses of language. Language is used, for instance, in small talk. Hundreds of phrases, such as "How are you?" "You know," and "Nice to see you," are actually conveying little meaning at all. Almost any other phrase would serve the purpose equally well. No matter how important these utterances are for proper social behavior, for our purpose they are meaningless, and we should discard them from our consideration.

Language is also used rhetorically. Some people who use language in this way are politicians, poets, art critics, and software designers (including the author of this book) when they informally discuss their design decisions. In this use of language the meaning is not the literal meaning of the words but some vaguely related meaning, strongly dependent on context and time. In spite of exaggerations and understatements, though, this use of language permits transmission of ideas. In fact, our everyday use of language is mostly of this type, and we manage to get along fairly well. We are even able to discuss software design ideas, and within the limits described in the preceding chapters, we are able to create large software systems.

Another use of language is exemplified by legal briefs, government documents, and some technical (nonmathematical) reports, including most software design specifications. At this level language relies as little as possible on context, and it uses many specifically created words (jargon). While this use of language increases precision, its intelligibility for uninitiated persons is considerably decreased, thus creating the need for a plethora of specialists such as lawyers, tax accountants, government employees, and software system specialists.

Definitions

Now we arrive at the critical issue: All these specifically created words must be rigorously defined. By creating a sufficiently large number of definitions, can we create some form of language that is totally unambiguous? Unfortunately, the answer is no (Kershner and Wilcox, n.d.). For example, in an English dictionary many definitions are defined in terms of other words. Thus there must exist a few words whose meaning is primitively understood by everyone without definition; otherwise, we would end up with some basic word defined in terms of words that, in turn, are defined in terms of the original word—in other words, we end up with circular definitions. But circular definitions are useful if we have a basic group of words whose meanings can be assumed to be unequivocally known. All languages have a basis of these undefined words that can be used for the definition of other words.

Circular definitions are unavoidable

Similarly, mathematics uses undefined words whose meanings are assumed to be known to everybody. In mathematics, however, the number of words and related concepts considered undefined are kept very small, and the concepts defined by these words are very primitive indeed. Yet mathematical language is very general and at the same time very precise.

All we said above obviously applies to the description of software systems. Currently, design decisions are described in the computer world's version of the legal jargon, and hence we need specialists to deal with such language. However, the design problems of large software systems are of such complexity that even the highly specialized computer jargon is inadequate. Thus it is useful to seek a form of the mathematical language that is applicable to the description of software design decisions.

Programming languages are as precise as mathematics but only for commanding computers

Of course, in the computer field there already are languages that permit a level of precision comparable to that of mathematics: programming languages. However, their precision manifests itself only when they are executed by a computer. People do not have the same unequivocal understanding of the various commands of a programming language. For example, different implementations of the same language often show differences in function. Since the effects of these commands are, after all, expressed in some human language, their meaning is ambiguous. And this ambiguity may only be resolved by the actual testing of these commands. In tests, however, only the particular interpretation given in the specific implementation tested can be ascertained.

We thus must return to mathematics, at least to find a way to express the meaning of programming languages in a precise way.

THE NATURE OF THE MATHEMATICAL METHOD

The precision of mathematical language is one of the desirable attributes of mathematics we want to exploit for the design of software systems. Another attribute is the predictive power of mathematics, which gives us confidence in the results of scientific researches. Predictive power is based on the mathematical method.

The Development of Mathematical Thinking

Before we examine the mathematical method, let us briefly review what mathematics is. To some people, mathematics is arithmetic or the science of numbers. This aspect of mathematics was perhaps the first one to be explored and to be put to practical use. Kershner and Wilcox, in their book *The Anatomy of Mathematics* (n.d.), give us a humorous reason for the origin of the science of numbers: the desire of a primitive tribal chieftain to improve his chances of victory in battles against other tribes. They hypothesize that this unnamed genius observed that the victor in battles was usually the side that had excess warriors not engaged in one-to-one fights against opponents. Then, perhaps, this unnamed genius organized some form of friendly meeting with a tribe he wanted to conquer and suggested, as a sign of friendship, that each warrior of one tribe embrace a warrior of the other. Thus this chieftain could determine which tribe had an excess of warriors and hence which one was likely to be the winner.

Once this concept of one-to-one correspondence was born, real things could be put in correspondence with abstract things, making the real things easier to manage and manipulate. These abstract things were verbal utterances, which became the names of the first system of numbers. We still use this system of numbers, the natural numbers.

The next step in the development of mathematical thinking was logical reasoning. Logical processes allow us to predict properties, behaviors, and relationships of abstract objects without extensive experimentation. Historically, geometry was the first branch of mathematics that accepted the notion that most results can be obtained by logical reasoning. In geometry, and in most mathematics, rigorous, logical deduction of results is obtained from a rather limited set of primitively accepted facts called axioms. This deductive process, called the axiomatic approach, does not claim to obtain absolute truth but only to arrive at statements that are valid consequences of the assumed axioms and of all the rules of inference used for the deduction process. The science employing this process is called mathematical logic.

Steps in development: one-to-one correspondence, number systems, logical thinking

The Mathematical Method

The thrust of the modern view of the *axiomatic approach*—and the mathematical method—is to eliminate (or at least to reduce considerably) the use of intuition in constructing proofs, that is, in demonstrating the existence of conjectured properties from axioms. Intuition is removed by consciously avoiding to attribute any real-world property to words like *point* and *line*. A mathematical object is as defined in the axioms. If its name conveys some intuitive feeling about its properties, these feelings must be disregarded. In fact, erroneous results are introduced by the tacit reliance on some intuitive property not expressed precisely and therefore forgotten or misused in subsequent reasoning steps.

The key feature is the elimination of uncertainty caused by intuition

How does this discussion of mathematical thinking relate to software systems? Unfortunately, the relationship is negative. The cornerstone of the axiomatic approach—removal of intuition—is ignored in software development. Instead, designers rely on some informal or intuitive properties of programming language. In spite of the considerable ingenuity displayed during system design, the informal arguments are not easy to verify rigorously because of the absence of any theoretical background.

The above discussion should not be construed as a statement about the absolute superiority of formal logic over intuition. The point is, as Bronowsky (n.d.) put it, all scientific demonstrations, including mathematical proofs, are an act of persuasion. And experience with mathematics indicates that persuasion through formalism, including formal logic, appears to produce useful results. Mathematics has supplied much higher predictive power to sciences than nonmathematical thinking has. However, this statement is one about an experimentally observed fact only; it is not a statement about intrinsic superiority.

In the computer field the use of mathematical reasoning for demonstrations of software properties is often said to be impractical. The experience of the industrial world, however, suggests that the lack of mathematical thinking is what is impractical.

THE RELEVANCE OF THE MATHEMATICAL METHOD TO SOFTWARE DEVELOPMENT

How does the mathematical method apply to software problems? How does a software developer distinguish between the use of mathematical results to create a model of software system behavior and the use of the mathematical method to create the structure of the software system?

A software system is a collection of artificial entities that must cooperate to produce the desired behavior. These artificial entities are machine-stored items of information that guide computer mechanisms to manipulate this information. The problem in developing large software systems is to organize these entities in such a way that the resulting system will always behave as desired.

Verification process: state desired behavior of system and its support, then demonstrate that design works

Thus we have to find a verification process for design ideas that incorporates the following features. The desired behavior of the system is precisely expressed in some form that makes sense in the context of system use (the user requirements). This behavior is then compared with the proposed organization (the design idea) of the information stored in the system (the software system). Finally, the software system relies on existing mechanisms (the hardware system) whose behavior is known. Two things must be known for the above process, and they are out of the control of the designer: the given desired behavior of the system and the given behavior of the machine (the hardware system) that is to support the newly designed software systems.

Let us now briefly consider an analogy: a generic mathematical problem. The mathematician's task is to verify (mathematicians use the word prove) that a statement of a particular property of abstract objects is really true in a world where certain predefined axioms are assumed to be true. To do so, the mathematician first states this property in precise language. Then by using the axioms (also expressed in a precise language) and by applying the rules of inference of mathematical logic, the mathematician follows a step-by-step process of verifying the truth of a sequence of statements. This sequence, if it ends up in a statement equivalent to (or more general than) the original statement of the property, proves the truth of the statement. The essence of this process is the form "if-then." That is, any mathematical truth depends on the assumed truth of the premises.

In principle, a similar process can be applied to the design of a piece of software or an entire software system. Thus we state the desired behavior of the system in a precise form. We also express the behavior of the supporting mechanisms precisely. Once these two precise statements are available, we should be able to demonstrate, by using some rules of inference, that the design actually will behave as desired.

The purpose of this discussion has been merely to identify the analogous entities between the mathematical process and a software design process. The thesis of the mathematical theorem corresponds to the statement of the desired behavior of the system together with the proposed solution. The precise description of the behavior of the supporting machine plays the role that axioms play in mathematics. And lastly, relevant inference rules in both processes drive the developer's thinking in the creation of a step-by-step process of verification.

PROGRAM CORRECTNESS

In the late sixties Floyd (1967) proposed a scheme almost like the one sketched above to prove the correctness of programs. A few years later Hoare (1969) precisely identified a few axioms relative to some basic constructs of programming languages together with a few rules of inference that may be used to demonstrate the correctness of some programs.

The basic idea of the Floyd method is to express the purpose of the program in the formalism of first-order predicate calculus. Then all the rules of this formalism are available to prove the basic property that the program behaves according to the specifications. Floyd used the intuitive, informal understanding of the meaning of programming language commands and constructs to build his example proofs. Hoare discovered that these meanings can be expressed as axioms of a logic system, making the program verification process, at least in principle and within the limits of the proposed axioms, intuition-free and fully formal.

The above discussion gives only a general view of the principles needed for the introduction of mathematical rigor into software design. The details are many, and a considerable amount of technicality must be explained before even the primitive ideas of the Floyd-Hoare method can be introduced and exemplified. Thus many of the remaining chapters of this book present the many details of the rigorous methods of correct software design, which are developments of the original ideas of Floyd and Hoare. At this point we only want to remark that the Floyd-Hoare approach is a breakthrough in our view of software.

Before the introduction of these approaches, the only known way to establish what a program was supposed to do was to execute (in a real or mentally simulated environment) the various computations of the program. This execution is done by testing. But the number of these computations is tremendous, and as we will see later in more detail (Chapter 8), there is no easy way to reduce this number to reasonable levels and still obtain the goal of complete verification of the program's behavior.

The potential importance of Floyd's and Hoare's discoveries is that they permit us to consider a program as an intellectual object that can be studied in a purely abstract manner, independently from its execution. So design decisions about programs (and perhaps even about software systems) can be verified without being physically run on a machine. These techniques thus introduce into the software design process the predictive capabilities of a modern engineering design process. For this reason, in the next few chapters we will present the conceptual frame-

Programs are mathematical objects subject to rigorous analysis

work of the Floyd-Hoare method, together with an example, which we will use as the basis for the discussion of rigorous design methods that show promise for effective practical application.

We point out here that modern theoretical computer science uses the mathematical method in many ways and for many problems. The Floyd-Hoare method is but one of the many approaches to applying mathematical thinking in the computer science field, which today has mainly historical importance. We are interested in design for correctness because of its potential impact on both the productivity of the process and the reliability of the product. To this end we need many new concepts, which will be the subject of the next few chapters.

HIGHLIGHTS

Mathematics is the basic force behind the predictive power of modern engineering design. Similarly, the axiomatic method of mathematics is an effective way to attack the problem of verifying program correctness with respect to some specifications. A method that permits this verification was introduced by Floyd and Hoare. Following that pioneering work the mathematical method made headway in the computer science world, producing results of practical applicability that are the subject of most of the remaining chapters of this book. Thus we will see that, at least in principle, it is possible to introduce into the software design process methods and disciplines analogous to the ones used by modern engineering.

REFERENCES

Bronowsky, J. No date. *The common sense of science*. New York: Random House (Vintage Books).

Floyd, R. W. 1967. Assigning meaning to programs. *Proceedings of the Symposium in Applied Mathematics, Providence, R. I.* 19:19–32.

Hoare, C. A. R. 1969. An axiomatic approach to computer programming. *Communications of ACM* 12 (no. 10): 576–580, 583.

Kershner, R. B., and Wilcox, L. R. No date, *The anatomy of mathematics*. New York: Wiley.

CHAPTER FOUR

Fundamentals of Program Specifications

INTRODUCTION

In this chapter we introduce a few basic concepts needed for the verification of the correctness of a program without executing it. To accomplish this verification, we must express the program's meaning in some language different from the programming language. Following Floyd and Hoare, we will use for this purpose statements of the first-order predicate calculus. You do not need to be familiar with the first-order predicate calculus to understand what follows. We will discuss the relevant principles of predicate calculus later. For the purpose of this chapter you need to know only that the program is expressed in two forms. One is the familiar set of commands and control constructs of a programming language (the program text expressing *how*); the second is a series of statements in a mathematical formalism (the specifications expressing *what*). Assuming that one of these two forms is a faithful representation of the programmer's intentions and that we can demonstrate that they express the same meaning, we can conclude the program is correct.

This approach to program verification does not imply any concept of absolute correctness of the program. All it implies is that we can show the consistency of two descriptions of the same problem. This approach is completely in tune with the mathematical approach. In mathematics there is no absolute truth, only statements that are logically consistent with some assumed axioms.

The advantage of expressing a program in the predicate calculus formalism is that its meaning is expressed in a way that is completely independent of any step-by-step execution of a sequence of commands. In other words, the distinction between *what* (the specification) and *how* (the code) requires drastically different approaches in our way of thinking about programs, approaches that are complementary and thus useful in reducing errors (King, 1978).

THE MEANING OF A PROGRAM

If we are asked to describe the meaning of a piece of software, we usually describe the interaction of the program's actions with the user's environment. As an illustration, let's consider an analogy to banking systems. We can desribe a banking system by considering a typical sequence of operations of the bank teller. Suppose you ask for a withdrawal from your checking account. This request is checked as being legitimate; and if your balance permits it, a withdrawal is authorized or denied. Thus the description of the meaning of this banking system function is couched in terms of things known to the user, such as checking account number and withdrawal.

Similarly, the program that might realize this banking function can be explained by presenting a sample execution. That is, its meaning is described in terms of its interaction with the user's environment. Other program functions can be expressed similarly. In the software field the expression of all possible sample executions defines the meaning of the program. Expressing the meaning of a program by describing its possible execution is called an *operational description*.

The expression of the meaning of a program in user's terms is not the only possible way to fully express the meaning of a program. Another way is to describe this meaning in terms of programming language entities. To clarify the difference between these two ways, let us consider the banking example again. In programming language terms the checking account number becomes a string of bits or an integer. It may be that the programmer has identified this integer with a significant name, perhaps with "checking account number." But an interesting point can be made about this integer. In the real world a checking account number is an entity that can be compared with another one to find out whether they are the same. It can also be created or deleted. But it does not make any sense to add or subtract two checking account numbers. In the program representation, however, the checking account number now is an entity that can be operated on as an integer; i.e., it can be added to, multiplied with, or divided by another integer. Thus the programming language defines the meaning of this entity, checking account number, in terms of its being represented by a different entity, namely an integer.

The meaning of a program in terms of programming language entities

Two views of a program: user's and programming language

We now see that the meaning of a program can be expressed in terms of two different worlds. One is the world of the user, and the other is the world of the entities used by the programming language. Both expressions are important, and both are needed independently from the text of the program itself.

In this book the word *requirements* will be associated with the user (or any external) view of the meaning of a program (or system) and the word *specifications* with the expression of the requirements in computer terms.

The program verification technique introduced by Hoare and Floyd involves the specifications, i.e., the meaning of a program in terms of the entities used by the programming language. It does not consider the consistency of the user's view of the program (the requirements).

Usefulness of Formalism for Specifications

How useful is it to describe the program meaning in terms of the same entities used by the programming language? If it is possible to make the obvious mistake of adding two checking account numbers in the programming language formalism, it would be equally possible to express such an erroneous notion in the first-order predicate calculus formalism. What is the advantage of this double description?

The expression of the meaning of a program (its specifications) in the formalism of the predicate calculus, even though it is still in terms of the entities used by the programming language, is effectively independent of any concept of execution of commands in a real or an abstract machine. This concept is important because it allows us, in principle, to express the meaning of a program in such a way that the consistency of several possible implementations can be verified. Also, since the specifications are expressed in a form very different from the execution model implicit in the programming language, a new way of thinking about programs is introduced (King, 1978). One of the most frequent sources of errors in programs is that a portion of logic is missing (Boehm, 1981). The expression of the what of a program in such a different way is an effective way to reduce this source of errors.

Formalism allows verification of several implementations of a problem

We need to be familiar with some additional concepts before we can understand an example of specifications. These concepts will be introduced gradually, beginning with the next chapter.

Review of Concepts

Let us now recapitulate the concepts introduced in this section. We have three different ways to express the meaning of a program. We can describe its interaction with the real world, and when we do so, we use terms of the real world to define objects having certain properties, all assumed to be known. We can also describe the execution of the program on a machine. This description is analogous to (it could be exactly the same as) the description given by the program's text in some programming language. It is couched in terms of objects used by the programming language, and it assumes the knowledge of their properties. Finally, we can express the meaning of a program in a completely execution-independent way. And we can verify the consistency of a program text with this execution-independent description by using the techniques first introduced by Hoare and Floyd.

We still have to find out if there is any possibility of showing consistency between the description of the programming problem in user terms and this execution-independent description. Before we consider this subject, however, an introduction to the technique of program specification with the first-order predicate calculus is needed.

VARIABLES AND STATES OF A PROGRAM

Control and execution are two aspects of a program

If we examine a program written in any programming language, we can identify two aspects. One is the *control* of the execution sequences of commands, as manifested by statements such as **if-then**, **go to**, etc. The second aspect is the *execution* of commands, such as the assignment of the value resulting from the evaluation of $(X + 2) * 5$ to some variable. This latter aspect is manifested by the change of the value of the object identified by some variable name or machine address.

We can therefore imagine that for each program variable there is a *state*, which is its information content at any particular time. This state is identified by the variable value, which can be changed by the execution of a command. This change of state is particularly evident in a machine language, where each memory word content is modified by instructions and the final state usually depends on the state before the execution of the instruction.

Another example of the mechanism for this state change is the familiar assignment statement in most high-order languages. The state of the variable on the left of the assignment sign changes from its value before the assignment to the new value resulting from the evaluation of the expression on the right of the assignment sign. Note that the state of the variable after the assignment may or may not depend on the state before the assignment, depending on whether or not the variable is present in the expression on the right. For example, $X := 5$ puts X in the state $X=5$; $X := X+1$ puts X in a state equal to the one before the assignment plus one.

By considering the set of all the variables of a program (or the set of all possible storages of information in a machine), we can speak about states of a program and even of a complex software system. Let us consider the set of all the possible states a particular variable can assume. For example, any byte can assume values (in bit string terms) between 00000000 and 11111111. We usually have several variables of a certain kind. Hence it is convenient to define the set of potential states of the various kinds of variables in our program once and for all and then to refer to this definition for all the variables we have to manipulate in our program. This concept is very common in all programming languages, where all variables are defined as being of a certain type, such as integer, real, or files.

Let us now consider the set of all variables used by a program. For each variable we can identify a set of possible states, i.e., the set of its potential values. For example, if X is a letter, its values are $a, \ldots, z$. At any particular instant before or after the execution of a command, a set of states of all the program variables can be identified. Similarly, there is a set of states of these variables before and after any execution of the entire program, as can be visualized by considering a simple program made up of only an assignment, as in the example above.

THE STATE SPACE

There is an elegant way to define the states of a program. Let us assume that each program variable is associated with one of the axes in a many-dimensional Cartesian space, which we call the *state space* of the program. A point in this space is a *state* of the program. The *execution* of an elementary command is visualized in this space as a segment joining the state of the program before and after the command execution. Thus if only one variable, say X, is affected by a command, the segment representing its effect is parallel to the X axis.

The state space is the set of all possible values of all the program's variables

A complete computation is represented by a sequence of these segments. At each state (a point in the state space) there must be enough information to permit the command to execute and therefore determine the next state. The control of program execution is thus dependent on program states also. We can also relate the states in input and the states in output that represent a desired computation by defining those subsets in the state space that contain only the desired values.

Let us clarify these ideas with an example.

Example

We want to define a program that divides two numbers X and Y; the result of this division will be another number, say Q. We also know that every division may have a remainder, which we call R. The word *number* used to define X, Y, Q, and R should indicate precisely some set of possible values. For example, let us assume these values to be the four-digit positive integers from 0000 to 9999. We have thus defined a four-dimensional state space.

We also know that we cannot perform a division with a null divisor. Therefore we establish that the acceptable *input states* for the correct execution of our program are the ones for which the relation $Y > 0$ is verified (Y is the divisor). This relation defines a subset of the state space by excluding all the points, such as $X = 25$, $Y = 0$, $Q = 0$, or $R = 0$, for which $Y = 0$. The relation $Y > 0$ is the statement of a *condition* on the state space; it defines the states that are acceptable for the correct execution of the program.

To define what subset of the state space contains the collection of valid results, we use our knowledge about the result of division, i.e., the problem's requirements. We know that the remainder must be positive or null and less than the quotient and that the multiplication of the quotient by the divisor must be equal to the dividend plus the remainder. Or if we do not want to express this requirement in terms of a multiplication, we can say that the sum of the divisor Y with itself taken Q times plus the remainder is equal to the dividend. It is clearly much more precise to use mathematical notation to express the above requirement. We can thus write

$$R \geq 0 \textbf{ and } Q > R \textbf{ and } Q * Y + R = X$$

In this expression the word **and** is to be interpreted as the logical connective and. (We will print such logical connectives in boldface in this book.) We will define the meaning of the logical connectives with precision later. Each of the terms of the above expression can be true or false. We are stating that for a point in the state space to be a correct result of the division program, all three terms of the above expression must be true.

In most cases, to specify the valid *output states* of a program, we must relate the value of variables before the program's execution with the value after the execution. In the example above this requirement is not obvious because X and Y are not changed and the Q and R values depend on the initial values of X and Y. However, if we modify our state space definition by saying that the quotient at program termination will be stored in the same variable X that stores the dividend at the beginning, we can express the relation between the initial state of X (representing the dividend) with the final state of X (now representing the quotient). We can indicate the final values by a primed variable; i.e., X is the value before execution and X′ is the value after execution. If we use this convention, the specification of the division program with the quotient stored in X becomes

$$R \geq 0 \textbf{ and } X' > R \textbf{ and } X' * Y + R = X$$

Note that we must consider a variable value before and after the program execution since a variable represents some form of storage, which is changed by the program.

Conditions

Preconditions define states prior to execution; postconditions at program termination

The expression of the condition on the state space that has to be satisfied for the correct execution of a program is called a *precondition*. The specification of the states at program termination is called a *postcondition*.

We can specify the effect of a program by describing a condition on its state space defining those points that represent the desired outcome at the termination of all computations. The description of this condition is a statement about the variables of the state space, which may be true or false depending on whether or not the point is a state we desire as a result of the program executions. This statement, when expressed according to certain rules we will examine in detail later, is called a *predicate*.

Note that in the above example we have defined no particular *algo-*

rithm, i.e., no controlled sequence of commands, to perform the division. Any correct algorithm must respect the defined conditions.

Terms and Signs and Their Interpretation

Before we close this introduction of program specifications, let us consider the various terms we used in the statements of the pre- and postconditions in the above example. We used terms of the form Q > R containing the relational operator >. We also used signs such as * and +. We are implying that the meaning of these signs is known and that it is sensible for the things represented by the variables of the state space to be related to each other via the operations expressed by these signs. In other words, if we substitute for X one of its possible values, say 4795, we are able to state unequivocally the meaning of 4795 > 0; i.e., we can assert whether or not the statement 4795 > 0 is true.

In the world of computers, however, we do not use numbers but some representation of them in terms of other more computerlike things. Consequently, to correctly represent objects such as numbers in the computer, we have to know and to be able to express which operations are possible on the variables in the state space we used to define the meaning of the program. This consideration suggests the concept of data type.

DATA TYPES

We have seen that we need to associate with every variable in the state space the set of all the potential values this variable can assume. However, when we attempt to define this association precisely, we soon discover that it is not as straightforward as it might appear at first glance.

In the division example we defined the range of values of all variables as the four-digit strings from 0000 to 9999. This definition seems satisfactory. But in a computer each of these four digits may be represented by bytes of 8 bits, or the whole string may be a portion of a word of 32 bits. Our definition of the set of values allows us to say that we are able to recognize the valid representations of these values. This definition is analogous to the definition of whole numbers in mathematics. There are certain names, such as one, two, and three, and some rule for constructing the next number. These numbers may then be represented by sticks, pebbles, enemy warriors, symbols like 1, 2, 3, or even by some configuration of a computer storage.

Operations allow us to recognize different representations of the same concept

What makes it possible to recognize a string of digits (or a bunch of pebbles) as a legitimate representation of a whole number? The answer is the possibility of manipulating these representations in such a way that these manipulations produce the same effect as the operations on whole numbers. We can, in fact, add pebbles to a bunch of pebbles or modify computer storage by some operation, and when we interpret the result in terms of numbers, we recognize it as the result of an addition. It appears that if we want to define, with precision, what type of entity a variable in a state space is, we have to define the operations permitted on its value set. In this way we avoid the description of the value set by a particular representation.

Let us try this approach to definition with our version of the integers. We say that an integer can assume a value from a value set, which we do not have to define by enumerating its elements. Let us call this set G. This set may be imagined as infinite if we consider the integers of the mathematician, or it may be finite, i.e., a particular range of integers. In this latter case we may say that this set contains the two values "overflow" and "underflow," which take care of operations whose result values exceed the range. We also define integers as those things that can be manipulated by four operations, "add," "subtract," "multiply," and "divide." We would also like to use the relational operators "greater than" and " less than." Since we are defining our own integers we are free to stop listing the allowed operations at this point.

The next step is to examine each of the above operations a little closer. We know that we can add two integers and that we get a new one as a result of this operation. We indicate this operation by writing

$$\text{add:} \quad G \times G \rightarrow G$$

The above statement says that the operation "add" puts every possible pair of elements of G (the values of our integer) into one-to-one correspondence with one element of G. The term G $\times$ G indicates the Cartesian product of G with itself, i.e., the set of all the pairs that can possibly be constructed with elements of G. According to this definition, "add" will put the pair (2, 5), for example, which is an element of the set G $\times$ G, into correspondence with 7, which is an element of the set G. Or assuming G contains only the range (0, 9999), the pair (7527, 8125) in G $\times$ G will correspond to the value of G called "overflow."

Similar statements can be written for "multiply," "subtract," and "divide." However, if we try to express "greater than," we have to write

$$\text{greater than:} \quad G \times G \rightarrow \{\text{true, false}\}$$

In this case each pair of values corresponds to one of the two values of the set containing only (true, false).

This example tells us that to define operations on data, which can assume values from some predefined set, we may need to introduce another set of values. In the above example, to define our integers, we needed to introduce {true, false}, namely, the set of the Boolean values.

A data type is a set of values and operations defined on them

From this simple example we may define a *data type* as a set of values together with all the operations that put values of these sets in correspondence. Once data types are thus defined, the state space of a program (or of a software system) can be described by enumerating the variable names and specifying the data type for each variable. This approach is used by programming languages; i.e., when a variable is declared to be a certain type, it can be operated on only by a limited set of operations. Similarly, a repertoire of hardware machine instructions can be defined by the definition of its data types. For example, memory words might be considered as a data type, with their set of possible bit configurations and the instructions allowed on them.

USER-VISIBLE FUNCTIONALITIES AS DATA TYPES

If the concept of data type were limited to the examples above, it would be useful only for clarification of some issues of programming languages and computer architecture. However, the applicability of this concept covers a much wider ground. In fact, a data type can also be used for the definition of a user's interface with a software system in terms of user-related entities.

Let us consider as an example a terminal operating in connection with an airline reservation system. The clerk at this terminal can enter a certain number of commands that affect the information stored inside the system and produce some response at the terminal. To a large extent, the commands at the terminal can be entered in any order, even though probably only a few sequences produce sensible responses. We can now identify the elements of a data type. Each command entered by the airline clerk is a data type operation. Its effect on the system is to put into correspondence values from various information repositories (sets of values), such as flight numbers, available seat numbers, and the display on the terminal. Note that this information is defined in terms of the user's application. Just as the data type operations in a programming language create the desired changes of states through a specific flow of control via the control constructs of the program, the operations on a system terminal can be used in appropriate sequences for some particular purpose, which can be regarded as the desired system state changes as seen by the user.

To recognize that the user's view of a software system is a data type is an important clarification about the nature of software systems. It is indeed cumbersome to describe what a software system is in terms of a program. We know the system is made up by programs, but we cannot easily relate the user's view of a software system with any particular prescription of a flow of control, which is the essence of all programs. As we noted above, the proper use of the system in the application world requires certain sequences of operations. These sequences are not specified explicitly by any program in the system but are conditions used for the correct arrangement of the programs in the system. Also, they are not the only sequences possible, and the system has to be designed to react to any sequence of use.

A system is a collection of mechanisms that realize one (or more) data type(s)

The introduction of data types allows us to separate the concept of software system from the idea of computer program. A computer program can be defined as the prescription for the flow of control of operations in a certain state space that satisfies some specifications. A system is a collection of mechanisms (which may be programs) realizing one (or more) data type. A design technique based on this definition is presented in Chapter 11 and following chapters.

THE MEANING OF DATA TYPE OPERATIONS

We introduced the concept of data type by considering the approach used by mathematicians to define objects such as whole numbers. It is interesting to extend the analogy and to see if we can gain some indication about how the "meaning" of the data type operations can be expressed. We used the word *meaning* here in the same sense that we used it when we introduced the concept of pre- and postconditions of a program.

In mathematics there are several ways to express the meaning of the operation on mathematical objects such as whole numbers. Thus the operations of addition or subtraction can be defined (1) by enumerating their results, (2) by defining their effect in terms of other operations, or (3) by describing a procedure to perform the operation. If we examine these three techniques, we can gain some insight into the possibility of using similar techniques for defining the meaning of data type operations.

Definition by Enumeration

To define the operations on numbers by enumeration is merely to enumerate the elements of the sets of values put into correspondence by the operations. If, for example, the operation

$$\text{multiply:} \quad G \times G \rightarrow G$$

Enumeration is one type of definition

is defined by tables, we have the familiar multiplication tables. The elements of the set G × G are chosen as the two entries into the table, and the result is an element of G. Because G is (for the mathematician) an infinite set, it would be impractical to list all the results. Therefore the mathematician limits the tables to the first ten numbers and supplies an algorithm to construct the results for other numbers. Actually, the tables define a different operation, say digit multiply:

$$\text{digit multiply:} \quad G^{10} \times G^{10} \rightarrow G^{100}$$

where G^{10} is the set {0, 1, 2, . . . , 9} and G^{100} is the set {0, 1, 2, . . . , 99}.

Definition by tables defines states in the state space by their enumeration. If we are able to limit the size of the set of the values of the data type, we can define the meaning of a data type in this way. An example is the data type "bit," which has a set of two values only, which can be operated on by **and**, **or**, and **not** operations, and whose results are usually described by tables.

Definition by Operations

The method of defining the operations by relating one operation to another uses the properties of some operation to produce a result related to results of another operation. For example, suppose one operation result is the inverse of another one; this fact may be used to undo what another operation did. We know that if we add a to b and then subtract b from the result, we obtain a again. We can express this operation in the form of an equation:

Equations are another type of definition

$$(a + b) - b = a$$

By writing down an appropriate set of these equations, we may be able to define the meaning of the operations. An extension of this idea (put in a precise mathematical form) is the basis of a technique used for the specification of the meaning of data types. It is called the *technique of algebraic specifications of data types* and was introduced by Guttag (1976) and Gouguen et al. (1975).

Definition by Procedures

The third technique for expressing the meaning of operations on numbers is to assume the existence of procedures that perform the operations. This technique is manifest in the currently well-entrenched habit of describing a software system by describing the programs that implement it.

The description of these programs, however, can be done in two ways. One description supplies the flow of control of the possible execution sequences of the operations of the hardware machine (or programming language) data types. The second description supplies the pre- and postconditions defining the admissible states in the state space made up of the variables used by the programs. In the first description we express one of the many possible implementations (how), while in the second we express the conditions to be respected by every possible implementation (what). These two ways correspond to the familiar description of procedures in a programming language and to the specifications of pre- and postconditions as outlined above.

The description of a procedure to perform the operation is a third form of definition

Note that in both cases we need to know the meaning of the data types (operations and values) used by the programs. That is, we have to accept that the meaning of the data types used by the programs is primitively known (e.g., by enumeration) or can be described in terms of more primitive types. In fact, we can always explain these types by using bits and bit operations.

HIGHLIGHTS

In this chapter we have introduced a few concepts that represent, from a different point of view, entities already familiar to the computer professional. The purpose of introducing these concepts in this form is to create a basis for an appropriate formalism in the process of system design.

A design discipline to adequately support the creation of software needs the use of formalism. We have indicated that this formalism may be parallel to the process of creating mathematical results. The work of Hoare and Floyd gives us an existing mathematical theory to precisely define the specifications of a program and to verify the consistency of a program text with its specifications. We have also indicated that the meaning of programming language constructs can be supplied as axioms to be used within the formalism.

The basic concept presented in this chapter is the state space, the collection of all possible values the program's variables can assume. In this space the meaning of a program can be expressed by two conditions defining the states required at the inception and the states desired at the conclusion of all computations. These conditions are, respectively, the pre- and postconditions of a program.

The idea of state space, in turn, required the definition of data types, which are fundamental entities for software system. We can also define the meaning of a system in terms of real-world entities by using appropriate data types. In addition, data types turned out to be useful in defining a different view of software systems. In this view a software system is an entity made up of programs but is not identified with them.

So far we have defined concepts mostly in English, with all the possible imprecision of human languages. In the rest of the book the language will become more symbolic, similar to the language of mathematics. Symbolism allows us to be brief and precise. All the concepts expressed thus far could have been described in less space and with more precision by using mathematical language.

Symbolism is an adjunct of formalism. And as we have said before, formalism allows us to rigorously verify properties of abstract entities. Once formalism is acquired, its abstract entities can become part of the informal language used for communication among designers, with considerable improvement in clarity and conciseness.

This last point is very important. Currently, communication among designers is not based on any understanding of the nature of abstract entities. In fact, most language used for design communication refers to implementation entities, which are not usually suitable for intellectual treatment. Thus demonstration of correctness must be deferred until the actual code is written and tested. However, formalism allows correctness to be verified in the design stage. The next three chapters consider the design of programs through the use of formalism.

REFERENCES

Boehm, B. W. 1981. *Software engineering economics*. Englewood Cliffs, N.J.: Prentice-Hall.

Gougen, J. A.; Thatcher, J. W.; Wagner, E. G.; and Wright, J. B. 1975. Abstract data types as initial algebras and correctness of data representations. In

Proceedings of the Conference on Computer Graphics, Pattern Recognition and Data Structures, pp. 89–93.

Guttag, J. V. 1976. Abstract data types and the development of data structures. *SIGPLAN Notices* 8 (no. 2):72–73.

King, J. 1978. Remark at the closing discussion of the IFIP Conference on Constructing Quality Software, Novosibirsk, USSR. In *Constructing Quality Software*, edited by P. G. Hibbard and S. A. Schuman. North Holland Publishing.

CHAPTER FIVE

The Programming Problem

INTRODUCTION

A software system is made up of programs. A considerable amount of research activity in the past decade has been devoted to studying the programming process. In this chapter we begin the presentation of some results of these research activities. We include here an example of a proof using Floyd's method.

We limit our discussion to small programs, typically the ones written and/or modified by only one person. These programs constitute the building blocks (modules) or larger programs and systems.

Since these programs are used as building blocks of large systems, their specifications may be expressed in terms of software-related entities such as computer words and some programming language's integers (which are not exactly the same as the mathematician's integers). We are not considering here the requirements for programming problems expressed in user terms. In other words, we assume in this chapter that the transformation of the real-world phenomena in computer terms has already been done.

Even though considerable differences exist between the design techniques for small and large programs, the underlying principles are essentially the same. In both cases we must clarify the concept of software specifications as separate entities from the executable code, and we must understand how to define the effect of programming language commands. These ideas are best illustrated first in the case of small programs.

MENTAL PROCESSES USED BY PROGRAMMERS

The creation of code is not entirely subconscious. Most programmers use consciously expressed arguments to convince themselves of the correctness of their decisions. However, these arguments are always informal and may be revealed as incorrect by later testing or by the system's use. Nevertheless, programmers do create correct programs, and quite often they do so by using a trial-and-error process and test runs. Thus there must be some precise thinking patterns used by programmers, even if in a subconscious manner.

The three processes are enumeration, mathematical induction, and abstraction

According to Dijkstra (in Dahl et al., 1972), programmers may use three mental tools in program design: enumeration, mathematical induction, and abstraction. In this chapter we will discuss only enumeration and mathematical induction. Abstraction in all its useful forms is the subject of most of the following chapters.

ENUMERATIVE THINKING

The mental tool of *enumeration* is the dominant tool used by programmers today. We use enumerative thinking any time we want to instruct ourselves or others about the execution of a series of activities. Consider, for example, the instructions for preparing a cake by using a cake mix. The instructions are actually the enumeration of the tasks that must be executed, one after the other; the cook is presumed to know how to perform these elementary tasks. A computer program may also be thought of as the enumeration of tasks (namely, instructions from its instruction repertoire) that we assume the computer knows how to execute.

Program Design with Enumeration

Let us go through an example of a program design emphasizing (perhaps even exaggerating) the use of enumeration. We will consider the problem of writing a program to search a list of numbers from left to right to determine whether or not a given number is in the list. This statement can be considered as the requirements for the program we are about to design.

At this point some programmers will give names to the entities identified from the requirement statement and then proceed to write a sequence of computer instructions (programming language statements) realizing the specified task. Others might skip the naming of the entities and begin by creating the instruction sequence; they would name the entities during the creation of the code when the need arose. In addition, a few problems of interpretation of the requirements might be explicitly put forth by some programmers, such as the interpretation of the meaning of left to right or what is intended by the word *numbers*.

Now assuming that the list of numbers is representable in computer terms as an array of integers whose indices range from 1 to 100, the application of the mental process of enumeration might follow these lines:

Enumeration is a step-by-step listing of the program's actions

- Load the index I (I is the name chosen for the index) with the lowest value (1).
- Compare L(I) (at this point a name for the list must be chosen; we chose L) with X (the given number) and see if they are equal.
- If they are, then print a message saying a match has been found.

- If there is no match, then increase I and continue to check whether the next element of A is equal to X.
- Proceed in this way until the whole array is examined.

Some programmers would consider the above reasoning as the design specifications. They may even use this explanation of the mental process as a comment within the program text.

Assuming the programmer is using FORTRAN, a program like the following one may result:

```
DIMENSION A(100)
I = 1
1 IF (X. EQ. L (I)) GO TO 3
I = I + 1
IF (I. LE. 100) GO TO 1
PRINT 2
STOP
3 PRINT 5, I
STOP
2 FORMAT (7H NO MATCH)
5 FORMAT (I2)
```

Remarks

We note two things about this program. First, some decisions were probably made at the very moment the code was written. For example, the message NO MATCH may have been decided at the moment the FORMAT statement labeled 2 was written. This decision is one made by the programmer and not discussed with the specifier. While this decision may appear to be unimportant (and certainly it is in this case), it illustrates the origin of some of the problems of lack of standardization for the messages exchanged by a large system with its environment.

A second point to note is that in some way the programmer decided to make the list L of a fixed length of 100. It is reasonable to assume that this decision was discussed by the specifier and the programmer, but it is also reasonable to assume that the rationale for this decision was not documented in any way. The subsequent program works only if the array L is exactly of 100 elements, and even though this decision may be perfectly satisfactory at design time, it may be unsatisfactory for subsequent specification changes. A good programmer would not have written that code.

All the above observations are of a general nature and refer to the interplay between specifications and code. For purposes of illustrating the use of enumeration as a mental tool for programming, it is also interesting to note the close correspondence between the structure of the enumerative thinking and the program as written in FORTRAN. But we do not know whether the structure of the thinking process is a consequence of the structure of the control constructs (IF, GO TO, etc.) of the programming language, or vice versa.

SHORTCOMINGS OF ENUMERATION

Even for a program of the size and simplicity as the one shown above, we may detect several limitations of enumerative thinking and the use of programming language constructs. For instance, it is possible that the decision of making the list of constant length may have been influenced by the habit of enumerative thinking. If we are to design this program for a list of variable length, our enumerative thinking becomes quite complicated.

The human mind operates well when enumerating a sequence of actions of finite and a priori known length. But when required to enumerate actions that can be repeated several times and that depend on other actions, the human mind encounters difficulties. For example, using enumerative reasoning to create the program shown above with a variable list size, say, of length N, we would substitute, in both reasoning and code, the symbol N for the value 100. But the resulting program would not work for a list of length zero (N = 0). In this case the modified program might continue to test whatever the compiler had put in memory in the area reserved for L against X. And it may happen that this area contains a number (or a representation) that can be considered equal to X, and thus the program may end up by giving the value of the location where this erroneous match occurred, or the program may not terminate.

An even more limiting drawback of enumerative thinking is the rapidly exploding complexity of the enumeration sequences with the size of the program. In general, we need a sequence of action for all possible program execution, i.e., a sequence for each possible state verifying the program's precondition. We intuitively feel that these sequences can be grouped, i.e., that we can define a typical sequence for properly chosen subsets of input states. But unfortunately, we do not know how to do this grouping in any reliable or rational manner except by following the control flow of the program. This grouping, however, does not support reliable thinking, because we may examine (or test) all paths of a program without detecting all potential errors. This subject is discussed in further detail in Chapter 8.

Enumerations of actions are grouped to make programs in a subconscious way

Another example of the limitation of enumerative thinking is the enumeration of the computations executed in a loop. In many practical cases the number of loop iterations depends on data values generated during loop execution. The enumeration of all computation sequences would thus be impossible. However, programmers do group these sequences in some way when they conceive a program, and often they construct correct loops. Nevertheless, this mental process is intrinsically unreliable because it is based on some inexplicable power of the human mind.

Therefore we conclude that we should rely on enumeration for short, straight-line sequences only. And since enumeration is a mental simulation of computer runs, this basic limitation applies to all design methods that rely on any form of code execution for verification.

The interpretation of enumerative thinking in terms of states in the program state space may help to illustrate the inadequacy of enumeration as a design tool. Enumeration, as used by most programmers, is the mental arrangement of a list of actions, i.e., computer commands. Each of these actions, however, produces an outcome—namely, a state—that depends not only on the nature of the action but on the state existing before the action is performed. These states can be grouped in sets, which are all correctly transformed by a sequence of commands. Consequently, if we enumerate states, we may avoid the uncertainties we have pointed out above.

As an example of enumeration of states, consider the sequence

```
(0 ≤ X ≤ 100)
 X := X + 1;
(0 < X ≤ 101)
 Y := X / 2
(0 ≤ Y ≤ 50)
```

where the expressions in parentheses indicate the possible values of the variables X and Y. If these expressions are a correct indication of our intentions, then the program's steps

X := X + 1   and   Y:= X/2

are correctly performing the desired transformations of states.

The mere enumeration of actions X := X + 1 and Y := X/2 does not supply any information about the purpose of these actions. Enumeration applied to states, on the other hand, is an effective way to design some programs in a reliable manner. But we still have to determine in which cases and with which additional techniques enumeration of states can be used for reliable program design.

MATHEMATICAL INDUCTION

The second mental tool indicated by Dijkstra as essential to programming is mathematical induction. Its application is very useful for the design of program loops. However, mathematical induction is not as natural a mental process as enumeration.

Definition of the Induction Principle

Let us review what *mathematical induction* is. In general, the induction principle may be defined as follows:

1. The basis for induction is to establish that a certain element p of a set S satisfies a relation R.
2. The induction step is to show that if a generic element y of S satisfies R, so does $T(y)$, where T is some sort of transformation in which another element of S satisfies R.

3. If the basis and the induction step are proved, then any element derived from p by any number of applications of T also satisfies R.

Mathematical induction is a loop verification tool

The induction principle is the foundation of the verification method proposed by Floyd (1967). It is also the foundation of the constructive approach for the design of loop programs proposed by Dijkstra (1976), which we will describe in detail in the next two chapters. Its conceptual importance is that as a thinking pattern, it does not require the mental execution of a sequence of command, therefore permitting the design and verification of loops that may be executed any number of times, depending on the particular values of data. Once mathematical induction is applied to states described by the relation R of the definition above, it is an effective mental tool for the design of sequences of iterations in a general and execution-independent manner.

Example of Program Design by Use of Induction

We will illustrate how the thinking pattern of mathematical induction can be applied informally to the problem of list searching treated above. To apply induction, we have to identify a set of objects for which we want to prove a relevant property of states. The list L is clearly a set of this kind. The property we must prove is that the program terminates in a state for which a portion of the list between the leftmost element and the one that precedes an element for which X = L(I) satisfies the property X ≠ L(I). This portion may be the whole list, in which case the element equal to X does not exist. Clearly, this property is satisfied by an empty list. We can use this fact as the induction basis.

Now let us consider the transformation

```
I := I + 1
```

(we use the assignment operator := to indicate the substitution of the current value of I with its next in the sequence of integers). If we assume that a portion of the list from the induction basis up to the current element has been constructed by repeated applications of I := I + 1, and that at each transformation the property X ≠ L(I) is verified, then the fact that now L(I) ≠ X is also verified proves that the portion of the list for which the desired property is verified spans through the element indexed by I + 1.

If this reasoning extends to the whole list, we terminate with a no-match situation. Otherwise, the index bounding the portion of the list for which X ≠ L(I) is the index locating the element of L matching X.

Now we can write the following program text:

```
I := 1;
while I ≤ N and X ≠ L(I) do I := I + 1 od
```

Note that we used an Algollike language to emphasize that the use of induction as a thinking pattern is encouraged by control constructs such as **while do**.

We have presented a very informal way to use mathematical induction. The most important consideration is the explicit definition of a property that must apply to any number of elements of L. We have actually defined the states of L before the execution of I := I + 1 as those that verify the properties X ≠ L(I) for all elements L(J), with J defined as 1 ≤ J ≤ I. These states can be specified in a semiformal way by writing

for all J [if 1 ≤ J ≤I then X ≠ L (J)]

This statement describes the program states before the execution of I := I + 1 by a relation that will only be verified by the correct program states.

We can express the specifications of this program as a postcondition written in a language close to the language of predicate calculus:

for all J [if 1 ≤ J < I then [X ≠ L(J) and I ≤ N]] and X = L(I)
or
for all I [if 1 ≤ I ≤ N then X ≠ L (I)]

We are stating the fact that the program may terminate in what are two different categories of states for L. In one of these categories an index I in the range 1 ≤ I ≤ N identifies L(I) = X, and for all the elements of L indexed by a J in the range 1 ≤ J < I, the property X ≠ L(J) is verified. Thus we are sure that there is no element on the left of I matching X. The second category of states for L says that for all indices I in the range 1 ≤ I ≤ N the property X ≠ L(I) is verified. Actually, this second case is identical to the first case when I is equal to N + 1.

These two categories are important from the external user's point of view. In fact, the user may ask for different output messages to identify these states at program termination. This example illustrates that we may show a simple correspondence between the requirements and the specifications we have written if we add to the above expression appropriate terms for identifying the output message content. The program text would have to be augmented accordingly.

Program design through the explicit identification of properties of states

The point we want to make here is that by using a mental pattern that does not rely on the creation of a sequence of actions, we have identified a unifying concept for program design—namely, the verification of the property X ≠ L(I) for a portion of L that may very well be an empty list or the whole list. The presentation of specifications in a precise language such as the predicate calculus, which does not specify an execution sequence but only the required states, may help programmers recognize unifying properties of this sort. Note also that the emphasis of thinking has shifted from consideration of control sequences to consideration of the structure of manipulated data.

We now have at our disposal some mental patterns typical of mathematics. One is the use of the induction principle. Another is the consideration of a sequence, independent of its size (in this case the list L containing zero or more elements), as an entity that does not need to be analyzed element by element in order to establish properties about it. Also, we do not need to introduce numerical examples to make our point. And finally, we have the use of the formalism of predicate calculus (as yet not fully introduced), which permits precision without verbosity.

AN EXAMPLE OF PROGRAM PROOF: FLOYD'S APPROACH

At this point let us see how the program we have designed can be proven correct with respect to its specifications written in the language of predicate calculus. We will use the Floyd method, because we have not yet discussed how the meaning of a programming language can be precisely defined (which is required in the Hoare method). The Floyd approach relies on the intuitive understanding of the meaning of the programming language constructs. Note that the previous discussion about mathematical induction and enumeration as mental patterns for program design also used an intuitive understanding of the meaning of the programming language constructs.

Floyd's proof: Does the program text execute the state transformations?

Floyd's method requires the programmer to define the predicates describing the correct states when the flow of control reaches certain points of the program. Floyd calls these predicates *assertions*. The *proof* consists in determining whether the text of the program between two assertions actually executes the state transformation specified by the assertions.

The Program

As an example, let us consider the search program presented previously (written now in FORTRAN and using N as the upper limit). The statements below labeled A1, A2, A3, and A4 are assertions specifying intermediate states of the program. The assertion

A3 **OR** A4

is the program postcondition. If we can show that the program terminates in a state satisfying either condition (or both), we will have shown that the program is correct with respect to this postcondition. The assertion

A 1: N ⩾ 1

is the precondition needed to avoid the possible erroneous executions indicated above for an empty array L. The program text augmented with assertions (we omit the STOP, DIMENSION, and FORMAT statements) is as follows:

A1: N ⩾ 1

A2: 1 ⩽ I ⩽ N **and** F(I − 1)

```
1 IF (X. EQ. L(I)) GO TO 3
  I = I + 1
  IF (I. LE. N) GO TO 1
  PRINT 2
```

A3: F(N)

```
3 PRINT 5, I
```

A4: F(I − 1) **and** X = L(I)

For brevity we have used F(I) to indicate the property that no element of L up to and including L(I) is equal to X. Property F(I) could have been written in full as

for all J [**if** $1 \leq J \leq I$ **then** $X \neq L(I)$]

It is evident that F(0) is always verified (an empty list does not contain any element equal to X).

The Proof

The application of mathematical induction for the proof is to show the correctness of the loop. The entire proof is presented here to illustrate the Floyd technique of program proving.

The program is broken down into pieces, each corresponding to a sequence of states, initiating in a state defined by an assertion and terminating in a state defined by another assertion. The proof involves showing that the commands in each of the pieces realize a correct sequence of states, starting and ending with the given assertions.

We can write the following pieces of program text together with the names of the assertions defining the desired states before and after their execution:

```
1 A1 {I = 1} A2
2 A2 {X = A(I)} A4
3 A2 {X ≠ A(I); I = I + 1; I ≤ N} A2
4 A2 {X ≠ A(I); I = I + 1; I > N} A3
```

We use the semicolon (;) symbol to indicate the sequencing of the actions listed within the braces ({ }).

Line 1 is the portion of the program transforming states defined by A1 into A2. Line 2 is the portion of the program corresponding to the case for which X = A(I) in the statement

```
IF (X. EQ. A(I)) GO TO 3
```

ending up at the point labeled 3 with assertion A4. Lines 3 and 4 correspond, respectively, to a loop iteration ending with the need for another iteration or with the end of the array L.

Each line can now be proven separately.

Line 1:

if $N \geq 1$ **and** $I = 1$ **then** $1 \leq I \leq N$ **and** $F(I - 1)$

For I = 1, I − 1 = 0; therefore F(I − 1) = F(0), which is true by definition. Also, because N ⩾ 1 and I = 1, 1 ⩽ I ⩽ N is verified.

Line 2:

if 1 ⩽ I ⩽ N **and** F(I − 1) **and** X = L(I)
then F(I − 1) **and** X = L(I)

which is obviously true.

Line 3:

if (1 ⩽ I ⩽ N **and** F(I − 1) **and** X ≠ L(I) **and**
I′ = I + 1 **and** I′ ⩽ N) **then** 1 ⩽ I′ ⩽ N **and** F(I′ − 1)

(Recall that I′ is the value of I after the assignment I = I + 1.) By substitution of I + 1 into I′, we have

if 1 ⩽ I ⩽ N **and** F(I − 1) **and** X ≠ L(I) **and** I + 1 ⩽ N
then 1 ⩽ I + 1 ⩽ N **and** F(I)

By definition, F(I) is equivalent to [F(I − 1) **and** X ≠ L(I)]. Also 1 ⩽ I ⩽ N **and** I + 1 ⩽ N verifies 1 ⩽ I + 1 ⩽ N.

Line 4:

if (1 ⩽ I ⩽ N **and** F(I − 1) **and** X ≠ A(I) **and** I′ = I + 1 **and** I′ > N) **then** F(N)

Substituting I + 1 for I′, we obtain

if (1 ⩽ I ⩽ N **and** F(I − 1) **and** X ≠ A(I) **and** I + 1 > N) **then** F(N)

Because 1 ⩽ I ⩽ N **and** I + 1 > N, we have I = N.

Thus by the definition of F(I) and by replacing I with N, we have

F(N − 1) **and** X ≠ A(N)

which is equivalent to F(N).

Remarks About the Proof

It is useful to note a few points in the proof (verification) process shown above. First, we note that the form of each line verification is that of a logical implication represented by statements of the form

if P then Q

This form is the classical form of a mathematical theorem, and what we have actually done is to produce informal proofs for one theorem per line. However, we have not explicitly stated some axioms we used. For example, we have split the IF statements in the two possible outcomes because we know informally that this is the meaning of a FORTRAN IF. In fact, the symbols we have written in braces represent an interpretation of the program based on our knowledge of FORTRAN, which may be imprecise.

Another point is that we have shown the program to satisfy the specifications if it terminates. But a wrong loop can cause the program to run forever, and we have not shown that this program terminates. Therefore we can state only that for all cases (input states satisfying the precondition) for which the program terminates, the program will terminate in a state satisfying the postcondition. This type of verification is usually called *proof of partial correctness*. It is also possible to verify a program for so-called *total correctness*. In that case we show that the program, for all states satisfying the precondition, terminates in a state satisfying the postcondition.

We are not arguing here about the practical applicability and usefulness of the verification process shown in the example. We are not even asserting that by this process we are mathematically sure a program will behave as desired when used in practice. The point of this example is simply that we have reduced a program to an intellectual object that can be subject to analysis independent of its execution. This example should be compared with the enumeration of action steps, which relies on the execution of the program for its verification. Since we are searching for possible ways to construct mental models that can be advantageously used by the software designer to verify design ideas before their implementation, this proof technique is a significant step toward that objective. The pattern of mathematical induction is thus the first mental tool that has shown a possibility of avoiding the exploding complexity of enumerative thinking, as evidenced by the fact that we were able to treat the correctness of loops without being confused by the examination of all possible iterations.

Program proving is more important for the new view of the programming process than for its application

Finally, we note that the proof has been split into sequences of statements and assertions that follow the program's flow of control. However, no specific values of the program's variables are used for the verification. The reasoning is quite general and applies to all possible values of the variables. Thus an example of a computation for one of the program pieces does not guarantee the correctness of that piece for all potential input states.

HIGHLIGHTS

Programs are currently conceived by using a mental pattern (enumeration) that matches the technique used for their verification (testing by executing the code). However, the introduction of the concept of states permits us to use enumeration of states and mathematical induction for program design, independent of any execution consideration.

The use of mathematical induction permits us to design loop programs in an execution-independent way. This idea is the basis of Floyd's proof process, which verifies the consistency of a program with its specifications. An example of Floyd's style of proof was presented in this chapter.

REFERENCES

O.J. Dahl, E.W. Dijkstra, C.A.R. Hoare. 1972. *Structural programming.* London and New York: Academic Press.

Floyd, R. W. 1967. Assigning meaning to programs. *Proceedings of the Symposium in Applied Mathematics, Providence, R.I.* 19:19–32.

CHAPTER SIX

Programming Language Constructs

INTRODUCTION

In the preceding chapters we discussed the need to express a program's meaning independently from the program text. We have also said that the meaning of a program can be expressed by using sentences of the predicate calculus. Before we proceed, we must make these concepts precise. So in this chapter we are going to discuss two languages that allow us to specify what a program is supposed to do. One is the language of predicate calculus, and the second is a programming language called guarded commands.

THE LANGUAGE OF PROGRAM SPECIFICATION

Any language is based on three elements (Carnap, 1939). One is *pragmatics,* i.e., the area of its use. The second element is *syntax,* i.e., the set of rules that allow us to decide whether or not a sentence of the language is, in fact, a sentence of the language. Finally, the third element is *semantics,* i.e., the interpretation of sentences in terms of things and actions in the language's pragmatics.

Three elements of language: pragmatics, syntax, semantics

We are concerned here with a language for the specification of the effect of program executions. The pragmatics of this language is the set of concepts we discussed when we introduced the idea of state space. What we need now are syntax rules and semantics of the language that have plausible interpretation in terms of the state space.

Let us assume it is possible to write a sentence S in some precisely defined syntax that contains the names of some (or all) of the variables of a program. Suppose also that once the names of these variables are substituted by their values as given at a precise point of the state space, there is a unique way to interpret S as true or false. If we can make this interpretation, we have a way to specify subsets of states in the state space (which represents the pragmatics we are concerned with). Note that this procedure is exactly what we have done in all the program specification examples we presented earlier. What we do not have yet is a syntax and useful rules for the interpretation of these sentences.

Let us define the most elementary entity in our language, the term. A *term* is a sentence containing only symbols indicating variables of the state space, symbols indicating specific values of these variables (constants), and symbols of operations that are valid for the types of the variables. All of these symbols are arranged in such a way that it is possible to interpret a term as being true or false for any point of the state space. For example, for a three-dimensional state space with variables X, Y, and Z, where X, Y, and Z are integers in some appropriate range and the symbols $\leqslant$, $\geqslant$, $+$, $-$, and PRIME ( ) indicate legitimate operations on integers, the following sentences are terms:

$$X \geqslant Y \qquad \text{PRIME (X)} \qquad X + Z \geqslant Y$$

To give an interpretation to the meaning of the terms (such as the ones shown here as examples), we need only evaluate them for all points in the state space. For example, for the point X = 5, Y = 40, and Z = 18, the first and the last sentences are false and the second one is true, according to the usual interpretation of the symbols used.

Terms can be combined by using the logic connectives **and**, **or**, **not**, $\Rightarrow$ (the implication symbol, which can be read "implies" and can be interpreted as a way to express the familiar statement "if this, then that," or "this implies that"), and $\Leftrightarrow$ (the equivalence symbol, which can be read "if and only if") to form predicate expressions. Note that we print the words **and**, **or**, and **not** in boldface to indicate that they are logical connectives, which do not necessarily have the same interpretation as that in common English usage. The truth value of a predicate expression is established by application of the following rules given in tabular form, where P and Q indicate terms or predicate expressions, and t and f indicate true and false, respectively:

P	t	t	f	f
Q	t	f	t	f
P and *Q*	t	f	f	f
P or *Q*	t	t	t	f
$P \Rightarrow Q$	t	f	t	t
$P \Leftrightarrow Q$	t	f	f	t
not *P*	f	f	t	t

For example, $X > 0$ **and** $Y = 5$ evaluates as true only for Y equal to 5 and X nonzero. As another example, $X > 0 \Rightarrow Y = X$ is true if either $X > 0$ and $Y = X$ or $X \leqslant 0$ and Y is either equal to or different from X.

Formulas containing logic connectives are usually not evaluated in any particular order. That is, the truth value of P **and** Q can be established by evaluating either P or Q first, and the result is the same. However, there are situations for the connective **and** for which it is useful to establish an order. Typical is the case where the variables of Q may have no defined value if *P* is false. In those cases, to avoid considering undefined values, we use the symbol **cand** (conditional **and**) to indicate that the term following the connective should not be evaluated when the term preceding it is false.

It is useful to be able to state properties valid for all the possible values a variable can assume. To do so, we use the universal quantifier **for all**, followed by the names of the variable (or variables) we want to consider. The quantifier precedes the expression containing the quantified variables delimited by square brackets. For example:

Quantifiers help us state properties

for all X [X ⩾ 0 **and** X > Y]

The truth of this expression can be evaluated only by considering all the possible values of X. It will be true only if the expression in brackets is true for all values of X.

Another quantifier symbol is the existential quantifier **for some**, and it states that for at least one value of the quantified variable, the quantified expression is true.

A sentence constructed according to the above rules is a *predicate*.

PREDICATE EXPRESSION OF PROGRAM SPECIFICATIONS

Let us now proceed to the interpretation of these predicates in terms of a state space. Each predicate defines a subset of the state space for which it is true. The precondition of a program is a predicate defining the subset of states accepted as legitimate input. We have seen that often the postcondition of a program requires us to relate, for some variables, the values in input to the values in output. In this case a predicate using variable symbols such as X or X′ defines a subset of the Cartesian product of the state space with itself (i.e., the set of all the possible pairs constructed by associating to each point of the state space all points of the same state space).

The constant predicate T, which is true everywhere, defines all the possible states of the state space. The constant predicate F, which is false everywhere, defines no state in the state space. In other words, since the state space represents the whole universe of the objects that can be manipulated by the program, T defines this whole universe, and F is the empty set. If a program is to be specified with a precondition accepting any state in the state space, T is clearly the predicate that correctly represents this condition.

Predicates define subsets of the state space

There is a correspondence between conditions on the state space expressed by predicates and the set of states. For example, if the predicate p defines the set of states P and the predicate q defines the set of states Q, the conjunction of p with q, p **and** q, defines the states in the set intersection of P with Q. Analogously, p **or** q defines the union of P and Q; p ⇒ q defines the fact that P is included in Q, and **not** p defines the complement of P, i.e., the set of all the points of the state space that are not elements of P.

We can use this correspondence between predicate definition and the set of states as an aid in writing the program specifications, since set theory is usually a more familiar formalism than predicate calculus. Following Hoare (1969), we use the expression

$$p\{S\}q$$

where p and q are predicates and S is a program, to indicate that the program S, when it terminates, will terminate in a state satisfying q, if it is initiated in a state satisfying p. The formula p{S}q defines the partial correctness of S. For example,

$$Y > 0 \textbf{ and } X > 0 \ \{Q := X/Y\}\ X * Y = Q$$

defines a simple division program.

Let us consider a predicate r ⇒ q (r implies q). This predicate means that the set of states satisfying r is a subset of the set of states satisfying q. If we can prove that

$$p\{S\}r$$

and if we assume r ⇒ q, then we have also proved p{S}q. This fact is easy to verify if we consider that all states defined by r are also defined by q.

We can describe the predicate r as a *stronger* condition than q, because it restricts the set of acceptable states more than q does. Conversely, we can define q as a *weaker* condition than r. Thus the above statement can be rephrased as follows: A program whose correctness has been shown for a given postcondition is also correct for any postcondition weaker than the one used for its verification.

For example, if we can verify

$$T\ \{Q := X/Y\}\ X * Y = Q$$

we have ensured the partial correctness of the program for the specifications indicated above. Note, however, that for Y = 0 the division's operation is not defined, which may be an indication of nontermination.

Conversely, if a program is verified as correct for some precondition, it is also correct for all preconditions stronger than the one used for the verification.

TOTAL CORRECTNESS OF PROGRAMS

Program verification for total correctness can now be defined. Given a program S and a postcondition r, we find its *weakest precondition*, i.e., the condition defining all initial states and only those initial states that ensure termination in states satisfying r. This weakest precondition is a predicate function of both S and r and is indicated as

$$wp(S, r)$$

It is clearly possible to define a dual problem. Given a precondition p and a program S, we find its *strongest postcondition*, i.e., a predicate that defines all states and only those states that the program will satisfy at termination when initiated in a state satisfying p. This strongest postcondition is a function of S and p and is indicated as

sp(S, p)

The concepts of weakest precondition and strongest postcondition were introduced by Dijkstra (1976).

To show total correctness, we must demonstrate a few important attributes of the weakest precondition and of the strongest postcondition. We have discussed the need for a pair of predicates to specify the meaning of a program, but we have also found that this pair is not unique because we can replace the precondition or the postcondition with a stronger or a weaker one without affecting the outcome of the possible verification. The introduction of the weakest precondition (or of the strongest postcondition) defines the limiting point of the series of conditions, all representing the correct program. We have also defined the weakest precondition and the strongest postcondition as depending on the program text and a predicate representing the sets of input or output states only. Thus we can use the concept of weakest precondition to describe the meaning of individual statements of programming languages since any statement is also a program text. This technique is actually the one Dijkstra used in defining a simple but useful programming language. We will discuss Dijkstra's language in the next section in some detail, omitting the more technical aspects.

THE MEANING OF PROGRAMMING LANGUAGE CONSTRUCTS

In most of the informal definitions of a language construct, such as

if S1 **then** S2 **else** S3

the meaning is defined in an operational way by describing a typical execution. For this example we say: First the truth value of the Boolean expression S1 is evaluated; then if S1 is true, the statement S2 is executed; otherwise, S3 is executed. Besides describing the meaning of **if-then-else** by enumerating possible computation, we actually define a class of computation effects. According to the nature of the particular statements S1, S2, and S3, the effect of the execution of **if-then-else** is different. We can say that we are defining the meaning of a program scheme that will become a concrete program only when a particular interpretation is given to the symbols S1, S2, and S3.

Execution-independent semantics of language constructs

We can define the weakest precondition of program schemes representing significant programming language constructs by using a formula that contains predicate symbols defining pre- and postconditions of the noninterpreted portions of the scheme. In the usual definition of program language constructs the execution of statements indicated by uninterpreted symbols such as S1, S2, and S3 in the example is mentioned. In a definition of the weakest precondition of language constructs, pre- and postconditions of statements such as S1, S2, and S3 will also appear as uninterpreted symbols.

Note that in this way the semantics of programming language constructs is defined without any knowledge of the data types manipulated by the statements, which are indicated only by symbols. That is, the semantics are applicable to very vast classes of possible interpretations of these symbols. Actually, the description of a programming language construct is the definition of the effect (weakest precondition, potential computations) of the control structure imposed by the constructs on some statement symbols. Each of these symbols can refer to a large program or to a single machine instruction whose ultimate semantics can be defined only by reference to the manipulated data types.

Defining the weakest precondition of most of the existing programming language constructs is a very difficult task because some of the features of these languages are not easy to describe. However, it is possible to describe some basic language constructs, which, in turn, permit the description of any practical programming task. By using these constructs, we can create program descriptions that may later be implemented in one of the available programming languages. The programming task is considerably clarified once the program is defined for a simpler language, thus permitting it to be rewritten in the desired programming language with a very low risk of introducing errors.

This technique is analogous to the common practice in the past (and today, too, in some cases) of producing a flowchart of a program and then coding it. We are not saying that this intermediate step is indispensable in practice. But we consider it convenient for our purpose of explaining a program design technique. For some programmers (including this author) the description of an algorithm in a simple language facilitates the design process of thinking about an algorithm without being overwhelmed by the characteristics of a specific programming language.

In the following sections our purpose in presenting this simple programming language is not only to teach the semantics of it but also to show a way of thinking about programs without considering their execution on a machine. Since this point of view forms the basis of all the rigorous methods for the design of both programs and large software systems, the mastery of this simple programming language is very important.

GUARDED COMMANDS

In the Floyd method (see Chapter 5) for proving the correctness of programs, we prove simple theorems stating that portions of the program once started in a certain set of states terminate in the desired set of states. These proofs use the intuitive meaning of the programming language. What we are introducing here is a set of axioms, like the ones used in mathematics, to make these proofs as rigorous as possible.

The language we describe is the language of *guarded commands* as introduced by Dijkstra (1976). The presentation in this section is mostly Dijkstra's definition of this language. Since we are not showing detailed mathematical proofs, we can dispense with the preliminary definition of the healthiness of the concept of weakest precondition. These conditions essentially state properties of the weakest preconditions, such as

$$\text{wp(S, P \textbf{and} Q)} = \text{wp(S, P) \textbf{and} wp(S, Q)}$$

Properties of this kind are needed to demonstrate the results we present in the following subsections without proof.

The Do-Nothing Axiom

The first statement of this programming language is *skip*. This statement is the no-operation statement. It is defined by

$$\text{wp(skip, R)} = \text{R}$$

which says that to terminate any execution of skip in a state satisfying the predicate R, it suffices to initiate in a state satisfying the same predicate R.

Therefore the definition of the weakest precondition for skip can be called the *do-nothing axiom*, which states the obvious fact that the correct way to do nothing in a state space is not to change anything in it.

The Axiom of Assignment

A more interesting axiom is the *axiom of assignment*. Let us consider the statement

$$x := e$$

where x is a variable and e is an expression that returns a value of the same type as x. We also assume the evaluation of e does not have side effects. In other words, only the state of x is changed by the execution of the statement.

Thus we can define the axiom of assignment:

$$\text{wp}(x := e, R) = R\ (x \leftarrow e)$$

This axiom says that the weakest precondition for any assignment to terminate in a state satisfying R is defined by a predicate constructed from R and by substituting to all the occurrences of x the expression e. For example (for x an integer),

$$\text{wp}(x := x + 1, x \geq 5) = x + 1 \geq 5 = x \geq 4$$

If we have a value for x, before assignment, greater than or equal to 4, by replacing this value with the result of its sum with 1, we obtain a resulting state of x that satisfies the condition of being greater than or equal to 5.

Other examples are as follows:

$$wp(x := 0, x < 10) = 0 < 10 = T$$

Here it doesn't matter what the initial state is; the statement will respect the postcondition.

$$wp(x := y, x + y = 5) = (2y = 5)$$

The statement will terminate correctly only if 2y is equal to 5 before its execution.

The Axiom of Concatenation

Now that the assignment and the do-nothing axioms have been introduced, we are able to write and prove one-line programs. However, one-line programs are not very powerful. To change this undesirable state of affairs, we introduce the *axiom of concatenation*. Given two statements S1 and S2, we indicate with S1;S2 the language construct whose meaning is defined by

$$wp((S1;S2), R) = wp(S1, wp(S2, R))$$

This formula says that for S1;S2 to terminate in a state satisfying R, S2 must be initiated in a state that allows its termination in a state satisfying R. But that means S2 must be started in a state satisfying wp(S2, R). Thus wp(S1, wp(S2, R)) defines the states for which S1 terminates in a state satisfying wp(S2,R), thus ensuring the termination of S2 in a state satisfying R.

The Axiom of Selection

For the next two constructs we need to define some syntax. Let us define, as a *guarded command set*,

$$B \rightarrow S$$

where B is a Boolean-valued expression called *guard* and S is any statement, which could be called a *guarded command*. A *guarded command list* is

```
  B1 → S1
□ B2 → S2
     ⋮
□ Bn → Sn
```

By inserting the logical brackets **if-fi** and **do-od** into a guarded command list, we can create two programming language statements (called IF and DO):

```
IF:   if  B1  →  S1
              ⋮
      □   Bn  →  Sn
      fi
DO:       B1  →  S1
              ⋮
      □   Bn  →  Sn
      od
```

You may already have some intuitive idea of the meaning of these statements, but we refrain from explaining them now. We will instead supply first the weakest precondition of IF, which can be called the *axiom of selection*:

```
wp(IF, R) = B1 and wp(S1, R) or
            B2 and wp(S2, R) or
            Bn and wp(Sn, R)
```

It is important to understand the significance of this formula because it contains the expression of some unusual features of the IF statement. If only one of the guards, say Bi, is true, the formula indicates, as the weakest precondition of IF, that predicate defining the set of states for which both Bi and wp(Si, R) are verified. This condition corresponds, in terms of program execution, to saying that the command Si, corresponding to the sole guard evaluating as true, is executed. But let us suppose that two guards Bi and Bj are true. In that case the weakest precondition of the IF defines the set of states that permit the correct termination of either Si or Sj in a state satisfying R. In terms of program execution this condition corresponds to the execution of either Si or Sj, because both of them will supply correct results.

Nondeterminism

The IF statement introduces *nondeterminism* in a programming language. This feature was used by Dijkstra because in some cases difficult algorithms can be correctly designed in a simpler way if only those choices indispensable for their correct development are made. Let us illustrate this point further by examining a very simple example. The following program satisfies the postcondition:

$$z = \text{MAX}(x, y)$$

with z, x, and y integers and MAX(x, y) representing the maximum between x and y. The program is

```
if x ≥ y  → z := x
fi
□ y ≥ x → z := y
```

When x = y, either one of the guarded commands can be executed with correct results. Forcing a choice between the two commands could be dictated by efficient operation of the implementing software, but it is not a factor for the correctness of the algorithm. Since we, like Dijkstra,

Nondeterminism avoids overspecification

are using the guarded command language to describe program designs that can be implemented in various languages, we should not be forced to express decisions that do not concern correctness such as implementation-independent execution efficiency. The correctness of the particular implementation will be ensured by the faithful representation of the design in the available language. Considerations of implementation-dependent performance will be part of this later stage of development. For example, the above program can be efficiently and correctly implemented as

```
if x ≥ y then z := x else z := y;
```

The feature of nondeterminism is of fundamental importance for concurrent programs. This issue will be discussed in additional detail in Chapter 16.

Simultaneous Assignment

Another useful form of nondeterminism that we will use to some extent in the rest of this book is the *simultaneous assignment*. Its syntax is

$$U_1, U_2, \ldots, U_n := e_1, e_2, \ldots, e_n$$

where U_i ($i = 1, 2, \ldots, n$) are variable names and e_j ($i = 1, 2, \ldots, n$) are expressions such that e_j returns a value of the type of U_i for $i = j$.

The meaning of this construct can be informally expressed as the assignment of the value returned by the e_i to the corresponding variable U_i. But we further assume that these assignments are performed simultaneously. The semantics of this construct is rather complex and beyond the scope of this book. The interested reader may consult Gries (1978) for a complete description.

In this book we will use the simultaneous assignment every time we do not want to specify any order of execution for a number of assignments. In other words, if we write

$$X, Y := X + 1, 0$$

we mean that the operations $X := X + 1$ and $Y := 0$ can be performed in any order. In this way we can specify a desired state transformation without imposing any unnecessary ordering of execution.

The Axiom of Iteration

The *axiom of iteration* defines the semantics of DO. Dijkstra presented this axiom as the weakest precondition for DO, but its formulation is too complex to be useful in program design. In its stead we present a rule of inference of much simpler formulation and of effective practical application. This rule of inference is called the *loop invariant theorem*, and it can be proven as a theorem when the axiom of iteration is assumed.

The loop invariant theorem

It actually defines a precondition slightly stronger than the weakest precondition, but for all practical purposes this difference is immaterial.

Let us indicate with BB the disjunction of all the guards of DO, i.e.,

BB = B1 **or** B2 **or** . . . **or** Bn

The loop invariant theorem is stated as follows: Let IF be the construct built by using the same guarded command list used for DO but with the **if-fi** brackets. Let P be a predicate such that

P and BB $\Rightarrow$ wp(IF, P)

is verified for all states of DO execution. Then we can conclude that for all states,

P and wp(DO, T) $\Rightarrow$ wp(DO, P and not BB)

The expression wp(DO, T) indicates the weakest precondition, which describes all those states for which the DO statement terminates in any state of the state space (T defines the universe).

Rather than give an interpretation of the formula above in familiar program execution terms, we will interpret the meaning of the loop invariant theorem in state transformation terms. The loop invariant theorem has the characteristic form of a mathematical theorem. If something is true, then something else will be true. The "something" here is the formula

P **and** BB $\Rightarrow$ wp(IF, P)

This formula states that if at least one of the guards is true (BB is true), then the loop body will initiate and terminate in a state satisfying a predicate P. The loop invariant theorem states that if this formula is verified, then the whole loop initiated in a state verifying P will terminate in a state verifying

P **and not** BB

Thus at termination all guards will be false, and the postcondition that can be guaranteed by the application of the invariant theorem is

P **and** BB

The predicate P is called the *loop invariant* since it is to be verified at loop initiation, at loop termination, and before and after any execution of the loop body. Of course, the predicate P is not to be verified during the execution of individual commands within the loop body itself.

Note that if the DO construct is reduced to one guarded command, it behaves exactly like the familiar iteration construct **do while** of such languages as PL/I and Algol.

Loop invariant theorem supplies a design method

The importance of this theorem is that it can be readily transformed in a design procedure for loop programs. All the needed elements for the presentation of this procedure are already stated in the theorem itself, except for a way to ensure the termination of a DO construct in any state. However, this termination procedure is easily found. Let us assume that the number of iterations the loop is going to execute is n ($n \geq 0$). At each iteration this number is reduced by 1, but at no time will n be less than zero. Let us imagine that we can find an integer-valued function of the variables involved in the DO execution that can be shown to be greater than or equal to zero at loop initiation and such that its value is strictly reduced at each iteration and at termination cannot be negative. The existence of a function with the above properties is proof of the loop termination. The intuitive justification for the above termination function is that it behaves as the counter of the number n of iterations considered above.

HIGHLIGHTS

In this chapter we have introduced two languages. One is the language of predicate calculus, and it is used to define states for program specifications. The second is the language of guarded commands, a simple programming language that shows the unusual characteristic of potentially nondeterministic execution. This latter language has been defined in its semantics exclusively in terms of state transformations by the use of the weakest precondition of its constructs.

The guarded command language presents the unusual feature of nondeterminism. Nondeterminism is a natural conclusion of the way the semantics of the selection and iteration constructs are introduced. A theorem concerning iteration, called the loop invariant theorem, appears to be a good candidate for the basis of a design method for loop programs.

REFERENCES

Carnap, R. 1939. *Foundations of logic and mathematics*. Chicago: University of Chicago Press.

Dijkstra, E. W. 1976. *A discipline of programming*. Englewood Cliffs, N.J.: Prentice-Hall.

Gries, D. 1978. The multiple assignment statement. *IEEE Transactions on Software Engineering* SE–4 (no. 2): 89–93.

Hoare, C. A. R. 1969. An axiomatic approach to computer programming. *Communications of ACM* 12 (no. 10):576–580, 583.

CHAPTER SEVEN

Program Design

INTRODUCTION

In the preceding chapter we introduced all the elements necessary to describe the program design technique introduced by Dijkstra (1976), which he called a *calculus of programming*. The basic idea behind Dijkstra's calculus is to use proof-of-correctness techniques not to verify a program already created in some way but to guide a step-by-step, explicitly conscious process of program design.

This idea is clearly attractive for our purposes. In Chapter 1 we pointed out the lack of disciplines in software development to support the intellectual creation and verification of design ideas, disciplines that are so effective in modern engineering. Dijkstra's calculus is directed toward the realization of a technique that, at least for programs (not necessarily for large software systems), supplies the needed discipline for verifying the design of programs by intellectual analysis before testing the product.

In this chapter we will discuss the Dijkstra calculus relative to small programs, such as those created by one individual. These programs are typically the building blocks of large systems. Assuming that the specifications of the program are correctly defined, the difficulty in the kind of programs we will discuss in this chapter is mainly in determining a correct (and efficient) algorithm. Dijkstra's calculus is a very effective technique for this purpose.

A SIMPLE EXAMPLE

We will introduce Dijkstra's technique by examining a simple example in detail. Let us consider the problem of writing a program that performs the division of two (positive and nonzero) integers. We used this example to illustrate the definition of pre- and postconditions in Chapter 4, and we repeat the reasoning here for convenience.

The Problem

The first step of a design process is to establish a suitable state space from the problem requirements. In this case the requirements can be expressed as follows:

- Write a program that divides one positive nonzero integer by another.

State space definition

The state space clearly needs two objects: X, the dividend, and Y, the divisor. Also, we know that a division produces (returns) two integer values: Q, the quotient, and R, the remainder. So these two objects are part of the state space. The fact that X and Y are defined in the informal requirements as positive and nonzero is expressed in the precondition by stating

$$X > 0 \textbf{ and } Y > 0$$

Any integer values respecting this precondition are good inputs. The postcondition is constructed by using what we know about the division of two integers:

- Q times Y is equal to X minus the remainder:

$$X = Q' * Y + R'$$

- If the remainder is negative, the above statement does not describe the results of an integer division. Consequently, we have to write

$$X = Q' * Y + R' \textbf{ and } R' \geqslant 0$$

- If the remainder is greater than Y, the above statement does not describe the results of an integer division. The predicate

$$X = Q' * Y + R' \textbf{ and } R' \geqslant 0 \textbf{ and } R' < Y$$

  indicates this last consideration.

This last expression represents the results of an integer division only if we also state that X and Y are positive and nonnull, as we have stated in the precondition. Therefore the full expression of the integer division postcondition is

$$X = Q' * Y + R' \textbf{ and } R' \geqslant 0 \textbf{ and } R' < Y \textbf{ and } X > 0 \textbf{ and } Y > 0$$

Inspection of the pre- and postconditions shows that while the postcondition is a rather strong constraint on the possible output values, the precondition is rather weak. In fact, only a single value of each variable at a time will satisfy the postcondition, while any pair of positive nonnull integers (as infinity of values) will satisfy the precondition. The final program will be one or more (probably several) constructs concatenated into a sequence that will produce an ordered sequence of states, the initial one satisfying the precondition, the last one satisfying the postcondition.

Solving the Design Problem

To build the sequence of constructs (i.e., to solve the program design problem), we can start from the input state and postulate some intermediate state that can be obtained from the input. Then we use this new intermediate state as input and build another state. We continue in this way until a state satisfying the postcondition is obtained.

Forward and backward program construction

An alternative method is to work backward, starting from the output definition, then defining an input, which in turn becomes a new output, etc., until a state satisfying the precondition is obtained.

In the forward process we have to determine, at every mental step, a construct that will eventually bring us to the determination of a condition equal to or *stronger* than the given postcondition. In the backward process we have to reach a condition equal to or *weaker* than the given precondition.

A strong condition by nature contains more information than a weak one. Consequently, it seems easier to construct a weaker condition from a stronger one (which can be viewed as a removal of information) than to create a stronger condition from a weaker one (which requires the creation of new information). This idea will become clearer as we proceed with this example.

Let us attempt the apparently easier backward approach. We can weaken the postcondition by removing the term $R' < Y$. That is, we are now assuming that a state satisfying

$$(X = Q * Y + R) \textbf{ and } (R \geq 0) \textbf{ and } X > 0 \textbf{ and } Y > 0$$

has already been reached (in some magic way) from a state satisfying the precondition. The reasoning that brings us to the choice of the condition above is highly subjective. In fact, it may have been chosen because of some previous imprecise knowledge we already have about the algorithm. On that ground it seems reasonable to remove from the postcondition the term $R' < Y$ and try to solve the problem of moving from a state defined by the resulting condition to the state that does respect the postcondition. But this choice is not automatic: It represents a highly creative part of the design process. We could indeed have chosen the intermediate state as defined by a relation obtained by removing the term $R \geq 0$:

$$(X = Q * Y + R) \textbf{ and } (R < Y) \textbf{ and } X > 0 \textbf{ and } Y > 0$$

However, any attempt to build a program according to this choice would probably present enough difficulties to discourage the continuation of the attempt.

Going back to the condition of the first choice as the intermediate state definition, we note that if we are in a state for which $R > Y$, it seems reasonable to attempt to reach an output state that satisfies the term $R < Y$ by reducing the value of R by subtracting Y from R. In doing so, if Y and R are positive, we would make a step toward the postcondition if we had not violated the first term of the intermediate state condition, since now

$$X \neq Q * Y + R$$

To reestablish the truth value of the term

$$X = Q * Y + R$$

after R has been decreased by Y, it is sufficient to increase Q (again assuming Q is a positive number) by one. We have therefore determined that the following program segment,

$$R := R - Y; Q := Q + 1$$

when initiated in a state satisfying

$$X = Q * Y + R \textbf{ and } R \geq 0$$

will terminate in a state satisfying the same predicate. Also, it appears to be a step toward a desired output state. But a desired output state is reached when R < Y. Therefore it is clear that the following loop is the appropriate solution:

$$\textbf{do } R \geq Y \rightarrow R := R - Y; Q := Q + 1 \textbf{ od}$$

provided that R, Q, and Y are positive numbers.

APPLICATION OF THE LOOP INVARIANT THEOREM

Let us examine this example in light of the loop invariant theorem. We had a postcondition R, which we split into two parts: the loop invariant

$$P = (X = Q * Y + R \textbf{ and } R \geq 0)$$

and

$$\textbf{not } BB = (R \leq Y)$$

Consequently, BB is R > Y. A program segment has been constructed that terminates in a state satisfying P when initiated in a state also satisfying P. Note that between the two assignments P is not satisfied. We have also ensured that at each execution of this program segment, we get closer to a state satisfying not only P but also **not** BB (the desired postcondition).

We have thus determined that the above loop will terminate in a state satisfying R when initiating in a state satisfying P (the loop invariant). Since the invariant P we have determined is not a weaker condition than the required precondition, we may now proceed to create program segments that will terminate in P when started in a state defined by the given precondition (or a weaker one).

It is now simple to determine the next segment that will bring us to any input state that satisfies the required precondition. Recall that all our reasoning thus far required that R, Q, and Y be positive numbers. Thus we actually must have stated the following at loop initiation:

$$(X = Q * Y + R) \textbf{ and } (R \geq 0) \textbf{ and } (Q \geq 0) \textbf{ and } (Y \geq 0)$$

Let us assume the value Q = 0. The verification of the term

$$X = Q * Y + R$$

imposes R = X, which in turn imposes $X \geq 0$. Thus the following program segment will create a state satisfying this new condition when activated in a state satisfying $X \geq 0$ **and** $Y \geq 0$:

```
Q := 0; R := X;
```

Since $X \geq 0$ **and** $Y \geq 0$, the given precondition is weaker than (is implied by) $X > 0$ **and** $Y > 0$, the program is correct for the required specifications. So our design task is successfully completed.

However, we have not yet shown that the loop always terminates. We have only determined that we move toward the desired postcondition by the execution of the loop body. So before we accept the results of the above process, we have to find a function C and show that it is properly handled by the program under the defined conditions. A good choice for C appears to be C = R. In fact, R is a function of the program state variables that has a positive value at the input and at every cycle because it is equal to X and initialization, and $X > 0$ according to the precondition. Also it is reduced only by subtraction of positive nonnull values of Y. It will have the value $R \geq 0$ (as stated in the postcondition) at termination.

Demonstration of termination

Note that the above reasoning about termination forces us to require $Y > 0$ in the precondition of the program, because for null or negative Y, C is not reduced at each iteration. Without termination considerations we verified that the postcondition

$$(X = Q' * Y + R') \textbf{ and } (R \geq 0) \textbf{ and } (Q \geq 0) \textbf{ and } Y \geq 0 \textbf{ and } X \geq 0$$

is satisfied by the designed program when initiated in a state satisfying $X \geq 0$ **and** $Y \geq 0$. Since this precondition is weaker than the given one, we may have concluded erroneously that the program was correct. In fact, we had shown only partial correctness, i.e., that when the program terminates, it terminates correctly. The precise determination of the termination condition has shown that we need a stronger precondition for total correctness. Therefore we reach the conclusion that the weakest precondition $X \geq 0$ **and** $Y > 0$ is required—which is still stronger than the required one—and that hence the program always terminates correctly for the given pre- and postconditions.

A GENERALIZED PROCEDURE FOR LOOP PROGRAM DESIGN

By considering the above example, together with the precise definition of the loop invariant theorem, we can now define a generalized procedure for the derivation of correct loop programs from the specifications:

1. We determine, perhaps on the basis of an informal definition of the algorithm, that an iteration is needed.

2. We break down the postcondition into two parts: the invariant P and the negation of the loop guards, **not** BB.
3. We determine the termination function C from the knowledge of the guards.
4. We design the loop body code as the one that maintains the invariance of P and strictly reduces the termination function C, as shown in the example.

At this point a portion of a program that initializes the loop by establishing the loop invariant is usually needed. The precondition of this program portion must be weaker than (or the same as) the required precondition. This technique, when properly applied, allows one to design correctly terminating programs from the specifications in a semi-automatic way.

Once the correctness concern is removed, the designer can consider other concerns such as performance. By continuing to use this design technique, the designer can introduce any change dictated by performance into the program, without excessive difficulties.

Now we can deal with relatively small programs and also (in large measure) with requirements that can be effectively expressed (i.e., with reasonable assurance of being correct) by specifications written in the language of predicate calculus. However, the particular implementing language may behave differently from the constructs whose semantics were so precisely defined. Therefore we are not still at a point where we can say we have completely solved the programming problem. On the other hand, the mental approach we have used is more comprehensive and satisfactory than the one usually used, which enumerates the commands in a sample computation sequence.

Dijkstra calculus power is evident for algorithmically difficult problems

The power of the Dijkstra approach is not fully appreciated until more difficult examples are considered. So we now present a few examples presenting a higher degree of difficulty than the very simple one we used to introduce the method. By examining these examples, you will appreciate the full power of this approach for designing loop programs.

THE ARRAY DATA STRUCTURE

In the following example and in the rest of the book, we will extensively use the data structure array. We define an *array* (following Dijkstra 1976) as the association of zero or more elements of a certain type (they may even be other arrays) with an ordered sequence of integers that we call *indices*. We also have the following definitions, given an array A.

- A.lob is a function indicating the value of the lowest value of the indices.
- A.hib is the highest value of the indices.

- A.dom = A.hib − A.lob + 1 is the total number of indices of A.

Given an integer i such that

$$A.lob < i < A.hib$$

both i + 1 and i − 1 are indices of the array. We also state that for any array A

$$0 \leq A.dom \leq n$$

with n any (undefined) finite integer.

We also assume that the following functions are available for the manipulation of the array elements:

Functions for array manipulation

- A:swap(i, j), whose weakest precondition is

  $$wp(A{:}swap(i, j), R) = A.lob \leq i, j \leq A.hib \textbf{ and } R(A' \leftarrow A)$$

  The symbol R(A′ ← A) identifies a predicate of the same form of the predicate R with only the following substitutions:

  $$\begin{aligned} A'.lob &\leftarrow A.lob \\ A'.hib &\leftarrow A.hib \\ A'.dom &\leftarrow A.dom \\ A'(i) &\leftarrow A(j) \\ A'(j) &\leftarrow A(i) \end{aligned}$$

  This weakest precondition says that if i and j are in the range of indices of A, then A:swap(i, j) will terminate in a state for which the values of A(i) and A(j) are exchanged in the final array. Note that if i and j are not in the range (A.lob ≤ i, j ≤ A.hib), the weakest precondition is false. Therefore there is no guarantee of proper termination. In other words, the function aborts.

- A:hiext(x), where x is a variable of the same type as the elements of A. The weakest precondition is

  $$wp(A{:}hiext(x), R) = R(A' \leftarrow A) \text{ and } A'.dom = A.dom + 1 \text{ and } A'(A'.hib) = x$$

  where the following substitutions are to be effected in R:

  $$\begin{aligned} A'.lob &\leftarrow A.lob \\ A'.hib &\leftarrow A.hib + 1 \end{aligned}$$

- A:hirem, whose weakest precondition is

  $$wp(A{:}hirem, R) = R(A' \leftarrow A) \textbf{ and } A'.dom = A.dom - 1 \geq 0$$

  with the following substitutions:

  $$\begin{aligned} A'.lob &\leftarrow A.lob \\ A'.hib &\leftarrow A.hib - 1 \end{aligned}$$

  Note that if A.dom = 0, A:hirem does not terminate; hence it will abort.

Intuitively, the meanings of these functions are the exchange of the two elements in i, j for A:swap(i, j), the appending of x at the high end of A for A:hiext(x), and the removal of the element at the high end of A for A:hirem. We have presented the precise semantics of these functions to show how complex these function definitions can become when they are expressed precisely. This complication is real in the sense that these functions are doing complicated things. However, we do not perceive this complexity because our intuitive picture of an array does not require the listing of all the changes. We actually abstract those changes by using words such as *exchange, appending*, and *removal*, which, it is hoped, have a clear and identical meaning for everyone. Unfortunately, sometimes the meanings of words used to define data processing concepts are not universal and unequivocal. We then have to use definitions in terms of simpler entities that should be universally known. Here we used the concept of weakest precondition as the context in which to express the meaning of swap, hiext, hirem in terms of lob, hib, and dom, which we assume are unequivocally understood.

A SIMPLE PROGRAM DESIGN EXAMPLE

Let us now consider the problem of finding the greatest element in an array of integers.

Initial Design Steps

The first step is to define the state space, i.e., to give names and types to the variables of the program. We name A as the array to search for the maximum:

```
A: integer array
```

The type of A is indicated by the statement after the colon, namely, an integer array. We name M as an integer variable where the maximum will be stored:

```
M: integer
```

We also need an index, which will be an integer variable. Let us call it

```
i: integer
```

We can now transform the informal requirements to more formal expressions. In doing so, we may need more details from the source of the requirements.

The postcondition, expressed in English but using the symbols of the state space defined above, is as follows:

> For all indices i in the range of indices of A, the values A(i) are less than or equal to the value of M.

This postcondition is easily rewritten in predicate terms as

$$\textbf{for all } i\ [A.lob \leq i \leq A.hib \Rightarrow M \geq A(i)]$$

If we do not recognize any limitation on the input from the informal specifications, then the precondition T (the whole state space) is appropriate. Otherwise, we must include the possibility of an empty array (A.dom = 0). It is trivial but slightly more cumbersome to define the postcondition so that it covers the case of an empty array. Therefore for the sake of simplicity in this example, we assume the precondition

$$A.dom > 0$$

Definition of the Loop Invariant

Loop invariant as the definition of intermediate loop states

The next step in the design process is to split the postcondition into two parts: the loop invariant P and the guards BB. With an array structure the postcondition may represent a property that is applied to all the elements of the structure. In this case the property is $M \geq A(i)$. A straightforward way to obtain the invariant is to imagine that this property is applied only to a portion of the array. This portion can be the whole array as well as any part, even an empty portion, of the array. We can describe this situation by writing

$$\textbf{for all } i\ [A.lob \leq i \leq j \leq A.hib \Rightarrow M \geq A(i)]$$

This predicate for j = A.hib is identical to the postcondition. Also, for j = A.lob it identifies a single-element array, for which it is easy to see that $M \geq A(i)$ is verified. We then decide that this predicate is the loop invariant. We next define the loop body as the code that initiates and terminates in a state verifying this invariant while reducing the value of the termination function. Thus we have to determine this termination function.

The technique for inventing a termination function is to identify an appropriate counter of the number of iterations remaining at each state before termination. A function related to the size of that part of the array for which the property $M \geq A(i)$ does not necessarily apply is an appropriate one. Intuitively, if the desired property applies to the dashed part of the following figure, the counter is a measure of the size (in number of array elements) of the nondashed part:

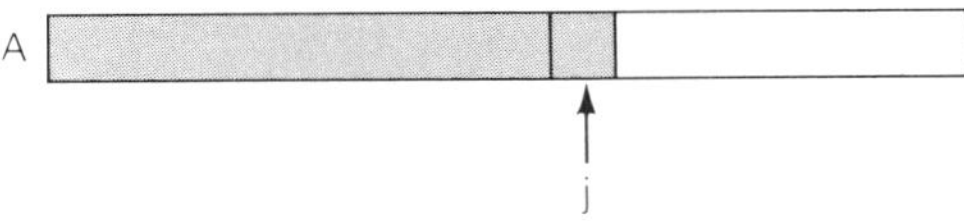

Consequently, the termination function can be chosen as

$$A.hib - j$$

It is clear that if at each iteration we reduce the value of A.hib − j, the shaded portion of the figure above will progress to cover the whole array.

Combining all this reasoning, we can now design the loop body:

```
j:= j + 1;
if  A(j) ≥ M → M := A(j)
□ A(j) ≤ M → skip
fi
```

To illustrate the design process, let us discuss the reasoning that demonstrates the correctness of the design of the above program. At termination of this program segment two things must be verified. First, the loop invariant is satisfied, and second, the termination function has been decreased. Let us assume that the invariant is verified for a portion of the array from A.lob up to and including the value of j. For the correctness of the final program to be obtained, the invariant must be considered as the precondition of the IF statement. At termination of the IF statement, clearly the invariant is verified for a portion of A including A(j), because if A(j) is greater than the value of M, the latter is made equal to A(j). By assuming that the invariant is verified up to and including j before the IF, we are now ensuring that if M is properly initialized, the execution of the above code will maintain the truth value of the invariant for all the subsequent iterations.

Design correctness follows the proper use of the method

We also see that the termination function A.hib − j is decreased by this program segment, since j is increased by the assignment j := j + 1. Therefore we have designed a loop body that satisfies the conditions for building a correctly terminating loop program for the given postcondition.

Note that we are exploiting the nondeterminism of the IF statement by not prescribing a choice between the two commands of the IF. Clearly, performance considerations will dictate a specific choice for the implementation. But here we are concerned only with correctness. The deduction process of the code from the loop invariant and the termination function does not suggest any choice.

Final Design Steps

The next step is to design the guards of the DO statement. From inspection of the loop invariant we see that in order to have correct termination in a state satisfying the postcondition, we have to ensure that the invariant must be satisfied up to a state for which j = A.hib. From the reasoning we used to build the loop body, we know that at termination of the loop body code, the invariant is satisfied up to and including a value of j that is greater by one than the value at initiation of that code. The guard j < A.hib will become false when j = A.hib. Since the invariant for a state for which j = A.hib is identical to the postcondition, this choice is a correct one. Thus the loop portion of the program is as follows:

Guards are designed to satisfy the postcondition for the chosen invariant

```
do j < A.hib → j := j + 1;
     if  A(j) ≥ M → M := A(j)
     □  A(j) ≤ M →     skip
     fi
od
```

This loop portion, when initiated in a state satisfying the invariant, is guaranteed to terminate in a state satisfying the postcondition.

The loop invariant we have used is a stronger condition than the given precondition. Thus we must design another segment of code to establish the invariant. It is evident that if j = A.lob and M = A(j), then the invariant is verified. Also, the termination function will be greater than or equal to zero. Thus the program segment

```
j := A.lob; M := A(j);
```

terminates in a state verifying the invariant. Its weakest precondition is A.dom > 0, as required.

Summary

As a system programmer struggling with uncertainties about the environment in which your program is supposed to execute or plagued by uncertainties of the interfaces, you may think that the above example is not relevant for your work. However, this method is very important both for design applications and for the purpose of this book. With this method we now can reason about programs without building a real one (and using it) to determine correctness. We have discovered conceptual entities that define important correctness properties, such as the loop invariant and the termination function. Admittedly, the above example is a very simple one, and it could have been created by the traditional enumeration of commands in an execution sequence, perhaps even without errors. However, note how the method (Dijkstra's calculus) allows the designer to be in complete control of the design process at all stages. All the reasoning steps can be explicitly formulated, and the correctness of the arguments can be checked by mental reference to the precise definition of the semantics of the language constructs. Furthermore, the process is not as tedious as the proof process introduced in Chapter 5. In sum, the correctness of the design of a program can be discussed along the lines presented above without requiring an excessive amount of effort or any particular skill on the part of programmers.

A DIFFERENT EXAMPLE OF THE LOOP INVARIANT: A BINARY SEARCH

For all the preceding examples the loop invariant was determined by imagining an intermediate state during the loop execution. It was easy at that point to transform the postcondition in a loop invariant, because all the examples dealt with arrays whose elements were transformed continuously to the desired final state by moving the index up or down toward one of the array's bounds.

A more difficult program design example

Not all problems are so simply attacked in practice, however. To illustrate a different situation, let us consider the case of a search in a sorted array containing all distinct elements, one of which is known to be equal to the value we are searching for. These conditions suggest that we use a more efficient search than a left-to-right (or right-to-left) scan of the elements of the array until the desired value is found. Incidentally, the requirement that the searched value exist in the array is not strictly needed for this exercise. Since it simplifies the exposition of the program, however, we will maintain it. (You may wish, as an exercise, to solve the slightly more complex problem for yourself.) This problem is usually called a *binary search,* and the solving algorithm is the fastest way to search all sorted arrays but the smallest ones.

Postcondition and Precondition

The postcondition of the program can be expressed in words (A is the array to be searched for a value equal to X):

> All the elements of A between A.lob and i − 1 are strictly less than X; all the elements between i + 1 and A.hib are strictly greater than X; and A(i) is equal to X.

In the language of predicate calculus, this statement is as follows:

for all h [A.lob < h ≤ i − 1 ⇒ A(h − 1) < A(h) < A(i)]
and
for all j [i − 1 < j ≤ A.hib ⇒ A(i) < A(j − 1) < A(j)]
and
A(i) = X

The precondition is expressed as follows:

for all j [A.lob < j ≤ A.hib ⇒ A(j − 1) < A(j)]
and for some j [A.lob ≤ j ≤ A.hib ⇒ A(j) = X]

The three terms of the postcondition define three separate regions of the array A. The first one, R1, defined by

for all h [A.lob < h ≤ i − 1 ⇒ A(h − 1) < A(h)]

Inspection of the postcondition indicates three regions of the array with different properties

delimits a portion (possibly empty) of A bounded by A.lob and the first element on the right of the element indexed by i, which in turn represents the second region, R2, made up by only the element A(i). All elements in R1 are not equal to X because they are defined as being strictly less than each other. Therefore, because the relations of all the elements in R1 are different from X.

A(i) > A(h) for h = i − 1

The same reasoning shows that all elements in R3 are different from X (and from each other) because R3 is defined as

$$\textbf{for all } h\ [i + 1 \leq h < A.hib \Rightarrow A(h) < A(h + 1)]$$

Loop Invariant

For the purpose of determining the loop invariant, let us now generalize these three regions. That is, we will weaken their definition by allowing the middle portion, R2, to contain some of the elements at the left and at the right of i. Thus R1 is defined by

$$R1\text{: } \textbf{for all } h\ [A.lob < h \leq H - 1 \Rightarrow A(h) < A(h + 1)]$$

where H is an index in the range A.lob to A.hib. Similarly, R2 is defined by

$$R2\text{: } \textbf{for some } h\ (H \leq h \leq K \textbf{ and } A(h) = X]$$

where K is an index in the range A.lob to A.hib. And R3 is defined by

$$R3\text{: } \textbf{for all } [K + 1 \leq h < A.hib \Rightarrow A(h) < A(h + 1)]$$

We see that for H = A.lob and K = A.hib, the definitions above reduce to the precondition, while (by construction) for H = K = i they become the postcondition. We therefore have a good candidate for a loop invariant. Assuming that we have reached a state satisfying this loop invariant, a step toward termination is to make K − H smaller, i.e., closer to zero, as it must be if H = K = i. The termination function is therefore chosen as H − K.

The following loop body code initiates in a state satisfying the invariant, reduces the termination function, and concludes in a state satisfying the invariant:

```
j := F(H, K);
if      A(j) > X → K := j - 1
     □  A(j) = X → skip
     □  A(j) < X → H := j + 1
fi
```

where F(H, K) is a function that chooses a value for j such that

$$H < j \leq K \textbf{ or } H \leq j < K$$

Typically, for performance reasons, F is the result of the integer division of K − H by 2 plus H, that is, the midpoint of R2:

$$F(H, K) = DIV(K - H, 2) + H$$

Now we can complete the loop by considering that at termination H = K. Therefore:

```
do H < K → j := F(H, K);
     if A(j) > X → K := j - 1
     □  A(j) = X → skip
     □  A(j) < X → H := j + 1
     fi
od
```

Final Program

The precondition is the same as the invariant, where H = A.lob and K = A.hib. Therefore, the whole program is as follows:

```
H, K := A.lob, A.hib;
do H < K → j := F(H, K);
    if  A(j) > X → K := j − 1
    □  A(j) = X → skip
    □  A(j) < X → H := j + 1
    fi
od
```

This example is clearly more difficult than the preceding one. The point here is that Dijkstra calculus is quite effective for the design of programs and is useful in practice for maintaining the intellectual grasp over rather difficult, even if (so far) not too large, program design problems.

TEXT-PROCESSING EXAMPLES

In this section we will use examples of text processing to show how a different choice for a loop invariant produces a different program.

The problem is to eliminate duplicate characters in a string of characters

An array of characters is given. Our problem is to write a program that eliminates the multiple instances of all characters present in the input array. For example, if the array in input is

a, r, r, a, y

the program must produce as output

a, r, y

The order of the characters in output is not required to be the same as the order in input. In the example above r, y, a would also be a correct result.

Precondition and Postcondition

No limitation of values at input is stated; therefore we have the constant predicate T as the precondition.

The first object of the state space to be recognized is the array to be manipulated:

A: character array

The postcondition must state the following facts (A′ is A after any program execution):

- All the characters in A′ are different.
- The domain of A′ is at most equal to the domain of A.
- All the characters in A′ were in A and vice versa.

The postcondition can be written precisely as follows:

let h, j: integer;
for all j, h [A'lob ≤ j, h ≤ A'.hib ⇒ [A'(j) = A'(h) ⇔ j = h]]
and A'.dom ≤ A.dom
and for all j [A'lob ≤ j ≤ A'.hib ⇒ [**for some** h [A.lob ≤ h ≤ A.hib **and** [A'(j) = A (h)]]]
and for all h [A.lob ≤ h ≤ A.hib ⇒,
[**for some** j [A'.lob ≤ j ≤ A'.hib **and** A(h) = A'(j)]]

Loop Invariant

Different loop invariants can be chosen

By inspecting the postcondition, we notice the use of quantifiers. This fact is a strong indication that the program will be realized primarily by an iterative construct. To design an iteration properly, we must search for a loop invariant. This search, as we learned in the previous example, can be effectively done by considering some property expressed in the postcondition and applied to the whole array that can be also expressed for a part of the array.

The postcondition states that all the elements of A are different. The usual trick to discover a loop invariant is to imagine that this property of containing distinct elements applies to only a part of the structure. In this case we may imagine this partial structure as shown in the following figure:

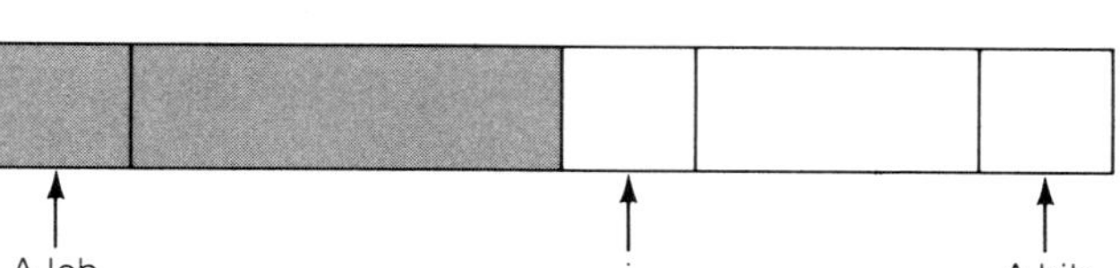

Here the dashed portion indicates that the elements it contains are different from each other. Our problem is to write code that extends the dashed portion to cover the whole array.

However, we still have to establish whether the generic A(i) (the first element after the dashed portion) is different from all the elements in the dashed portion. In other words, the property of the elements in the dashed portion may be different from each other only, or they may also be different from any element in the nondashed portion, i.e., A(i). Both conditions are acceptable because both produce the desired postcondition when the whole array is dashed. But the loop invariant *is* different, and it produces different code.

Program Design for the First Choice of the Loop Invariant

Let us develop first the loop invariant and the program under the assumption that nothing is known about A(i). That is, the property of being different applies within the dashed portion only. We can write the following loop invariant:

```
for all j, h [A'.lob ≤ j, h ≤ i − 1 ⇒ [A'(j) = A'(h) ⇔ j = h] ]
and A'.dom ≤ A.dom
and
for all j [A'.lob ≤ j ≤ A'.hib ⇒
        [for some h [A.lob ≤ h ≤ A.hib and A(h) = A'(j)]
and
for all h [A.lob ≤ h ≤ A.hib ⇒
        [for some j [A'.lob ≤ j ≤ A'.hib and A(h) = A'(j)]
```

With the above loop invariant we may define the termination function as the difference

$$A.hib - i + 1$$

which may be reduced in two ways, by increasing i or by decreasing A.hib.

The following code for the loop body assumes the loop invariant as the precondition produces output respecting the loop invariant, and always decreases the termination function:

```
j := i − 1;
do   j ≥ A.lob cand A(i) ≠ A(j) →
     j := j − 1
od;
if   j < A.lob → i:= i + 1
□    j ≥ A.lob → A: swap (i, A.hib);
                 A: hirem
fi
```

The loop body code respects the invariant

The justification for the above code is as follows: Since from the loop invariant we do not know if A(i) is equal to any of the elements in the portion (A.lob to i − 1), we must search in this portion for possible elements equal to A(i). This search is done linearly from the right (from j = i − 1) to the left (down to j = A.lob, inclusive). For this purpose, we use the code derived in Chapter 5 to illustrate the use of mathematical induction as a programming tool. Note the use of the connective **cand** to avoid the possibility of a test of A(i) with an out-of-bounds element when j < A.lob. The index j at termination of the search will be either less than, greater than, or equal to A.lob.

In the first case (j < A.lob) there is no element in the searched portion equal to A(i). Thus we can reduce the termination function by increasing i, therefore including (correctly) A(i) in the dashed portion of the figure shown earlier.

In the second case (j ≥ A.lob) we have to eliminate A(i), because it is a duplicate. We eliminate A(i) by exchanging it with the last element in the list, then removing it. This technique is legitimate because the order of the elements of A is not required to be preserved by the program execution. The termination function is reduced by the removal. The loop invariant is still respected since no change was made to the shaded portion of the figure, and the elimination of a duplicate character does not affect the property that all characters in A′ be present in A also. Notice that we remove A(i), but more elements of this value may still be present in the nondashed portion of the figure.

Program

With all these conditions in mind we can complete the program:

```
i := A.lob + 1;
do i ≤ A.hib →
    j := i − 1;
    do   j ≥ A.lob cand A(i) ≠ A(j) →
           j := j − 1
    od;
    if   j < A.lob → i := i + 1
    □    j ≥ A.lob → A:swap (i, A.hib);
                     A:hirem
    fi
od
```

A Different Solution for the Same Loop Invariant

An alternative code can be written by choosing a linear search from left to right. In this case since A(i) may work to terminate the program, a considerable number of comparison instructions may be saved by eliminating the test j ≥ A.lob from the search loop guard. The following alternative code is more efficient than the code above.

```
i := A.lob + 1;
do i ≤ A.hib →
    j := A.lob;
    do A(j) ≠ A(i) → j := j + 1 od;
    if j = i → i := i + 1
    □ j ≠ i → A:swap (i, A.hib);
              A:hirem
    fi
od
```

The concern for efficiency is an important one for programmers. The use of this method of program design allows the programmer first to derive a correct algorithm and then to analyze its performance and modify it to improve its efficiency of execution. A distinct advantage of this design method is that the intellectual grasp of the rationale demonstrating the algorithm's correctness will usually permit performance improvement modification with less risk of introducing errors. In the above example, even if the transformation is rather subtle, the correctness is easily demonstrated by reference to the reasoning used to derive the previous version.

The search for alternative solutions to a programming problem may be required by efficiency considerations

A NEW VERSION OF THE TEXT-PROCESSING EXAMPLE USING PROCEDURAL ABSTRACTION

A new loop invariant

As we said above, we may use a different choice for the loop invariant, producing a completely different program. In this choice for the loop invariant we assume that A(i) may have duplicates in the nondashed portion of the figure only. This assumption implies that all the elements in the dashed portion are different not only from each other but also from all the elements in the nondashed portion.

Formally, this new fact can be written as

$$\textbf{for all } j\ [A.lob \leq j \leq i - 1 \Rightarrow A(i) \neq A(j)]$$

As a termination function we take

$$A.hib - i$$

This new invariant will require a search for all the elements in the nondashed portion that may be equal to A(i), since all these elements must be removed from the array at each iteration.

A search for all the elements in an array equal to some datum is a slightly more difficult problem than the linear search for the first element we used in the preceding solution. Therefore we may decide to introduce a subprogram for this search. In doing so, we are able to defer its solution until the overall program structure is fully defined.

Procedural abstraction as a tool to abbreviate programs

This technique is a rather common programming technique, and it is called *procedural abstraction*. It consists of abstracting a piece of the program (usually not yet written) by substituting to its text its pre- and postconditions. In this way the overall structure of the program can be defined and its correctness demonstrated by using a shorter program text.

The following program segment maintains the new invariant and decreases the termination function if the subprogram SEARCH is written to respect the following pre- and postconditions:

```
SEARCH (A(i));
i := i + 1
```

SEARCH precondition:

$$A.lob < i < A.hib$$

SEARCH postcondition:

$$\textbf{for all } j\ [i + 1 \leq j \leq A'.hib \Rightarrow A'(i) \neq A'(j)]$$
$$\textbf{and } A'.dom \leq A.dom$$

The overall program (using SEARCH as a subprogram) can be written as follows:

```
i := A.lob;
do i < A.hib →
   SEARCH (A(i));
   i := i + 1
od
```

Note that the invariant is established by defining an empty dashed portion (i = A.lob).

The guard i < A.hib may require some justification, particularly in light of the fact (not yet clear) that i ≤ A.hib would also result in a correct program. From examination of the SEARCH precondition, however, we see that the guard i < A.hib is the right choice. The point is that as a consequence of A(i) not being equal to any element in the dashed portion of the figure at the state for which i = A.hib, the whole array becomes dashed, as required in the postcondition.

Design of SEARCH

The subprogram SEARCH requires a treatment similar to that of the main program. The problem is to search the portion of the array from i + 1 to A.hib for all elements equal to A(i). We supply in this example only a sketch of the specification and derivation for this program.

An appropriate loop invariant for SEARCH is found by the usual approach of imagining that only part of the iteration has been performed. In this case we imagine that the search has been performed for the portion between i and j of the part of A that must be searched. This choice is shown in the following figure:

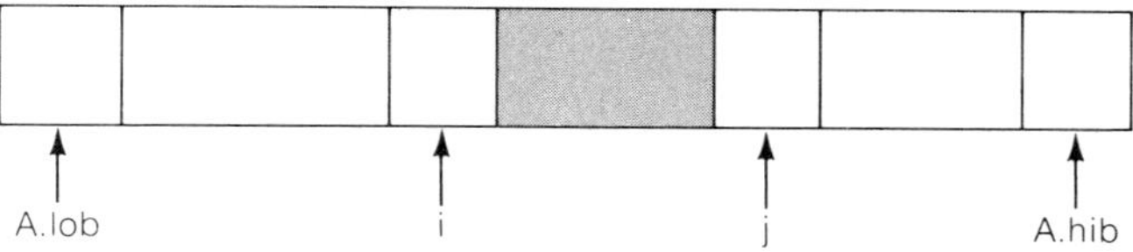

The dashed portion (between i and j) contains elements that are known to be not equal to A(i).

Formally, the loop invariant for SEARCH can be written as

for all h [i + 1 ≤ h ≤ j − 1 ⇒ A′(i) ≠ A′(j)] **and** A′.dom ≤ A.dom

As a termination function, we choose

A.hib − j

which can be reduced by both increasing j and reducing A.hib.

The following program maintains the loop invariant and reduces the termination function:

```
j := i + 1;
do j ≤ A.hib →
    do j ≤ A.hib cand A(i) ≠ A(j) → j := j + 1 od;
    if  j > A.hib → skip
    □ j < A.hib → A:swap (j, A.hib); A:hirem
    □ j = A.hib → A:hirem
    fi
od
```

As long as the inner loop—which performs a left-to-right search for an element A(j) equal to A(i)—is in execution, the termination function is reduced (j := j + 1) and the invariant is maintained (A(i) ≠ A(j)).

At termination of the inner loop, if A(j) is equal to A(i), A(j) is removed, thus reducing the termination function while maintaining the invariant (nothing has changed in the dashed portion).

Procedural abstraction is not sufficient for large-system designs

The last two examples we have discussed are much more difficult than the first one. Thus it should be apparent that Dijkstra's design technique may be applied effectively to programs of much more algorithmic complexity and larger size than the simple examples shown earlier. [For a large number of elegant and generally difficult examples, consult Dijkstra's (1976) book.] However, even with the use of procedural abstraction, it is not yet possible to imagine applying this technique to the task of designing a large software system. It is only possible to imagine that once the system is specified in its component parts, these parts, if they are not too large, can be designed as programs by using this technique.

APPRAISAL OF DIJKSTRA'S CALCULUS

By the introduction of Dijkstra's calculus we have gained the advantage of not being required to build and execute the program to verify a design decision. We also have at our disposal several concepts that permit us, for the first time, to discuss the correctness of a program on a rigorous basis. In addition, a description of the mental process used by the designer can be read, appreciated, and criticized by reviewers on a more solid basis than intuition, and program documentation could include a description of the reasoning used for the design of a program. Dijkstra's technique supplies a precise framework for this type of documentation. Thus this technique could be a significant step toward the introduction of engineering discipline in the programming craft.

Problematic features of programming languages limit Dijkstra calculus applicability

On the other hand, the technique is still far from solving some pressing issues of programming. One such significant issue is the presence of problematic features in currently used programming languages and systems. We have shown the application of the technique only by using the data structure array, as defined by Dijkstra, which is not a common feature of the implementation tools available to present-day programmers. Data types such as pointers and some mechanisms of parameter passing are far from being tractable with the same degree of rigor and elegance.

Expression of the program specifications in the language of predicate calculus helps reduce errors

Another negative consideration is that specifications written in the language of predicate calculus may be considered illegible by many practitioners. Also, errors can be (and are) introduced in the specifications, and their discovery is not an easy task. Furthermore, specifications usually contain more symbols and therefore may be considered more complex to write. However, this complexity reduces errors in the final product because it forces the designer to consider situations that are likely to be neglected when the problem solution is expressed exclusively in the programming language. In other words, the additional complexity of the specifications is not artificially introduced for the sake of formalism but reflects the true complexity of the programming problem, which the compact form of the programming language tends to hide. In this sense the use of specifications is a way to force the designer to extend attention to aspects that may have been otherwise neglected.

In summary, we have found a way of defining and documenting correct algorithms in the language of guarded commands. And it does not matter how difficult the algorithms are, provided they are not too large. We also have some properties of programs (such as loop invariants and termination functions) that are useful mental constructs for the design of correct programs. But if we had to stop here, the interest for the practical system programmer would be rather limited. Fortunately, we are now at the point where we can move toward the introduction of similar techniques that allow us to consider the design of much more complex systems, as we will see in succeeding chapters.

CORRECTNESS OF PROGRAMS DESIGNED USING A RIGOROUS METHOD

How effective are these methodologies, such as Dijkstra's calculus, in creating correct programs? It must be said immediately that these techniques will by no means make any designer an infallible creator of correct programs. Even persons experienced in the use of these techniques may produce incorrect program designs. Errors may be introduced in both the specifications and the reasoning used to support design decisions.

One possible specification error is to state postconditions that are actually weaker than required. This error happens when informally stated specifications are not explicit about some obvious features. For example, consider the informally stated requirements for the program that eliminates duplicate characters. The exclusion of the requirement to preserve, in the output, the order of the characters in input may have not been explicitly presented. In that case, if the intent of the requirements was to preserve that order, all the designs we presented are incorrect.

A common error is having postconditions that are too weak

Another example is the specification of a list-sorting algorithm that does not explicitly state that the final sorted list must contain all the elements of the list used as input. Because the expression of this last condition in the language of predicate calculus is very difficult, it is seldom expressed formally. But if this condition is not written, a program that constructs the elements of a sorted list in some arbitrary manner would be perfectly correct with respect to these specifications.

In practice, one of the most common sources of errors is the incompleteness of requirements, which is caused by the reliance on and the use of informal language for their expression. For all programs that are part of a large system, requirements are actually specifications of the functions required from the program to satisfy the overall system requirements. We will discuss, in Chapters 12 and 13, rigorous methods to organize these specifications. Since requirements may be incompletely expressed, they should be checked by appropriate test cases (see the

Informally expressed requirements are a cause of errors

next chapter). However, the effort to express the requirements as *what* the program is supposed to do seems to be much more effective in detecting incomplete requirements than the usual approach that skips the creation of formal specifications.

The use of informal arguments for the support of design decisions is another source of potential error. A designer may neglect some important property of the objects the program is to manipulate. However, even semiformal reasoning can be effectively checked by another person if it is based on precisely defined concepts. In this sense the use of programming methodologies such as Dijkstra's calculus could be quite effective.

There are a few examples in the literature of "correct" programs designed with the help of some modern rigorous methodology that are actually incorrect. An interesting description of some of these cases is given by Gerhart and Yelowitz (1976). However, the literature contains a much larger number of examples of correct programs derived by the use of rigorous methods.

Tedious formal proofs are causes of errors

The use of much more formal reasoning, such as supplied by formal logic, is possible. However, the tediousness of the process may be a deterrent to its use on the part of programmers. The obvious solution would be to have the computer perform the tedious part of the proof, possibly in an interactive manner. Some computer-based program verifiers are currently in an experimental stage [see, for example, the one described in Gerhart and Wile (1979)].

In summary, Dijkstra's calculus is a very effective method for producing correct programs of considerable algorithmic difficulty, provided the deduction process is carefully controlled by another experienced person or by the same designer at a later time. In other words, errors can be made, but they are usually found by critical inspection of the design. However, in spite of claims by supporters of these programming methodologies, it is not yet possible to dispense with testing programs created in this manner. The appropriate role of testing will be discussed in the next chapter.

HIGHLIGHTS

In this chapter, with the help of a few examples, we have illustrated a program design method, the calculus of programming conceived by Dijkstra, that uses the proof process as the essential mental tool. The importance of the approach is that it shows a valid alternative to the usual approach of program design by enumeration of actions that relies on the execution of test runs as the primary mental tool.

Dijkstra calculus requires the creation of formal specifications. The formal specifications are guides to the design process itself. The postcondition is used as the starting point for the determination of the loop invariant. In this method the postcondition is weakened in such a way that the weaker form represents an intermediate state for the program loop.

The examples here have shown that rather difficult programming problems can be attacked by this approach. However, both the examples presented and the experiences with Dijkstra calculus do not indicate that large-system design is facilitated by this approach. The main advantage of Dijkstra calculus is that it permits programmers to correctly derive programs of limited size, even if these programs are of considerable algorithmic difficulty. The use of procedural abstraction (a fancy name for the use of subroutines) permits the application of this approach to programs of more substantial size.

REFERENCES

Dijkstra, E. W. 1976. *A discipline of programming*. Englewood Cliffs, N.J.: Prentice-Hall.

Gerhart, S. L., and Wile, D. S. 1979. Preliminary report on the delta experiment: Specification and validation of a multiple user file updating module. In *Proceedings of a Conference on Specifications of Reliable Software, Cambridge, Mass.*, pp. 198–211.

Gerhart, S. L., and Yelowitz, L. 1976. Observations of fallibility in application of modern programming methodologies. *IEEE Transactions on Software Engineering* SE–2 (no. 3): 195–207.

CHAPTER EIGHT

Program Testing

INTRODUCTION

In this chapter we examine the testing process and its difficulties. We limit the discussion to the testing of an individual program. This simpler discussion allows us to introduce the essential concepts needed for understanding the problems of testing large software systems, a topic treated later in the book, after the characteristics of these systems are described in more detail.

Because of human fallibility, some errors may show up in a program even if the utmost care is used during design. Other errors may arise because of features of the environment, such as the effect of depressing a break key at the terminal, which are almost impossible to consider with precision in a design process such as Dijkstra's calculus. For these reasons programs must be tested—i.e., subjected to controlled experiments—to determine whether or not the design assumptions were fully representative of the real-world requirements and environment. This approach to testing is different from the one currently used.

The current approach to program testing is to use computer executions of the program to support the design process. In this way the designer's intuition is checked by the execution of test cases. In other words, the program is designed as a group of computations, and it is verified by the execution of one test case that is assumed to be representative of all computations in the program.

However, in the design approach we have introduced in the preceding chapters, particularly in the method of Dijkstra's calculus, the program's individual computations are not primary considerations. Instead, the definition of states and their transformation is the guiding concept of program design. In this case the purpose of testing is to check for misapplications and possible limitations of the design reasoning. This approach to program testing is analogous to quality control for engineering products. The purpose of quality control is to verify that the final product has no potential shortcomings due to erroneous design specifications and fabrication defects. Similarly, the purpose of program testing is to verify that the program has no remaining errors.

TEST CASE SELECTION

The reasoning behind testing a program is that once a particular computation—i.e., the processing of a particular state at input—is known to produce correct results, all other computations can be considered correct as well. The validity of this reasoning is trivially shown in the case when all the program's possible computations are tested. But this result implies that we must test the program for all the input states defined by the precondition. Of course, this testing would be impractical for even the simplest programs.

Selection of test cases ensuring correctness is an unsolved problem

On the other hand, our intuition and experience indicate that some computations—i.e., some states in the set defined by the precondition—are representative of a large number of similar computations. We therefore conjecture that a rather limited number of tests should be sufficient to completely verify the correctness of a program. This conjecture has been put in a precise form by Goodenough and Gerhart (1975). They proved a theorem that more or less states the above intuition in precise form. Unfortunately, nobody can determine guidelines for the selection of test cases that are representative of the whole program. To make the situation even gloomier, several recent attempts to solve this problem succeeded only in showing additional complications and difficulties that were not considered by Goodenough and Gerhart (e.g., see Weyuker and Ostrand, 1980).

The research on testing seems to indicate limitations on the use of testing as a correctness validation technique. But testing is currently the sole method used for the verification of design ideas. Thus we need some different approach, such as the one introduced in the preceding chapter, and we need to complement it with an effective test case selection technique.

PATH TESTING

A relatively common (but erroneous) belief is that successful testing of all the paths of the program flowchart, a technique called *path testing*, is a way to ensure a very high level of confidence in the correctness of the program. To show some of the problems with this approach, we will consider first a very elementary example. Let us suppose we have to test a program that squares an integer:

```
a := x * x
```

But for some reason the * sign has been typed as a +:

```
a := x + x
```

If we test the program for x = 0 and x = 2, we do not detect any error, because the values 0 and 2 give the same result when doubled as they give when squared. The point here is that all the paths (there is only one) of this program flowchart are successfully tested by the values 0 and 2, even though the program is incorrect.

Coincidental errors

This type of problem arises when some test results for an operation (such as $*$) coincide with those of another operation (such as $+$) for a subset of possible operands. Consequently, it is impossible to judge the correctness of some outputs unless all values causing ambiguities are known.

Another problem with this idea of testing all the program's flowchart paths can be seen by considering a program for the linear search (left to right) in an array of integers. Let us assume we have incorrectly written this program as follows:

```
i := A.lob;
do i < A.hib cand x ≠ A(i) → i := i + 1 od;
if A(i) = x → print i A(i) ≠ x → print "nomatch" fi
```

The program above is supposed to search the array A for the possible existence of an element A(i) equal to a given x. If we test this program with

x = 25, A.lob = 1, A.hib = 3, A(1) = 12, A(2) = 24, A(3) = 14

the program will correctly print "nomatch." If we test it again with

x = 25, A.lob = 1, A.hib = 3, A(1) = 12, A(2) = 25, A(3) = 14

the program will, again correctly, print i = 2; i.e., it found

A(2) = x = 25

Covering all program control flow paths doesn't detect all errors

These two test cases cover all the paths of this program's flowchart. In spite of these correct test results, the program is incorrect if we intend to use it as a search for a value of A(i) equal to x over all the elements of A. The following test case will show the incorrectness of the program:

x = 25, A.lob = 1, A.hib = 3, A(1) = 12,
A(2) = 24, A(3) = 25

Now the program will incorrectly print "nomatch," even though A(3) = x = 25. Thus we see that testing all the program's paths does not give us any assurance of correctness.

The type of error presented here is one that is promptly detected by textual inspection of the program. It is also easily avoided during design by use of Dijkstra's calculus.

Domain testing may ensure correctness in some cases

A considerable improvement on the approach of path testing is the attempt to determine sets of states that can be associated with various program paths. This approach has been exhaustively studied for programs using only real numbers as data types (White and Cohen, 1980), and it is called *domain testing*. Under a few limiting conditions it is possible to determine, for programs manipulating real numbers, a set of test cases that suffices to show correctness. However [see Pizzarello (1984) and the references listed there], this study points out another serious problem with the idea of exhaustively testing a program, namely, that the number of cases required even under limiting assumptions is still beyond any reasonable level for practical application.

In summary, path testing requires only a reasonable number of test cases, but it leaves serious doubts about the correctness of the program. Domain testing, in some cases and with considerable limitations, ensures correctness, but it requires too many test runs to be of practical use.

The technique of path testing is only one example of the current emphasis in the testing research community on attempting to show the correctness of the program without considering formal specifications (Pizzarello, 1984). With this assumption, the only available structure for determining test cases is the one supplied by the program text itself. But program text is a description of the potential flow of control (via its paths) and has very limited information about states and their transformation. Also, some of the required program functionalities may be missing in the text. It is impossible in the latter case to determine which test cases must be used to show correctness because the necessary information is not included in the sole source considered, namely, the program text.

THE PROBLEMS IN PROGRAM TESTING

We can clarify the shortcomings of test case selection as a correctness on verification procedure if we consider the two examples of erroneous programs above in light of the concept introduced in Chapters 6 and 7.

The first example (a := x + x instead of a := x * x) merely points out the insufficiency of test cases to detect potential ambiguities resulting from various operations of a data type. In this case it happens that the operations * and + for integers define the same output states for input states corresponding to the values 0 and 2.

The second example illustrates a program designed for a correct loop invariant but with an erroneous guard. This program would be correct, though, for a postcondition different from the one required by the problem specified. That is, it is correct for a postcondition that asks only for the detection of the leftmost match between x and the elements in the portion of A between A.lob and A.hib − 1. But the correct postcondition is not known because it is not expressed in any way.

Program proving and testing have different scopes

These two examples show that both the desired program and the incorrect program are actually correct with respect to a different set of specifications. If we use a test case that produces results in accord with specifications that we judge unsatisfactory, we actually discard both the program and its unsatisfactory specifications.

This result points out the difference in the scope of the testing process and the scope of the Hoare-Floyd proving process, even in a design-support form such as Dijkstra's calculus. The proving process scope is limited to a single set of specifications accepted as correct, a set used either for verification or for the direct derivation of the program text. The scope of testing, in contrast, ranges over several potential pairs of program text–specifications because it attempts to establish the correctness of one of several potential pairs by inspecting their results in light of some external knowledge of the real-world problem. In this sense no program verification or design technique can ever substitute for the testing process.

On the other hand, these pairs of program text and specifications are very close to each other. The sets of states defined by the postconditions usually intersect each other extensively. It is this closeness of all these pairs that contributes to the testing uncertainty, because a large number of test cases for an unsatisfactory program support the erroneous belief in its correctness by supplying satisfactory results.

This situation is illustrated in Figure 4. Two specification–program pairs P1 and P2 are depicted by the areas PRE1 (the precondition of P1), POST1 (the postcondition of P1) and PRE2, POST2. Assume P1 is the desired program and P2 the one actually written. A computation executed by P2 initiating in the intersection of PRE1 and PRE2 terminates in the intersection of POST1 and POST2 and thus is judged correct. If this judgment is extended to all computations of P2, there is the possibility that another input in PRE2 terminates in a state (such as x in Figure 4) that is not a desirable one. Consequently, P2 must be changed to become P1 and therefore correct. Note that the arrows in Figure 4 do not represent program paths. They are only computations, and two or more computations (arrows) may be realized by the execution of the code in one path.

Thus we see that two practical problems arise in program testing. One is the absence of a method that permits us to determine a set of successful tests that characterizes a correct pair of specifications and program text. The second problem is that when we move from a pair of specifications and program text found to be erroneous to a new pair, we know no way to make this move as a step in a rationally defined iterative process convergent to the desired pair of program text and specifications.

PROTOTYPING

We have assumed that during the testing process it is always possible to judge if the outcome of a test is satisfactory. However, in practice this judgment cannot always be made. The judgment of a satisfactory outcome must be based on some comprehension of the real-world requirements, and this knowledge is not always at hand. That is, some requirements that sounded good before the construction of the program do not look so good when the computer execution is examined. For example,

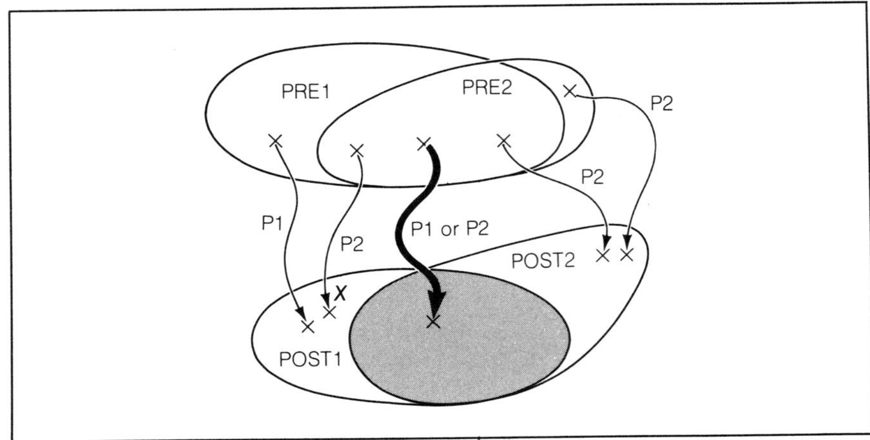

FIGURE 4 PROGRAM TESTING

a module of a large system may be tentatively specified at design time, but because of uncertain knowledge about the function of this module, actual experimentation shows the need for changes in the specifications.

Prototyping as a tool to reduce uncertainty about requirements

In those cases involving a relatively high degree of uncertainty about how to judge the outcome of testing, it is advisable to design, implement, and test a *prototype*. The prototype may be a simplified version of the final program, obtained by concentrating on the program functions relevant to the experimentation. For example, if the uncertainties are relative to a user interface, as is often the case, the interface may be simulated by the use of sample results. In this way the necessary calculations and processing for the preparation of the user-visible results may be reduced to almost nothing. Also, in prototype experimentation there is no reason to verify, for all possible cases, the prototype's correctness with respect to the specifications that are under experimentation. One case is often enough to determine the viability of some specifications in the real world of the application.

Clearly, a prototype is most useful when it can be economically created. If it cannot be, the prototype development is almost equivalent to final product development. However, in light of our previous discussion of the testing process, experimentation with prototypes is useful even when their development is as complex as development of the final product. The reason is separation of concerns. The development of a program is much more efficient when a considerable level of certainty about the validity of the specifications exists, particularly when design methods such as Dijkstra's calculus are used. Also, the refinement of a program for performance is suitable only when reasonably solid specifications are available.

The interest in prototyping has increased considerably in recent years in the computer science research communities ("Rapid Prototyping Workshop," 1982). This interest may soon generate results that can be applied in practice. However, prototyping is currently not used by most contemporary U.S. and Japanese software development organizations (Zelkowitz et al., 1983).

SOURCES OF UNCERTAINTY

In the discussions on testing we have mentioned several sources of uncertainty intrinsic in the process of program development. Because of the practical importance of this subject, it is useful to recapitulate these sources of uncertainty.

Specifications do not reflect the requirements

A program must be specified with precision in the language of the predicate calculus in order to be correctly designed (in the sense of Hoare-Floyd, the program must be consistent with the specifications). But these specifications may be an imperfect description of what the real-world requirements are, and therefore some experimentation may be needed to ensure that the specifications are indeed satisfactory. So specifications and requirements result in one source of uncertainty.

The use of Dijkstra's calculus will produce correct programs with respect to the specifications. In particular, if a review of the design is performed, this approach is quite likely to ensure program design correctness. However, it is a process performed by humans, and hence it is fallible. Thus we have another source of uncertainty.

Certain implementation features, such as depressing a specific key at a terminal or some exceptional conditions, may be cumbersome or impossible to deal with in the framework of a rigorous design process such as Dijkstra's calculus. The response of the program to these implementation features is another source of possible erroneous program behavior and of uncertainty.

Testing is an uncertain process

All these sources of uncertainty must be reduced to a reasonably low level by testing either a prototype or the final product. The problem, however, is that the process of testing introduces another significant source of uncertainty, because we do not have a method for selecting all those test cases that ensure correctness for all possible inputs.

In this chapter we are considering individual program testing. Most programs are parts of a system. Anticipating the analysis that will be presented in the following chapters, we can state that errors in individual program specifications are actually design errors of the whole system. Thus if we can find safe ways to design a large system, errors in the specifications of individual programs (the modules) will be greatly reduced. It is within this perspective that the importance of program design methods as a way to reduce the effect of major sources of uncertainty peculiar to individual programs should be evaluated. Consequently, from the point of view of individual programs, once the specifications are made more certain by some system design technique, the role of tests boils down to reducing the uncertainty deriving from human fallibility and from some possibly unpredictable effect of the implementation. Note, however, that when a rigorous design method is not used, the role of testing extends to cover the elimination of the uncertainties of an unreliable program design approach.

PROBABILISTIC CORRECTNESS

Let us concentrate now on the problem of testing an individual program (i.e., modules of a larger system). This program is very likely to be correct, because it was designed for correctness according to a rigorous method such as Dijkstra's calculus, with respect to some precisely stated specifications. These specifications, in turn, are very likely to be the desired specifications, because they were determined according to a rigorous system design method—a method we do not know about yet since it is the subject of the rest of this book. Our problem is to find a test case selection approach that supplies, if not complete certainty, at least a very high probability of not declaring as correct a program that is, in fact, incorrect.

The usual approach to solving problems of too vast a complexity for direct attack is to introduce probabilistic concepts. Typical examples are the study of the properties of fluids in statistical mechanics and the use of opinion polls for the study of social behavior of human populations. In this light the testing problem can be restated as follows: What is the set of test cases that gives a certain probability of correctness for a program within a preestablished level of confidence?

Because we have no knowledge of how the set of input states can be partitioned in subsets verifiable by a single test run, we may use a testing-by-sampling approach. In this approach we generate n different test cases by picking, within all possible input states of the program (as defined by the precondition), n cases at random. This approach, first proposed by Duran and Wiorkowsky (1980), is analogous to the sampling of voters' opinions before presidential elections. A few randomly chosen cases are used to extrapolate the opinion of a much larger population of voters.

Testing by random sampling

Assume that we test a program that may be still incorrect, with a probability Q, for n randomly chosen cases. For all these tests the program will behave satisfactorily with a probability of

$$P = (1 - Q)^n$$

It follows that the upper bound of confidence on this probability within a level of significance α is

$$\mathrm{UB}(Q) = 1 - \alpha^{1/n}$$

It should be noted that the value of UB(Q) *does not depend on the size of the sampled population.*

To get an idea of what these formulas indicate, let us assume $n = 50$ (i.e, 50 randomly chosen tests are performed with satisfactory results) and $\alpha = .95$ (i.e., we have 95% confidence in the result). Then

$$UB(Q) = .0582$$

In other words, the program that passes these 50 tests has a probability between 0 and .0582 of still being incorrect. This result is valid with a level of significance of 95%.

This result is very interesting. Most readers would agree that 6% probability of rain in a weather forecast means practically the certitude of good weather. However, let us consider a few practical points. Most programs conceived as they are today would not pass 50 randomly chosen test runs without a problem. Of course, they would execute for even more than 50 runs, but usually with inputs coming from a few subsets of test cases chosen by the programmer. The randomness of selection extends the probability of covering all the subsets of inputs necessary to show the correctness beyond some unavoidable bias on the part of the program's author.

Random selection avoids the programmer's bias in test case selection

However, 94% probability of being correct for a program integrated in a large system is not that high. In fact, if we have a system made up of a hundred programs all tested as above to ensure a probability of 94% of being correct, the probability of the system's being correct is only 1.6%. In other words, the probability of correctness for a large system requires a successful series of runs for the whole system, and it cannot be based on unit test results alone (see Chapter 16). However, the independence of UB(Q) from the size of the tested program or system allows us to obtain the same high level of confidence for the system with a limited number of test cases. So if the system passes 50 test runs, it will have a probability of 6% of being incorrect.

Another practical point is that most people are edgy about purely statistical considerations. What kind of assurance do we have that program errors do not present precise patterns of behavior defying the randomness assumption of the above formula? What kind of assurance do we have that very subtle program errors are also caught by random testing with the probability indicated above? That is, the concept of probability is essentially experimental (von Mises, 1957). So we should not trust any prior probabilistic inference if we do not have some experimental evidence to support it.

Fortunately, we have experimental evidence. A series of tests on real programs, together with simulation studies (Duran and Naftes, 1981; Bell, 1983), support the claim of effectiveness of random testing. Duran and Naftes (1981) report that a very subtle bug introduced in an algorithmically difficult program was repeatedly found by random test cases. Bell (1983) reports that by using random test cases, he was able to find an average of three logic errors per hour during the first three days of testing. The software tested in this case was rather large (actually, it was a software system according to the definition in this book) and had been thoroughly checked and tested by the developers before being subjected to random testing (Bell calls this random testing "Monte Carlo debugging").

These results support the validity of random testing as a quality assurance tool. Even though in this chapter we focused on individual programs, the random-testing approach is easily extended to a system test, and most of the above discussion applies equally well to software systems. We will discuss the specific system issues for system testing in Chapter 16.

HIGHLIGHTS

In this chapter we have examined the program-testing process. In practice, programmers use test runs to support the program creation process. In this way both the text and its specifications can be verified by test runs. However, this test process is highly intuitive, and it does not supply any definitive verification of program correctness.

To remedy this problem, researchers have focused on the determination of a set of test cases that ensure the correctness of the program. However, the problem is a very difficult one and is far from being resolved. In the few cases where a test case selection suffices for correctness verification, a very large number of test cases are needed, making it impossible to apply these results in practice. Because of this difficulty, testing should be used in conjunction with a rigorous design method to verify the program for all the errors introduced by the fallible human designer.

The most promising approach to testing as a verification tool is the random selection of test cases. For correctly designed programs this approach supplies a satisfactory level of confidence for programs of any size.

REFERENCES

Bell, R. C. 1983. Monte Carlo debugging: A brief tutorial. *Communications of ACM* 26 (no. 2):126–127.

Duran, J. W., and Naftes, S. 1981. A report on random testing. In *Proceedings of the 5th International Conference on Software Engineering, San Diego, 1981,* pp. 179–183.

Duran, J. W., and Wiorkowsky, J. J. 1980. Quantifying software validity by sampling. *IEEE Transactions on Reliability* R–29 (no. 2):141–144.

Goodenough, J. B., and Gerhart, S. L. 1975. Toward a theory of test data selection. *IEEE Transactions on Software Engineering* SE–1 (no. 3):156–173.

Pizzarello, A. 1984. A view of program and system tests. In *Proceedings of the 3rd Phoenix Computer and Communication Conference,* pp. 158–173.

Rapid prototyping workshop. 1982. *ACM SIGSOFT* (Software Engineering Notes) 7 (no. 5).

von Mises, R. 1957. *Probability, statistics and truth.* New York: Dover.

Weyuker, E. J., and Ostrand, T. J. 1980. Theories of program testing and the application of revealing subdomains. *IEEE Transactions on Software Engineering* SE–6 (no. 3):236–246.

White, L., and Cohen, E. I. 1980. A domain strategy for computer program testing. *IEEE Transactions on Software Engineering* SE–6 (no 3):247–257.

Zelkowitz, M. V.; Yeh, R.; Hamlet, R. G.; Gannon, J. D.; and Basili, V. R. 1983. Software productivity survey of industry. University of Maryland report, College Park, Md.

CHAPTER NINE

Reading and Understanding Programs

INTRODUCTION

A program is subject to modification during its life cycle. To accomplish modification work, programmers must understand the program's meaning; i.e., they must be able to derive its specifications from the program text itself. We discuss this problem in detail in this chapter.

The importance of this problem becomes evident when the maintenance phase of a software system is considered. During such phases an existing system has to be modified either because a malfunction has been detected or because an extension in its capabilities is needed. And at the base of all such maintenance work is the activity of reading programs with the purpose of understanding their meaning. Programs must be read because almost universally no written specifications exist that can be used reliably for this purpose. So reading and understanding programs represents a large percentage of the work done by the programmers involved in maintenance.

We have pointed out that writing a relatively small program cannot be considered the same as developing a large system, even in its essentials. But a system is made up of small programs, and therefore these programs are constructed as part of the software system development process. Analogously, the maintenance of a software system cannot be reduced to the activity of reading and understanding short programs only. However, reading and understanding small programs is a basic step in system maintenance. Consequently, as we have done for program writing, we will discuss reading and understanding relatively small programs without being concerned (for the time being) about the details of the large systems that these programs may be a part of.

TECHNIQUES FOR UNDERSTANDING PROGRAMS

The technique currently used to read and understand a program is (almost universally) a mental simulation of computer runs. Actually, it is hard to imagine any other method being used, because the only information available, the program text, is by its nature intended for execution on a machine.

Code comments may be unclear and out of date because of changes

In most cases the program text is augmented by comments. These comments are written by the program's author to explain some of the design decisions made. They reflect the writer's particular way of thinking, his or her cultural background, and the ability to express, clearly and concisely, what often is a complex technical issue. But very often comments are merely a paraphrase of the code itself, written in a human language. For example, maintenance programmers commonly find a comment such as "get the next entry" associated with the completely clear operation of increasing the value of a machine register.

This example is not to be construed as a discouragement of putting comments in the code. Quite the contrary. We would like to see, along with the code, a fully rigorous description of the design process, possibly done along the lines of the technique presented in Chapter 7.

Unfortunately, programs and comments are written in various ways, and no general rule exists for writing comments. Furthermore, the very process of program modification intrinsic to the maintenance phase often reduces the usefulness of the code comments. Thus when the program text is modified, the comments may not be modified to reflect the design decisions made in the modification. This oversight is not due merely to sloppy working habits, though many times this is certainly the case. But the nature of programs is such that a very small change (in the sense of the number of text characters altered) may cause a substantial revision of the program's specifications. In this case the programmer may modify the comments close to the modified code, leaving intact other comments in parts of the program that are affected by the change but not modified. These comments thus become ambiguous or even incorrect. Over time, the result is a degradation not only of the clarity of comments but also of their correctness. Note that this deviation of the comments from program meaning is a danger present in any form of written specifications. Even if a program is designed (and fully documented) along the lines introduced in Chapter 8, there is no guarantee that the formal specifications are changed when the program text is changed.

For this reason, experienced maintenance programmers, working on aged code, do not rely on the clarity and the correctness of comments. They prefer to obtain the semantics of a program by direct interpretation of the text.

Program may be a part of the documentation

A possible solution to this problem of comments is a tool recently proposed by Knuth (1983). This tool, called WEB, permits the programmer to extract the source code from an exhaustive description of the design reasoning. For instance, with this tool a programmer would take the text explaining the design of the programming examples in Chapter 7 and use it as the sole source code for the program (note that this procedure is possible only if the programmer had a compiler for the guarded commands language). In this technique design documentation is the only product of the programming activity.

UNDERSTANDING CODE BY SIMULATED RUNS

As we have observed, the most natural thing to do with code is to execute it. When execution is done mentally, the effect of that particular run is obtained. In turn, the effect of a particular run is usually generalized to a class of computations, and thus a mental picture of part of the whole program effect is obtained.

In analogy with the enumerative way of thinking used by the program's creator, when program readers are required to describe the meaning of a program, they usually express a sequence of action steps relative to the computations whose effect they thought they understood. In other words, even if the meaning of a program has been obtained by some process of abstraction (intuition) and not by execution of computations, the verbalization of this meaning is still expressed as a sequence of execution steps.

Verbalization of ideas helps in discovering inconsistencies

The purposes of verbalization of a program meaning are, first, to reduce the potential deception of the intuitive thinking process and, second, to communicate the meaning to other maintenance programmers, whose work may be affected by this knowledge. (To justify the first statement, think about how often a brilliant intuition has been proven wrong when an attempt to put it down in writing was made.)

The current approach to program understanding uses actual test runs of the unmodified and the modified program. Test runs are considered the definitive method for checking the validity of a guess about the meaning of a program. These tests, in some cases associated with core dumps, are the tools that supply state information about the examined computation. Unfortunately, as we noted for program writing, this process is expensive, and it is also inadequate for showing the meaning of a program with an acceptable degree of completeness.

In terms of our discussion about testing (Chapter 8), the job of the maintenance programmer is to attempt to re-create whatever design theory was in the mind of the original designer on the basis of some disjointed observations of test computations. If we assume, as is often the case, that that theory was never consciously expressed and may very well be erroneous, it is not hard to understand both the difficulty and the uncertainty of the maintenance programmer's work. But we have found a discipline that permits us to frame program design decisions in rigorous principles. Are these principles of any help in the activity of program reading and understanding? This is the issue we turn to now.

CREATING FORMAL SPECIFICATIONS FROM A PROGRAM TEXT

Understanding the program specifications does not require execution of the code

In a recent paper Basili and Mills (1982) presented a report about the use of the principles of program proving (the ones introduced in Chapters 6 and 7) for understanding and unequivocally recording the meaning of an existing program. The technique does not require any mental execution of the program but relies on the semantic definition of the programming language constructs.

In the following subsections we present an example to illustrate this technique. Even though the technique has had only limited application to practical cases to date, its effectiveness is quite impressive. The only prerequisite to understanding the technique is a degree of familiarity with the approach of program proving and design through formal specifications, as presented in the preceding chapters. The example follows the general lines of the Basili and Mills approach, but several variations and shortcuts were introduced by this author.

The program example is short but far from trivial (Gries, 1977). It presents considerable algorithmic difficulties, and it requires a rather strong precondition. For this latter reason a program of this type is similar to the ones that are components of a large system. In fact, the precise determination of pre- and postconditions is necessary for the successful modification of a module in a large system.

The Design of the Social Security Problem Program

Before we introduce the technique, we present the deduction of the program from its specifications by using Dijkstra calculus. In a sense, we are giving the solution to the problem in advance. But this procedure may clarify the steps used in constructing specifications from a program text. For readers who wish to test their ability to understand the program before examining the technique, the program text (written in PL/I) is presented in Figure 5. (For some reason, which was not recorded by the author, the program was called "The Social Security Problem.") Readers who wish to skip the design description, which is usually not available to maintenance programmers, may want to proceed directly to the next subsection.

The problem is as follows: Given three files A, B, and C (representable as arrays of integers), sorted in ascending order, and assuming that all three files contain at least one element with a common value, write a program that determines the indices of this common element in all three files.

If we call i, j, and k the indices for A, B, and C, with I, J, and K the indices corresponding to the common element, the program postcondition can be written as follows (we assume A.lob = B.lob = C.lob = 0 and A.hib = imax, B.hib = jmax, and C.hib = kmax):

[A(I) = B(J) = C(K) **and**
0 ≤ I ≤ imax **and**
0 ≤ J ≤ jmax **and**
0 ≤ K ≤ kmax **and** i = I **and** j = J **and** k = K] **and**
for some i, j, k [0 ≤ i ≤ imax **and** 0 ≤ j ≤ jmax **and** 0 ≤ k ≤ kmax
and A(i) = B(j) = C(k)] **and** [(A, B, C) are sorted in ascending order]

```
dcl   A(0:100) fixed dec (10),
      B(0:100) fixed dec (10),
      C(0:100) fixed dec (10),
      i fixed (4),
      j fixed (4),
        fixed (4),
i,j,K, = 0;
do while A(i) < B(j) or B(j) < C(K) or C(K) <
A(i);
      if A(i) < B(j) then i = i + 1 else
      if B(j) < C(K) then j = j + 1 else
      if C(K) < A(i) then K = K + 1;
end;
```

FIGURE 5 THE SOCIAL SECURITY PROBLEM

The program requires a precondition (which is not to be altered by its execution and therefore is also part of the postcondition):

for some i, j, k [$0 \leq i \leq imax$ **and** $0 \leq j \leq jmax$ **and** $0 \leq k \leq kmax$ **and** $A(i) = B(j) = C(k)$] **and** [(A, B, C) are sorted in ascending order]

The design of the program is accomplished by deriving the loop invariant relation from the postcondition together with an appropriate termination function. In words the invariant can be described as follows:

For all the values of the indices preceding the current one, the values of the files element are less than or equal to the common value, and the files are sorted in ascending order.

These two conditions become the postcondition when $A(i) = B(j) = C(k)$ is verified. The termination function can be chosen as the value of

$$(I - i) + (J - j) + (K - k)$$

Now we can write the loop in the language of guarded commands:

```
do A(i) < B(j) → i := i + 1
□ B(j) < C(k) → j := j + 1
□ C(k) < A(i) → k := k + 1
od
```

It follows immediately that the invariant is always maintained when any of the loop guards is true. It's also trivial (from the precondition) to show that at each cycle the termination function is reduced in value.

The program is initialized by the statement

$$i, j, k := 0, 0, 0;$$

which (trivially) establishes the invariant.

The program can be implemented in PL/I as shown in Figure 5. Because of the short length of the program, no comments were added, other than the rather misleading title. For the implementation it was assumed that

$$\text{imax} = \text{jmax} = \text{kmax} = 100$$

Reading and Understanding the Social Security Program

Let us now consider the task of understanding the meaning of the program shown in Figure 5. It is convenient to transform the program into the guarded command language. This step is also suggested by Basili and Mills (1982), but they use a different program design language. In this particular case, since the program was originally written by using guarded commands, the transformation is already accomplished.

The program consists of the following two statements:

```
Initialization
  i, j, k := 0, 0, 0;

Loop
  do A(i) < B(j) → i := i + 1
  □ B(j) < C(k) → j := j + 1
  □ C(k) < A(i) → k := k + 1
  od
```

Reading and understanding follows a forward approach

In the application of Dijkstra's calculus to this program design, we started with the postcondition and built the loop's invariant (and termination function), and then we used the invariant as a postcondition to determine the initialization statement. We have seen (Chapter 7) that this order (from the postcondition back) is usually the most effective one for program design. When the program already exists, however, the inverse order is deemed more convenient.

The effect of the initialization statement, as determined by the knowledge of the axiom of assignment, is to make

$$A(i) = A(0) \textbf{ and } B(j) = B(0) \textbf{ and } C(k) = C(0)$$

Nothing more can be said about any relation among these values at this time. However, from the knowledge of the semantics of the loop construct, we know that whatever relation exists among A(0), B(0), C(0), it must also be satisfied by the loop invariant. As we noted in Chapter 6 when we introduced the concept of loop invariant, the axiom of iteration is actually a weaker condition than the loop invariant theorem. This assumption may bring us to the determination of a stronger precondition for the whole program. This assumption's effect will be discussed later.

Under this assumption we know that the conjunction of the loop invariant with the negation of the loop guards is the postcondition. Thus, let us assume that the guards are all false at the first iteration; i.e.,

$$A(0) \geq B(0) \geq C(0) \geq A(0)$$

Because of the property of transitivity of greater than, the above relation is reduced to

$$A(0) = B(0) = C(0)$$

But this relation can be generalized to any index i, j, k because of the invariant theorem for a loop. Thus at termination

$$A(i) = B(j) = C(k)$$

We can conclude that the program stops when the current element values of A, B, and C are equal.

The next step is to complete the determination of the loop invariant by examining the loop code. Let us assume that we had executed a certain number of iterations up to some value of the indices i, j, k and that the guards are not all false; i.e.,

$$A(i) < B(j) \textbf{ or } B(j) < C(k) \textbf{ or } C(k) < A(i)$$

For any of the terms of this disjunction that are true, the corresponding array index is increased. This operation is considered as a step toward termination, which we already know occurs when A(i) = B(j) = C(k).

Now let us assume that we are in a state for which

$$A(i) < B(j) = C(k)$$

We can also deduce

$$C(k) > A(i)$$

Thus the only possible index to increase is i. If in so doing we obtain termination, then the value of A(i + 1) is greater than A(i), because

$$A(i + 1) = C(k) > A(i)$$

By applying the same reasoning to all other indices, we deduce

$$\textbf{for all } i, j, k\ [0 \leq i \leq imax \textbf{ and } 0 \leq j \leq jmax \textbf{ and } 0 \leq k \leq kmax \textbf{ and}$$
$$A(i) < A(i + 1) \textbf{ and } B(j) < B(j + 1) \textbf{ and } C(k) < C(k + 1)]$$

which is a statement of the fact that A, B, and C are sorted in ascending order. It immediately follows that if the three arrays are sorted in ascending order, then no other triple of equal-value elements, except the one found at termination, exists, for all indices less than the ones that point to this triple.

Because neither the loop nor the initialization create or exchange elements within the three arrays, it follows that both the sortedness of A, B, C and the existence of an element of common value in all three arrays are also parts of the program precondition.

No mental execution of the program was ever needed

Note that in all the above reasoning the program was never mentally executed. Also, no knowledge beyond some familiarity with the concepts used for the deduction of a program from its functional specifications is needed. Thus it appears reasonable to infer that the deduction of the meaning of a program (pre- and postconditions) from its text does not require more labor and skill than its design.

Appraisal of the Technique

We have seen an example of deduction of specifications from a program text. The technique exploits the concepts used in Dijkstra's calculus for the design of programs. Knowledge of the semantics of the constructs permits a deduction of predicates defining the states of the program, which are supposed to be correct inputs and outputs.

The technique supports the derivation of the pre- and postconditions at the same level of precision used for the rule of inference. As an illustration of this point, note that to construct the meaning of the loop, we used the invariant theorem. We know (Chapter 6) that the loop invariant is not, in general, the weakest precondition of a loop but a slightly stronger condition. In fact, in the example above we determined, as a precondition of the loop and consequently of the entire program, the statement that A, B, and C are sorted. You probably noticed that the program would work correctly under a slightly weaker precondition, namely, that all elements of A, B, C at indices less than I, J, K must be less than the common value A(I) = B(J) = C(K) but not necessarily sorted.

In general, this consideration should not be a potential source of error. It is unlikely that a designer would exploit the minor differences between the loop's weakest precondition and the invariant. However, users of the technique should at least be aware of this possibility.

Programming language features may be an obstacle for the application of the technique

Note also, in the technique presented above, that we have "translated" the PL/I program in the language of guarded commands. We had to do that because we do not have precise definitions of the semantics of PL/I constructs. From admittedly limited experience we believe that this type of translation should not be difficult. However, we have not given any rule or guidance as to how this translation can be done with reasonable hopes of correctness. So this step is an arbitrary one and may be a cause of mistakes. Furthermore, a program using more complex data structures such as pointers may be not usefully (or easily) translated. The issue of the complexity of the semantics of the operations on pointers is not changed by the translation of the control structures of PL/I to guarded commands. Consequently, it is not necessarily true that the elegance of the process of construction of the specifications, as illustrated above, is always shown in practice.

In spite of these remarks, this technique is an important step in the creation of a rigorous basis for large software system maintenance. It brings the process of program understanding to the same level of rigorous intellectual control as the process of program design by use of Dijkstra's calculus. It may even be more effective if the programs were originally designed by using predicate calculus and documented in the language of guarded commands. In this case the technique would allow the exact reconstruction of the meaning of the program. It appears, then, that this approach may be a substantial factor in improving productivity in the maintenance of software systems.

From the conceptual point of view the idea of understanding a program without mentally (or physically) executing it is a real breakthrough in the goal of introducing discipline into the software development process. Because the technique is very recent, however, we have to wait until more data is collected to fully evaluate its practical utilization.

HIGHLIGHTS

A basic step in modification work is to understand the meaning of a written program. Because changes during a program's life cycle may not be reflected in the comments or the written specifications, this understanding is essentially a process of reconstructing the specifications from the text.

Reconstruction of specifications can be done by simulated mental execution of the program. However, this process is intrinsically unreliable. A more efficient method, as illustrated in this chapter, is to use an approach similar to Dijkstra's calculus to derive the formal specifications of the program from the program text. This technique may have a great impact on maintenance work in the future.

In the approach illustrated in this chapter, we interpret the program's statements in terms of specifications by exploiting the fact that the postcondition of one statement is the precondition of the next statement. By having state information from the guards of some statements (IFs and DOs) and by knowing such properties as loop invariants, we can use a step-by-step forward process to reconstruct program postconditions.

REFERENCES

Basili, V. R., and Mills, H. D. 1982. Understanding and documenting programs. *IEEE Transactions on Software Engineering* SE–3 (no. 3): 270–283.

Gries, D. L. 1977. Verbal presentation at the Conference on Research Directions in Software Technology, Providence, R.I.

Knuth, D. E. 1983. Literate programming. Stanford University Report no. STAN–CS–82–981, Stanford, Calif.

CHAPTER TEN

The System Development Problem

INTRODUCTION

We are now at a point where we can initiate the study of large software systems. A frequently posed question is: Is the large size of software systems an attribute created by the requirements or a consequence of poor development practices? In this chapter we address this question by examining the factors contributing to the size of software systems and some difficulties induced by large size.

Size of any engineering product can be (and usually is) measured by the number of elementary components of the product. In this sense an airliner is a larger product than a dishwashing machine, since it is made up of a larger number of different pieces. For software we choose to measure its size by the number of source lines of code (as defined in Chapter 1) that represent its implementation. This way of measuring size is somewhat analogous to the method used by other engineering products.

Size differences among software systems exist in part because of different development practices and developer skills. But the size of a software system is also dictated by many other factors, such as user requirements, available hardware, and error handling. Therefore size comparisons between different systems should consider all these factors. When they are, little size reduction will be obtained for software written to solve what are intrinsically large and complex problems.

FACTORS CONTRIBUTING TO THE SIZE OF SYSTEMS

As we have just mentioned, many factors contribute to the size of a software system. In this section we will consider four major factors that make large systems large: *user requirements, hardware data types, the system's need to handle exceptions,* and *programming languages.*

User-Visible Functionalities

One cause of large size is the fact a large system must perform many functions, which in turn require a large quantity of code for their real-

Large size is a consequence of the complexity of user requirements

ization. The resulting system grows in complexity with the number of user-visible features. An example is a compiler for languages such as COBOL or PL/I, which is usually larger than the compiler for FORTRAN or Algol because of the larger quantity of source language features that must be taken into account by the compiler. Large size here is clearly the consequence of the vastness of requirements for user-visible functionalities.

A characteristic of this type of complexity is that the underlying structure of the system usually has a large number of separate parts, each realizing separate user-visible functions (see Figure 6). However, these functions need not be fully independent of each other; in fact, as we will see in the next few chapters, the interaction of these functions is a major concern in the correct design of large systems. Nevertheless, these functions are recognized as diverse user-visible endpoints, and they increase the size of the software system.

Hardware Data Types

Another source of increased size and consequent development complexity, hardware data types is best illustrated by a simple example. Let us consider again the program we designed in Chapter 7 to determine the maximum element of an array of integers:

```
j := A.lob; M := A(j);
do j < A.hib →
   j := j + 1;
   if A(j) ≥ M → M := A(j)
   □ A(j) ≤ M → skip
   fi
od
```

Now suppose that the operations A(j) ≥ M and A(j) ≤ M, i.e., the

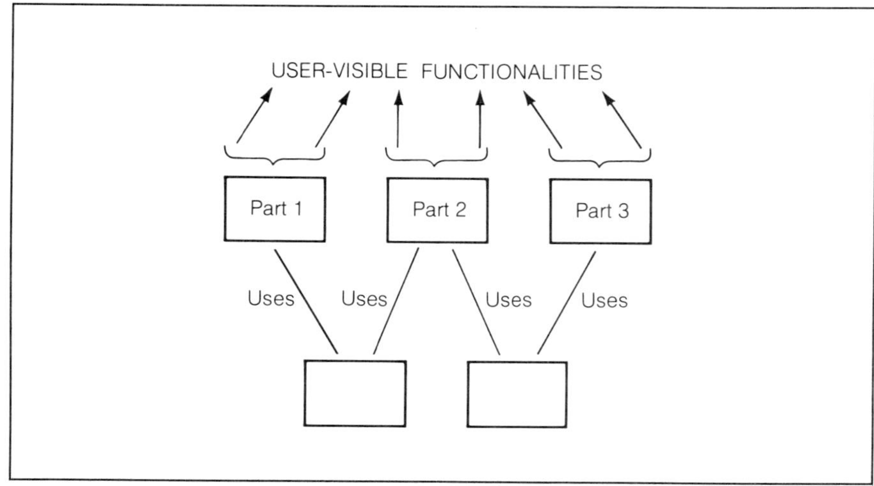

FIGURE 6 STRUCTURE OF LARGE SYSTEMS

Large size is caused by the presence of certain data types in hardware

comparison of two integers, cannot be performed directly in the hardware available. By the term *hardware* here we mean any existing supporting system, such as programming languages, operating system functions, database managers, any other available system software, and the actual machine. We assume that it is possible to perform comparisons only one digit at the time, except for array indices, which we assume can be compared and increased by a single operation.

If we try to rewrite the program for this new assumption, the text presented in Figure 7 will result. In this program A(j) and M are arrays of digits; b is a Boolean function indicating whether A(j) ≥ M, i.e., b <=> A(j) ≥ M; and A(j)(k) is the *k*th character of the *j*th element of the array A, i.e., A is an array whose elements, named A(j), are also arrays, whose elements in turn are named A(j)(k).

As an illustration of the increase in size, consider the single assignment M := A(j), which now becomes the following loop program:

```
k := A(j).lob;
do k ≤ A(j).hib →
   M:hiext (A(j)(k));
   k := k + 1
od
```

```
j := A.lob; k := A(j).lob;
     do k ≤ A(j).hib →
     M:hiext (A(j)(k));
     k := k + 1
     od;
     do j < A.hib
     j := j + 1;
     if A(j).dom > M.dom → b := true
     □ A(j).dom < M.dom → b := false
     □ A(j).dom = M.dom →
          b := true; i := M.lob; k := A(j).lob;
          do i ≤ M.hib and A(j)(k) = M(i) →
                    i := i + 1; k := k + 1
          od;
          if i > M.hib → skip
          □ i < M.hib and A(j)(k) > M(i) → skip
          □ i < M.hib and A(j)(k) < M(i) → b := false
          fi
     fi;
     if b → k := A(j).lob;
          do k ≤ A(j).hib →
          M:hiext(A(j)(k)); k := k + 1
          od
     □ not b → skip
     fi         od
```

FIGURE 7 PROGRAM SIZE GROWTH

Notice that the length of the text in Figure 7 can be shortened by creating a procedure for this repetitious part of the program text, which "moves" A(j) into M.

In this example the repetition is obvious. But in real software systems, code performing the same function often is repeated with, perhaps, minor variations so that the repetition is not so obvious. This repetition causes a considerable increase in program size (and its complexity). Yet the user-visible functionality supplied by the program is not changed. The program at termination still supplies (in M) the largest value (this time represented as an array of digits) of the numbers in the array A.

If we analyze this example in more detail, we see other interesting effects resulting from the changed assumptions about the hardware that is to execute the program. For instance, the pre- and postconditions would be also changed and would become more complex, because now we would have to express the idea of the maximum in terms of the comparisons of digits in a string. Also, the precondition must now express the fact, previously ignored (and irrelevant), that the string of digits in A and M do not have nonsignificant zeros. Note that if this condition is not met, the program shown in Figure 7 would be incorrect, because it uses the property (obvious for humans but subtle for a computer program) that a longer string of digits is always the representation of a number (integer) greater than a number represented by a shorter string. This property is true only if there are no zeros to the left of the first significant digit and if the integer zero is represented by one digit only. If we remove these assumptions, the resulting program will become even longer and more complex.

Handling Exceptions

Exception handling increases system size

All the code we have examined thus far assumes that the elementary state transformations, i.e., the operations on the hardware data types, are executed correctly. Of course, this assumption is not valid in practice, because it is possible that the outcome of these operations may be wrong. The code needed to react to these exceptional conditions represents a very large percentage of software systems. Even though it is executed very seldom because of the infrequent occurrence of exceptional conditions, it is essential for the system's satisfactory operation.

The techniques for dealing with exceptions are usually used for *fault tolerance*. As the name indicates, the basic purpose of fault tolerance is to permit the system to continue to work even when unexpected system states are reached. Fault tolerance study is beyond the scope of this book. In fact, this book is rather concerned with the subject of *fault intolerance*, i.e., techniques for the elimination of errors (exceptional conditions are usually but not exclusively errors).

Even though our concern is with fault intolerance techniques, we cannot ignore exceptional conditions and assume that the probability of errors will be zero. In fact, hardware can physically fail, code text can be incorrectly typed on a keyboard, and specifications may not consider some rare situation in the real world of the application. For these reasons exception handling must be part of any software system.

Hardware-detected exceptions

Let us look at some examples to see how code for exception handling affects the size of the system. To react to an exception in software, a hardware feature may interrupt the sequential execution of the code upon detection of an abnormal state during the execution of an operation. Once the normal sequence of the flow of control is interrupted, the control is transferred to some predefined memory position, where the code written for handling the exception resides. This code's first concern is to save the state of the computation at the instant the exception occurs. That is, once the exception is dealt with, the flow of control must return to the interruption point to permit resumption of the regular computation. Obviously, this activity requires quite a bit of code.

If the exception is an error, it is not always possible to overcome the undesired effects in the program state at interruption time because it is likely that the error occurred several states (steps of computation) before its detection. With this type of exception some safe state preceding the state where the error was manifested needs to be constructed. The usual (and quite often the only possible) way to construct a safe state is to store information relative to states during regular computation execution; upon recognition of the error, the program rolls back the computation to this safe state and then resumes. Saving safe states also requires quite a bit of code.

Software-detected exceptions

A second way to react to exceptions is based on software only, and it deals with both the detection of unsafe states and with the restoration of safe states. Restoration is essentially the same as in the case above. Error detection, however, requires code that at the completion of certain operations will check the state for its legitimacy. As an example, consider the operation of checksum used in some system software to verify the correctness of an I/O operation. The information contained in a record, which may be the object of both read and write I/O operations, can be interpreted as an array of binary numbers. The numbers are added to each other after a modification, and the resulting value will be written together with the record's information content. At a later time, when the record is read, the addition is performed again, and at this time its result must match the value recorded at write time; otherwise, something went wrong during the I/O operations. More sophisticated techniques, based on the same principle of creating redundant information in data structures, are used to detect errors in linked lists and other information structures.

Thus exception handling contributes to the size of the resulting code. Also, it is likely that a large system that contains code for a large number of user-visible functionalities requires different exception-handling code for different functionalities. In other words, there is a snowball effect that tends to increase the system size at a higher rate for those systems that are already large, because the vastness and variety of their requirements produces vast and varied requirements for exception handling.

Programming Languages

The growth of a program's (and consequently a system's) size may be caused by the data types in the programming language being conceptually too far away from the ones visible to the end user. This factor could be used as an argument in support of the idea (see Chapter 1) that different programming language implementation of the same problem could result in different system sizes. This statement is clearly true whenever the contribution of the data types available in the programming language is a significant proportion of the conceptual gap between data types the system is supposed to cover. Examples are numerical computation programs written in FORTRAN or Algol and text manipulation problems implemented in a suitable text editor. However, the gap between most of the required capabilities of a modern system and the ones supplied by a modern programming language is often so vast that in many cases the effect of the programming language on the total size of the system is very minor.

Much more important for its effects is the availability of system functions such as those supplied by an operating system or by a database management system. We can call these functions *environmental functions.* These functions are actually data types conceived in such a way that they support frequently required user-visible functionalities. If these data types are equally available through packages of different programming languages, size differences between implementations in these different languages will probably be very minor.

Environmental functions have important effects on size

Some programming languages, though, include data types specialized for the solution of a certain class of problems. For instance, in the early sixties very specialized programming languages were introduced to permit the expression of problems in terms very close to the specific problem area. Examples of these languages are COGO, for the solution of coordinate geometry problems, and STRESS, for the solution of problems of engineering analysis of elastic structures. More recent examples include application generators, which attempt to make available data types suitable for the solution of relatively restricted classes of applications.

In all these cases, however, some development organization must design and code the software that supplies these desired capabilities in terms of less suitable data types. These development systems are usually the large systems that are the subject of this book. In other words, the trend discussed above will make it possible for programmers to develop applications of relatively small size, because the large-scale system has already been developed by some other organization.

SYSTEM DESIGN BY ENUMERATION OF SUBROUTINE CALLS

Let us consider now current development techniques that are used to cope with difficulties generated by large size. The large size of a software system often dictates that many different persons be involved in development. This fact imposes the modularization (subroutines) of the code.

Software systems viewed as large programs

We may think of a program's subroutines as being written by different authors, while the main program is written by someone overseeing the development. Then according to this view, a software system is merely a large program. And the process of writing a main program that coordinates a large number of subroutines is similar to the development work of a large software system. This view, however, is fallacious, as we will see in the rest of this section.

The problems with this approach are numerous, but we will limit the discussion to the most evident ones. We will return to this subject in the following chapters, after other techniques have been introduced.

Exploding Complexity of the Large-Program View

To show why this approach is ineffective, we will correlate this view of a large system to the view of a program generated by enumerative thinking, as discussed in Chapter 5. Thus we suppose that a program conceived as a set of computation sequences is the model for the view of a large system as a series of subroutine calls. The enumeration of actions to be performed during the execution of each of these computation sequences is facilitated by the abstraction of a sequence of a large number of more elementary actions, in which each action is represented by the subroutine call.

The meaning of each subroutine has to be expressed, even if informally, in terms of a transformation both relevant to and understandable at the level of the main program. In our discussion of procedural abstraction we found that the pre- and postconditions of the abstracted portion of the whole program must be written in terms of objects of the state space of the whole program.

In an informal approach, as in the one normally used by software developers, the subroutine's pre- and postconditions are not explicitly expressed. In their stead a specific computation (one of the many the subroutine is potentially capable of performing) is described as the meaning of the subroutine when called by a specific computation of the main program. Other main program computations evoke different computation sequences in the subroutine, and the description of the meaning of the whole program is thus obtained.

The meaning of a subroutine depends on the invocation

This process is illustrated in Figure 8. Computation sequence a invokes the subroutine in such a way that its execution will activate a computation along the control path x. When the subroutine is invoked during computation b, the corresponding activity of the subroutine is an execution of a computation along the path y. In this way the meaning of the whole program as a set of enumerations of subroutine calls from a main program becomes an enumeration of subroutine actions that are not necessarily the same for all the enumerations.

We see, then, that this situation makes it rather difficult to describe what a subroutine is supposed to do. That is, a large program has numerous control paths, each of which may evoke an even larger number of computations. Suppose the designer of the whole is conceiving the pro-

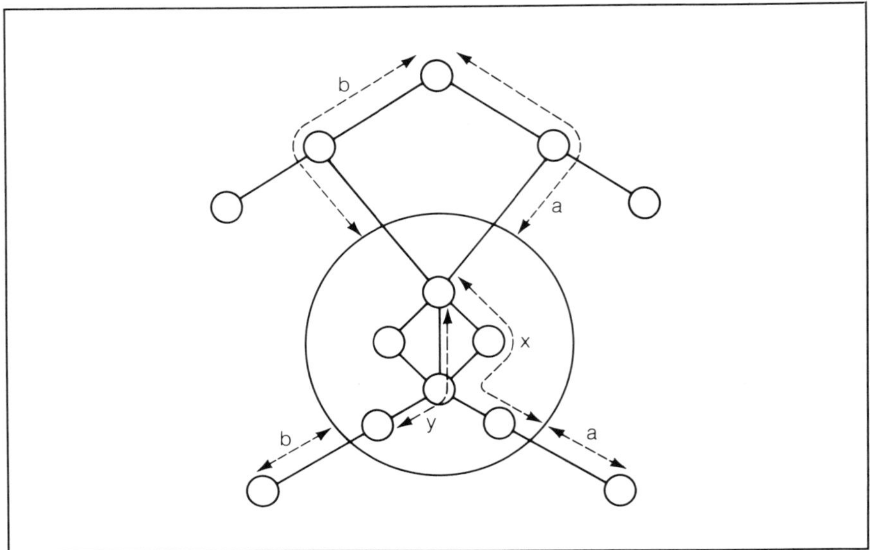

FIGURE 8 CALLING TREE OF A PROGRAM WITH SUBROUTINES

gram by defining these paths as sequences of subroutine calls. To describe the requirements for a specific subroutine, the designer has to be able to collect the various paths' descriptions of the subroutine from all the possible calls. But we know from our discussion about tests in Chapter 8 that the description of sample computations along the program's control paths by no means supplies the full meaning of a program.

If the above process has to be described precisely by using a formalism, an impossibly large amount of work will result. And, in fact, this is precisely what happens when a system informally conceived is implemented. The formalism of the implementation language forces a precise description of the computation sequences. However, because of the lack of precise definition of the intent of these computation sequences (i.e., specifications), the formalization of the system in programming language is usually incorrect. Only through a long and expensive testing process does product reliability become acceptable.

Coupling via Data

With global data it is impossible to consider subroutine invocations in isolation

Another problem, coupling via data, is caused by the above view of a software system. We have seen that the meaning of a program (as well as of a subroutine or a single computer instruction) is effectively expressed as the state transformation of the data manipulated by the program. In considering the effect of a subroutine, the programmer may describe the state changes of the data that are passed and returned as parameters at subroutine call time. The subroutine, however, may change the state of other data that are globally known to the whole (or a large part of the) system. This change of state may (and usually does) affect both other subroutines and the meaning of other subroutine invocations. In this way the effects of the action of a subroutine propagate invisibly to others and are not describable by the approach of enumeration of subroutine calls.

An obvious solution to this problem is to completely avoid this interaction of the various parts by eliminating storage of data accessible globally. However, there are some practical reasons for not using this solution. The most obvious one is that global data cannot be avoided because it is dictated by the problem. For example, in a banking system the database containing the information relative to the customers is intrinsically global data; it must be accessed by the action of inquiry for a checking account balance, by the action of modifying the available credit amount, and by many other necessary actions as well. But suppose that, in theory, we can conceive of a system organized so that customer information is stored with (and manipulated by) the code that performs a particular action. The resulting system may show an unjustifiably high amount of redundantly stored information, which, in turn, may cause both performance and consistency problems. For example, the customer name (or ID) would be repeated wherever information relative to her accounts is stored. Any change on this ID must be performed in all those places or inconsistency will result.

Distributed system architectures

Systems designed according to this architectural concept are usually called *distributed systems*. In a distributed system any information update has to be performed wherever the information is stored. This change requires a mechanism for the communication, to all the modules owning a copy of the information, of the occurrence of the change together with the transmission of the changed value for each update.

There are situations in which distributed system architectures that minimize (or exclude) global data are both desirable and possible. The approach to the design of these architectures, though, requires the introduction of new concepts, which will be discussed in detail in Chapter 16.

SYSTEM INTEGRATION

It is difficult for designers to put together correct specifications for individual modules from the global requirements of a large system by using enumerative thinking, as we have seen in the preceding section, because of the difficulty of controlling the interaction of sequences of computations via global data. The effect of the resulting erroneous module specifications is to increase the cost of the system phase called system integration (data relative to integration were presented in Chapter 2). In fact, system integration represents the first time, in the current software development process, that the design of global properties of a system can be rigorously verified. All tests of separate modules before integration can only ensure that the individual modules work satisfactorily with respect to their specifications, which may be both erroneously conceived and misinterpreted by the programmer.

Integration is the first phase of system development when the global system properties are verified

To see the scope of the problem, let us consider an analogy: the final assembly phase of a mechanical product. In this phase separately built parts are brought together to create subassemblies, and then these subassemblies are brought together to create the final product. This operation is almost completely free from mismatches, even in the case of a very large mechanical assembly such as a ship or an airplane. No mismatches occur because the size of each separate part was determined in the first design phase by a precise evaluation of an overall view of the machinery, carefully verified by a rigorous design discipline. These mechanical systems may present functional defects; i.e., some portions may not perform as required. But there will be no mismatches of parts or subassemblies in the degree shown in a software system, even for one-of-a-kind products such as a bridge or a ship.

An analogous situation for software systems would be if the integration process demonstrated performance shortcomings together with a few misinterpreted requirements but no unexpected behavior of the whole caused by a mismatch of the parts of specifications. However, in large software systems it is quite common for fundamental design assumptions, affecting the entire system architecture, to be found to be erroneous at the integration stage. If something of this sort happened in the case of a bridge or an aircraft carrier, it would make the evening news. The lack of rigorous verification of the overall system design before the assembly of the parts appears to be the reason for the costly integration problems.

The analysis of the causes of the high cost of the system integration phase will be completed in Chapter 16, after we have introduced some fundamental concepts of system design in the following chapters.

THE USE OF FORMAL SPECIFICATIONS

The point we are making is that the specifications for the parts of a software system should be in terms of system states, i.e., in terms of data values instead of the flow of control of specific computations. Because the various modules of a system interact with each other in a rather intricate manner via global data, the specifications of the system parts must be in terms of these data elements instead of the calling sequences of procedures. Specifications should be written this way not only for supporting rigorous and formal techniques but also for supporting informal arguments. A mental construct such as enumerative thinking along the paths of a program calling tree does not facilitate visualization of the interaction via global data, and therefore it is not an effective method for large system developments.

In Chapter 5 we indicated that even in the case of a single program, enumerative thinking is not a reliable way to conceive algorithms. However, an individual programmer may find it effective to use code as a vehicle to express design decisions and to verify decisions by test runs.

The test runs have the effect of clarifying, in the designer's mind, the various points of the design.

This procedure is not effective in a large system however. The system design has many different parts, each to be mastered by a single human mind. Furthermore, the interaction of these parts is not explictly shown in the programming language, because data are made global through some system program (such as a linker or a database management system). Even if the system conception is stored in a single mind (a chief programmer, a system designer), the sheer amount of details involved in the myriad of interacting paths and global data states makes it impossible for that one person to arrive at a smooth integration.

If we now attempt to apply a formal technique for the system design, we must attempt to express the meaning of the subroutine calls by writing pre- and postconditions. These pre- and postconditions could be written as predicates involving data that are local to the subroutines as well as global data. Once these predicates are written, we can apply Dijkstra calculus to design the subroutine code correctly. However, the design correctness of these subroutines is merely a demonstration of the consistency of the code with the specifications.

From what we have discussed so far, we have no way to be sure that each subroutine's pre- and postcondition represents the correct role of the subroutine in obtaining the desired global goals of the system, i.e., the user's requirements. This subject will be treated extensively in the following chapters. The reader should be cautioned, however, not to expect a quick and easy solution to what is a very difficult problem.

HIGHLIGHTS

We have examined the sources of large size in software systems. These sources fall into two broad categories. One involves the vastness of user requirements, which include the ability to tolerate exceptional execution conditions such as errors. The second involves the intellectual gap between the capabilities of the hardware (its data types) and the required capabilities (the user-visible data types). Neither of these categories can be eliminated, and hence large software systems are a fact of life. Designers thus must learn how to cope with their developmental problems.

The current approach to the design of large systems is based on the mental enumeration of subroutine calls. However, this approach is incapable of covering in any controlled manner all the potential computations a system is to evoke. Another problem in current approaches is that correct design specifications are not supplied to module developers, creating difficulties in system integration.

To use a formal approach such as Dijkstra's calculus, we must have precise specifications that are supplied for all modules. The creation of these specifications from the overall system requirements is the key problem discussed in the following chapters.

CHAPTER ELEVEN

Data Abstraction

INTRODUCTION

In this chapter we introduce a concept, data abstraction, that permits the programmer, at least in principle, to reduce the exploding complexity of specifications to manageable proportions.

We have already used the word *abstraction* for the technique of abbreviating the text of a program by the use of procedural abstraction. This technique makes a program text shorter by omitting all the coding details of a procedure. It concentrates the meaning of the procedure in its name and in the list of parameters passed and received. Of course, the effectiveness of this abbreviation relies heavily on the intuitive meaning of the procedure name. And to obtain the precise meaning of the procedure, we must either look at its code or look at the pre- and postconditions if they are available. Furthermore, if pre- and postconditions are available and written in a rigorous form, the quantity of detailed information needed to understand the procedure is of the same order of magnitude of the details in the procedure code itself.

But as we have seen, pre- and postconditions have the advantage of providing comprehensive understanding of the procedure without requiring mental execution of the procedure text. The problem of the exploding size of specifications still exists, though. So if we want to make any progress toward the creation of a rigorous technique to design large systems, we must find a practical solution for reducing the specification size.

Modern science and engineering can describe the behavior of large ensembles without being overwhelmed by details. The key idea behind the techniques used in science is to abstract essential features from the real-world phenomenon. Then they are used to create a model of reality that behaves reasonably close to the phenomenon and can be used to predict real-world behavior. Examples of this form of abstraction are the perfect gas law in physics and the perfectly elastic structures postulated by construction engineers.

A promising and similar form of abstraction for application to large system designs is the technique of data abstraction. The idea here is to abbreviate the representation of a piece of data instead of the procedural text of a program. That is, pre- and postconditions are expressions of relations among data values. If we can make complex assertions about data states concise enough to be intellectually manageable and at the same time precise enough to be used in a rigorous process of program derivation, we have clearly made considerable progress toward the goal of effective large system design.

ABSTRACTING CONCEPTS FROM DETAILS

The purpose of data is to store some meaningful information. Thus a mental concept can be represented in a written (stored) form as a sequence of characters (data). The concept, however, and its representation are not the same thing. It is the processing ability of the reader's mind that transforms the written text into the concept it represents.

Details may obfuscate the meaning

But a profusion of details can make even familiar things not intellectually manageable, as shown by an example presented by Hofstadter (1980). Suppose you must obtain the meaning of a piece of English prose by listening to all its words spelled out in their component letters. You would find very difficult, perhaps even impossible, to determine the meaning in this way. A similar problem in understanding is encountered when the words in a phrase are shuffled as though they were following the construction rules of a foreign language.

It is the abstraction of the details of the various letters of a word and of the various disjointed words of a phrase that makes human languages understandable. Similarly, we usually abstract from a plethora of details when we talk about a software problem.

What we have to do, then, is find out how informal, intuitively understandable ideas can become a rigorous mental process to support the design of a large software system. We have seen that precise definition of design concepts requires formalism, i.e., a precisely defined language to express these concepts. As usual, we have to ground this formalism in the real world (pragmatics), we have to supply a proper syntax, and we have to describe its semantics in terms of the basic pragmatic concepts.

The following sections present the process of creation of this formalism from the analysis of some simple real-world concepts and in terms of data abstraction.

ABSTRACT DATA TYPES

In Chapter 4 we defined the concept of data types. We also indicated that we can define data types from various points of view. Thus user-visible capabilities can be expressed as data types wholly in terms of real-world information and functions of its manipulation. Also computer entities such as machine instructions and storage can be interpreted as data types as well. It follows that we may be able to postulate a sequence of data types in such a way that different degrees of detail of the same software system are shown. A first informal presentation of this idea was made by Dijkstra (1970), who used the metaphor of a necklace to describe the above sequence.

Abstract Machines

As we have seen, a large conceptual gap exists between real-world data and its computer representation. But the program designer need not fill in this gap in one jump. Suppose we postulate some abstract machines that supply more suitable data types. Then the big leap can be reduced to a series of much shorter and more manageable ones. Of course, the nonexistent but desirable machines must be defined with the same rigor and completeness as a real machine.

A real machine has the undeniable advantage of being usable for running programs and therefore obtaining information about its functionalities. So the description of our abstract machine must be such as to supply complete information about its functionalities without requiring any experimentation.

To this end, we are now going to show how such artificial entities, which we call abstract machines [following Dijkstra's terminology, as introduced in Dahl, Dijkstra, and Hoare (1972)] can be invented. These machines will permit the organization of the design of a large system in such a way that both specifications and code can be broken down in steps of sufficiently small size to be intellectually manageable.

Defining the Abstract Machine's Data Type

To define the nonexistent but desirable machine, we must define the range of potential values of the data types for that machine. Recall that a data type is defined by its range of values and by the operations that can manipulate these values. But very often we do not know how to define this range of values.

Abstract machine's data types as a representation of a piece of reality

For example, suppose we are required to represent the books in a library as a data type. It is impossible (or utterly impractical) to enumerate all the possible titles, authors, publishers, and catalog numbers. On the other hand, if we define the books in a library as those things that are represented by a character array (which is clearly a possibility), we dismiss all the bookish properties when we process these arrays. In fact, character arrays may represent so many things besides books that no information about books and libraries can be extracted from them if no additional definitions are used.

In this sense we must ignore, at first, the computer representation of some real object, such as a book. Instead, we attempt to define a data type that captures all the properties of books we can gather from observations of reality. We can state, for example, that two books are different when either title, author, or both are different and that therefore if two books are different, they have different catalog numbers. Conversely, we can assert that if two books have the same catalog number, they cannot be different. Our knowledge of these (and similar) properties of books permits us to define the data type "book" without being required to enumerate all possible values of the type "book" and without reference to any hardware representation. Of course, we must be able to define what we mean by *different* and *same* in the context of these not-yet-represented bookish entities.

The key is to use all the information we have gathered from observations of the real world. For example, a value of the type "book" may be characterized by the combination of five other values: author, title, publisher, number of copies available, and catalog number. These components are observable for all books in a library.

Data Type Structure

A data type for which we cannot enumerate a range of values is called an *abstract data type.* However, all the structure necessary for the proper understanding and/or manipulation of the data type values must be sketched. The words *proper understanding* and *manipulation,* of course, are not yet defined precisely. We will define them later in this book. In the meantime, however, it is possible to state that we want to use these abstract data types in the same way that we use the "concrete" hardware data types, namely, to construct correct programs. Therefore we must be able to define enough structure to prove properties about programs that use these abstract data types. Continuing the discussion of the book example, this structure may be sketched in two ways, both very significant for all abstract data types.

The *first way* to sketch structure is to note that "book" is made up of author, title, etc. Thus without bothering to define the range of values of the five components, we know that each value of "book" will always be a quintuple of values, each one being required only to be in the not-yet-defined range of each component. Clearly, the definition of this quintuple is a form of representation of the type "book." However, it is a characteristic of the book we obtain from the real world, not one dictated by some consideration of hardware data types. Note, however, that not all these quintuples represent real books.

Identification of components and definition of relationships among them

The *second way* the structure may be given is more subtle, and it does not entail any form of representation. By using the adjectives *same* and *different,* we have stated certain relationships between the undefined values of the various components. These relationships may actually condition the definition of the operations that manipulate objects of the type "book." For example, suppose an operation, say "borrow," reduces the number of copies available, and another one, "return," increases this number. Then borrow will not be permitted to reduce the number below zero, and the subsequent application of borrow and return must not change the number of copies available.

Both ways of sketching structure are needed to convey the concept of book at the level of detail we chose to present. These properties, derived from the knowledge of the real world of applications, are actually axioms in the logical system we are going to use to demonstrate the correctness of the programs using abstract data types.

NOTATION FOR DATA TYPES

To formally express the first way of defining abstract data types, we need to introduce some notation. The notation we will use to indicate that a particular type is defined as being formed by several components is as follows:

```
<type name>:<component list>
<component list>:(<name>:<component__type>, . . . ,
<name>:<component__type>)
```

Here the dots indicate the presence of any needed number of components of the type. For example, the type "book" can be indicated as follows:

```
book:(title:string,author:string,
     publisher:string,cat__no:string,
     quantity:integer)
```

Notice that each component of a book has to be of a certain type. If no component has been identified, we will indicate this fact by using the key word **abstract** instead of a component list:

<type name>: **abstract**

Clearly, the types of the components may, in turn, be made up of other components or simply be **abstract.** However, in the component list we cannot use the key word **abstract** in place of a type name, because it is not a type name itself. It simply indicates all types that are not showing their potential components. If we were to allow the use of **abstract** in place of a type name, it would be impossible to distinguish one abstract type from another.

DATA OBJECTS AND TYPES

Before we proceed with more technical details about abstract data types, we note that whatever the characteristics of the type "book" are, they must apply to all books, no matter how different they are. These properties define equally well (within the scope of our design) Melville's *Moby Dick* and Stoy's *Denotational Semantics.* Actually, these characteristics define the abstraction of all the books in the world. In other words, the data type defines the concept of book, but it does not identify any particular object or set of objects of that type.

Data objects are instances of a data type

Because our system, to do actual work in the real world, has to deal with objects and not with concepts (we want to borrow from the library a copy of *Moby Dick,* not the concept of the book), the abstract data type definition applies to all the objects in the system, but it must not be considered as the definition of any object. When we want to identify a specific object, we have to say, for example,

MD:book

which defines an object of the name MD of the type "book." In this way we may indicate the various components of MD such as the author, title, publisher, and quantity. These components may assume different values that may be represented in various ways, but they all must satisfy all the properties defined for the type "book."

Let us consider now an object of the type "book" that we choose to name DS:book. The object DS may have an author, Stoy; a title, *Denotational Semantics*; a publisher, NIP Press; a catalog number, CS–42–1840; and a quantity, one. Note again that words like Stoy and NIP Press give only one value of the component of the type "book." And they have sense only because we are looking at a specific and utterly familiar representation, i.e., a string of characters. Another object of the same type may be called MD:book and at that particular state for which DS had the value *Denotational Semantics* etc., MD has, for example, the value

Melville, *Moby Dick,* Benjuin Books, FICT–88–4570, ten

We want to be able to discuss relations between MD and DS without using any representation at all for these values. We want to eliminate representations because of our well-justified concern that excessive details may result in needless complexity of specifications and programs.

Set of states can be defined independently from the type representation

Assume now that we want to select books of a particular subject. We may imagine that selection is done by examining some sequence of digits in the catalog number or, in a more sophisticated manner, by examining the title and author. But if we select books in this way, we may end up relying on some form of representation of the components of the objects of the type "book." We can avoid this difficulty by relating an object of the type "book" with an object of the type "subject," which we may still consider as abstract. To do so, we create an operator, say

subject_is

which, once applied to an object of the type "book" and to an object of the type "subject," will return true or false according to the particular values of these objects. For example, for DS:book and S:subject we can write

(DS) subject_is(S)

to describe all the states for which DS is a book classified as of the subject S.

At this point, you may be convinced that we are playing with words. That is, the interpretation of "subject_is" does not appear to be feasible without referring to some representation of the book-components in terms of familiar primitive data types (such as numbers and alphabetic characters). The way out of this dilemma is to introduce properties of the operator "subject_ is" that define it sufficiently without showing unnecessary representation details. This statement is similar to the one we made about the second way of giving structure to an abstract data type. However, that statement referred to relationships among the operations permitted for the manipulation of objects of the type "book." Now we are making a statement about relationships between sets of values of components of certain objects of an abstract data type. Since we know that the effect of operations can be described as state transformations, what we are doing here is defining properties of relevant sets of states.

SPECIFICATION OF ABSTRACT DATA TYPES

State space for abstract data types

The preceding discussion pointed out several intuitively understandable characteristics of abstract data types. Now, in order to define the semantics of our formalism, we must give precision to the concept by describing these intuitive characteristics in terms of some precise model. In the following discussion we will use the familiar state space model to supply organization to abstract data type specifications.

Assume that a system S is made up of several data objects A, . . . , Z, each one an abstract data type (not necessarily the same). We know that we can define a space that describes all the states of the system. Let us consider one of the objects, say H, and let's assume that this object is of the type

T:(C1:t1, . . . , Cm:tm)

i.e., it has m components. The object H defines a subspace of the whole state space of S. Each of the subspaces defined by the abstract objects are the sets of all the states the object can assume. If the object H is of Type T (which we defined as having m distinct components), and if the set of all the states of its generic component (i = 1, 2, . . . , m) is Gi, the operations on the type T for the specific subspace of H can be defined as follows × (indicates the Cartesian product of sets):

$$f1{:}G1 \times G2 \times \ldots \times Gm \rightarrow (G1 \times G2 \times \ldots \times Gm) \times (G1 \times G2 \times \ldots \times Gm) \ldots$$

In other words, a set of m abstract values in the subspace of H is transformed in a set of other m abstract values in the Cartesian product of this space with itself (see Chapter 4). Some of these transformations can be identities (no change at all in the abstract value).

If the type T did not contain any component, the operations on T are simply defined as transformations over the set of abstract values of T, which we may call G (as we have seen in Chapter 4):

$$f1{:}G \rightarrow G \times G$$

If the operations on the abstract data types of S are defined as above, we find that no change of state of an object H can influence a change of state of an object L, because each object is enclosed in completely separated sets of values (the subspaces defined by their type). This result is clearly an undesirable state of affairs because it represents a totally disjointed set of objects that have no way of exchanging information and hence cooperating with each other. We know that real-world systems are not built to operate in this way. Therefore we must extend the operation definitions above.

Parameters

Interaction between data types requires parameters

The necessary extension is to introduce *parameters* for the operations of a data type. Let us consider an operation f on type T. We can define values of some specific objects of some type, which must be available at initiation of each execution of f, and values of some specific objects returned by f at termination. These values are called, respectively, input and output parameters.

We insisted on defining the operation parameters as values because we want to emphasize that only one state of the input parameters is available for each execution of the operation. Also, only one particular state of the output parameters is returned for each execution. These definitions are not equivalent to the state transformations for an object of the type T. Even though we would characterize the execution of f as the transformation between states defined by a precondition and states defined by a postcondition, we are not putting any limitation on the number of possible intermediate states for the data objects of the type T. This definition of parameters imposes the restriction that no data object be accessible by two operations of different objects in our system while changes of states are performed on these objects. Note that most current programming languages do not enforce this rule for parameter passing when invoking a procedure but make available some common storage to both the callee and the caller of a procedure. The impact of this commonly used technique on system maintainability will be discussed in detail in Chapter 16.

A real-world example of parameters as defined above could be specific input values at a banking terminal to perform a transaction (or a portion of a transaction). These values (such as an account number) are made available to some operation on an appropriate system object and used to perform either changes in the object state or retrieval of some value of the current state of the object, then (possibly) returning a value to the terminal. The system has no way of affecting intermediate states of these values supplied or accepted by an operator. In other words, parameters as defined above are interpretable as messages exchanged between objects of some data types or between objects and the outside world.

Type Functions and Invariant

With all the above definitions in mind, a *data type operation* can be formally declared as follows:

<function name><function type>(<input parameters>)
returns(<output parameters>)

Here <function name> declares the name of the operation; <function type>, which may be **vfun, ofun,** or **init,** declares the kind of operation we define; and the two lists <input parameters> and <output parameters> are lists of the names and types of the parameters. The functions defined as **vfun** are such that the state of the data objects of this type is not modified by the execution of these functions. In other words, a **vfun** only reads the content of the object. Functions defined as **ofun** in general will modify the state of the object. Functions defined as **init** will create the object by setting it in a desired state from some predefined environment state. If needed, an **ofun** may be defined that sets the object in such a state that only an **init** function can make it available for further operations; this function is a delete function for the object.

The semantics of each data type operation may be defined by the usual pair of assertions, the pre- and postconditions. As we have indicated above, we have to create appropriate operators (such as "subject_is" in the book example above) among abstract type objects in order to write these pre- and postconditions. We will discuss the techniques of specifications of functions of abstract data types in detail later in this chapter.

A type invariant is a constraint to be respected by all the type's functions

Now we need to introduce one additional concept, which, again, is generated by observation of the real world. Certain properties of the data type's set of values are intrinsic to the type itself and must not be violated by the execution of any of the object's type functions. For example, let us assume that in a banking system the balance (a component of a type) of any account (an object of that type) cannot be "negative" (an abstract property not necessarily related to a potential integer representation of the balance). This global property can be defined by an appropriate predicate, and it is called the *type invariant.*

All type functions expect a state satisfying the invariant at their initiation and are required to leave the object in a state satisfying it at their termination. Only **init** functions initiate on states that do not satisfy the invariant relation, but they are required to terminate in states satisfying it. Of course, with the word *satisfying* we mean states describable by predicates that are equal to or imply the invariant. To avoid unnecessary complications, we assume that all delete functions, if they need to exist, will terminate in a state satisfying the invariant. That is, the object is not really deleted from the state space but only put in a quiescent state that is of no further use for the computations.

The type invariant concept is similar to the concept of loop invariant (Chapter 6). For a loop the invariant expresses the legitimate states before and after every execution of the loop body, i.e., before and after a transformation of states commanded by the loop body's code. The type invariant expresses the legitimate states for any execution of the type functions.

Syntax for Data Type Definitions

We now have enough elements to complete the definition of the syntax for the notation we will use to declare an abstract data type:

```
<type name>:(<component list>)
   let<object list>
      inv<assertion>
      ofun<function name>(<parameter list>)returns
         (<parameter list>)
         pre<assertion>
         post<assertion>
      .
      .
      .
      vfun<function name>(<parameter list>)returns
         (<parameter list>)
         pre<assertion>
         post<assertion>
      .
      .
      .
      init<function name>(<parameter list>)returns
         (<parameter list>)
         pre<assertion>
         post<assertion>
end<type name>
```

Specifications are written as predicates relating data objects

A further comment is necessary to justify the need for the key word **let.** The above syntax defines a type. Several objects can be of this type, but no particular object is declared here. Therefore to write <assertion>'s, which are predicates (probably constructed by using abstract operators), we need to use object names; i.e., it does not make any sense to construct predicates by using type names. Therefore in <object list> following the key word **let,** we list a series of dummy object names, which allows us to write assertions in a generic form valid for every object of that type.

An Example from Human Language

To reinforce the last point, let us make an analogy to human languages. The word *dog* may be interpreted as a type name. The property of this type may be applied to a large number of objects, each showing interesting properties. Also, these objects have names for specific individual identification. Thus when we want to refer to a particular dog, say Fido, we will call him by this name. But when we want to talk about a generic dog, we say "a dog," which is the human language equivalent of the dummy object declaration.

Let us use this analogy to present an example of the above syntax for the type "dog" (the declaration is, of course, facetious):

```
dog:(t:tail, h:head, hind:legs, front:legs, b:body)
   let a_dog:dog, you:human
   inv (a_dog) loves (you)
   vfun noise (a:anything)returns br:bark
      pre (a_dog) senses (a)
      post (br) is loud
   ofun dinner (f:food)
      pre (a_dog) hungry
      post not (a_dog) hungry
   init birth (m:dog)returns (m:dog,pup:dog)
      pre (m) is pregnant
      post not(m) is pregnant and (pup) is born
end (dog)
```

Even for this somewhat frivolous example, a few characteristics of the abstract data types (in the way we have introduced them thus far) are worth nothing. The **vfun**'s do not change the object value; therefore their postcondition is a predicate containing parameter names only. An initialization function, if it establishes its type invariant only, does not have to establish this fact explicitly in its postcondition, but it may state additional restrictions on the state space, possibly in its parameters. All postconditions (and all preconditions, except those for **init** functions) represent further restrictions over the states defined by the type invariant.

In this example, the invariant represents the fact that a dog loves us. According to the above definition, the only case for which this fact cannot be stated is when a dog is not yet born. A possible delete function in this example would be relative to a dog's death. But we can imagine that the type invariant after the death of the dog would still be satisfied, because we can imagine the dog still "loves us," at least in our memory.

SYMBOLIC EXPRESSION OF PREDICATES

Let us return now to software system design. In the example discussed above, we have used English words to establish relations between objects. We used these relations to define pre- and postconditions of functions of abstract data types. Now we must introduce a technique to permit the definition of relations among abstract objects in a precise way.

That is, if we want to use abstract data type functions as we use a computer instruction set, we must be able to rely on much more than the intuitive meaning of the words. The problem is to precisely explain a relation among data objects whose representation is both not known and not unique. Indeed, different implementations of an abstract data type are not only conceivable but also desirable—as, for example, in the case of accommodation of different hardware systems to implement the same user-visible functionalities. Therefore we need a way to characterize the meaning of the abstract predicates we use for pre- and postconditions of abstract data type functions that does not rely on any representation.

Symbolic expressions of predicates look like English sentences

Let us consider a predicate expressed symbolically, such as an English statement containing appropriate data object names and stating some properties of these data objects. Examples of these predicates are the quasi-English statements used in the "dog" example above. Here we wish to use the symbolic expression to abbreviate and to add intuitive meaning to what may be a cumbersome formula. As an example, let us consider the expression of the fact that an array, say A, of integers is sorted in ascending order. We may declare the meaning of this symbolic expression of a predicate as follows (we introduce another key word, **means**):

> (A:integer **array**) is_sorted **means for all** i
> [A.lob ≤ i < A.hib **and** A(i) ≤ A(i + 1)] **or** A.dom ≤ 1

Note that since the A(i)'s are integers, we can use the symbols ≤ and < with their usual and well-understood meaning.

After this declaration, we may use the abbreviated expression "is sorted" instead of the bulky formula on the left of the key word **means.** But if we know nothing about the representation of the components of the data object, we cannot write any detailed formula. In that case the only statement we can make is that the symbolic predicate **means abstract**; i.e., we don't know anything about its representation. To solve this problem, we introduce a completely different technique to supply meaning to abstract type functions without revealing anything about the representation of the data type. The technique is described in the next section and is called characterization of abstract predicates (Boyd and Pizzarello, 1978; Boyd, Pizzarello, and Wood, 1979; Parnas, 1972).

Characterization of Abstract Predicates

Let us introduce the characterization concept with a simple example. Assume that we have a file F about which we know only that it is made up of a number (zero or more) of records, which we have not defined in detail. We want to assert that at the end of a certain operation activated by the function SORT, the file is "sorted." In other words, we know that F looks like an array, but its elements are not further defined in their representation. Our problem is to explain the familiar concept of "sortedness" of a file in an unfamiliar fashion. However, since we have no knowledge of the content of the records, we cannot identify the key to be used for establishing the sortedness. Thus we have to invent some abstract predicate that relates objects of the type record; the predicate will behave just as the relational operator ≤ behaves for the integers.

Properties of the set of states defined by an abstract predicate are used for its characterization

Let us write the above informal explanation in the notation introduced earlier:

```
PREDICATES
let x, y: record;
   (x)precedes(y) means abstract
      {this predicate defines a nondescending order between records of
      a file}
. . . .
TYPES
   record:abstract;
   file:record array
      let i:integer; F:file
      ofun SORT
         pre F.dom > 0
         post F.dom = 1 or
            [F.dom > 1 and
               for all i
                  [F.lob ≤ i < F.hib ⇒ (F(i))precedes
                                          (F(i + 1))]
```

The informal comment following the declaration of precedes is not a sufficiently precise description of what we intend to define with "precedes." However, from our understanding of the idea of sortedness (perhaps by generalization of the sortedness of an array of integers), we can easily establish the following properties:

1. The statement (x) precedes (x) is always true.
2. If (x) precedes (y) and (y) precedes (z), then (x) precedes (z).
3. If (x) is not equal to (y) and (x) precedes (y), then (y) precedes (x) is false.

Note that these three statements are almost written in a precise assertion language, yet they are in English. Also note that another symbolic predicate appears to be needed, that is "x is not equal to y."

Perhaps we may write $x \neq y$ to identify "x is not equal to y" unequivocally. In fact, if x and y were integers, the meaning of $x \neq y$ would be unequivocal. But we do not know yet what x and y are. Thus we have to define what "is equal to" means. For example, suppose x and y are to be represented later as character strings. We do not know if "equal" means equality of all blocks in a string made up of nonblank characters or equality of all blocks in a string including blanks.

Therefore the characterization of the symbolic predicate "precedes" requires the definition and the characterization of the predicate "is equal to," which is done as follows:

1. (x) is_equal (y) if and only if (y) is_equal (x).
2. If (x) is_equal (y) and (y) is_equal (z), then (x) is_equal (z).
3. (x) is_equal (x) is always true.

Characterization Syntax

At this point we introduce the syntax to express the characterization of abstract predicates. We will then use it to characterize the predicate "precedes" as an example.

The generic form of the notation for predicate characterization is as follows:

```
<predicate declaration1>characterized by
<property__1, 1>,
    .
    .
    .
<property__1, n>;
    .
    .
    .
<predicate__declaration m>characterized by
<property__m,__1>,
    .
    .
    .
<property m, p>
or
characterized by
<property__1>,
<property__2>,
    .
    .
    .
<property n>;
    .
    .
    .
```

Here <predicate—declaration> is one or more declarations of symbolic predicates by using the key word **means.** Each group of characterizations is separated from the next by a semicolon (;). Each characterizing property in a group is separated from the next by a comma (,). The second form of the syntax for the declaration of a group of declarations is used to relate predicates whose declaration was done before the key word **characterized by.**

The properties for the abstract predicates "precedes" and "is equal to" introduced informally in the preceding section can now be expressed as follows:

```
let x, y, z:record;
   (x)precedes(y) means abstract;
   (x)is__equal(y) means abstract;

characterized by
   (x) is__equal(y) => (x)precedes(y),
   [(x)precedes(y) and(y)precedes(z)] => (x)precedes(z),
   [(x)precedes(y) and not (x) is__equal(y)] => not(y)precedes(x),
   (x)is__equal(y) <=> (y)is__equal(x),
   [(x)is__equal(y)and(y)is__equal(z)] => (x)is__equal(z),
   (x)is__equal(x)
```

The equality concept characterized above is the one used by mathematicians when they interpose the sign = between two symbols. In fact, the above characterization is a consequence of our knowledge of this use. Note, however, that x = y is independent from the actual representation of both x and y, even for mathematicians, for whom the representation of the objects indicated by symbols is not an important issue. The two expressions two = two or 2 = 2 are equally satisfactory representations of two values of the objects indicated by x and y. In the computer world, however, it is not clear whether tƀwƀo = two is a true statement or not (ƀ indicates a blank).

At this stage any decision about the issue of representation of objects in such a way as to satisfy abstract predicate properties is premature. But it is important to realize that no representation is precluded, provided that the prescribed properties are maintained. How to define this representation is the subject of the next chapters. At this point, to avoid useless and cumbersome notation, we will assume that the sign = has the meaning given to it by the mathematicians, i.e., the one of the abstract predicate "is_equal" defined above.

Abstract data types can be represented in many ways provided the characterizing properties are respected

As an additional example, let us consider a file that (at this level) is an array of records that are not further detailed. We want to specify a function for this file that, when given a record name, will return a Boolean, which tells us if a record with that name is in the file. Also, we want to specify the function that stores a record with a certain name.

First, we write the type declaration:

```
record:abstract;
file:record array
    let F:file
    vfun look (n:name) returns(b:boolean)
        pre T
        post (n)is_in(F) ⇔ b = true
    ofun store (m:name)
        pre T
        post (m)is_in(F') and
            F.dom = F.dom + 1
end file;
name:abstract
```

Next, to define the meaning of the two functions, we need to use the abstract predicate "is_in." To declare its meaning, we use the following declaration and characterization:

```
let m, n:name;F:file;
    (n) is_in (F) means abstract;
characterized by
    for all n [F.dom = 0 ⇒ not (n)is_in(F)],
    (n)is_in (F) and not (m) is_in (F) ⇒ n ≠ m
```

Note that the characterization shows only those properties we are aware of from our understanding of the problem. We have yet to see how these properties are to be used for the specification and the construction of software. These properties, however, are axioms in a proof system for the correctness of programs specified by the abstract predicates.

USE OF TYPE FUNCTIONS

Abstract data types are entities needed to specify and write the programs that comprise a system. In this section we describe some notation for the use of type functions when writing programs.

Type function compositions

Let us consider two data objects A and B of some type t. Let us assume that one of the **vfun**'s of t is named f, and it accepts one parameter x of type t1 and returns one parameter y of another type t2; thus we have

vfun f (x:t1) **returns** y:t2

Also, let us define another function of t, called g, as follows:

vfun g (p:t2) **returns** q:t1

To indicate that the operation indicated by f is performed on the object A, we will use the notation (consistent with the notation used for Dijkstra array operations; see Chapter 7)

A.f(r)

where r is the name of an object of the type t1 (see the definition of f above). The value returned by A.f(r) is of the type t2.

It is possible to consider A.f(r) as a symbol indicating the returned value, which must be of the type t2. It is thus possible to combine **vfun** as follows:

B.g (A.f(r))

This symbol, in turn, indicates the value returned by g when applied to B, using, as an input parameter, the value returned by f when applied to A, with r as the input parameter.

We further assume that the weakest preconditions of f and g are as follows:

wp(f, R(x, y)) (Because the function is a **vfun,** R is a function of the parameters x and y only.)

wp(g, R(p, q)) (Because the function is a **vfun,** R is a function of the parameters p and q only.)

The resulting composition B.g(A.f(r)) weakest precondition will be

wp(g, wp(f, R(x, y)))

which depends on f, g, r, and R only. The same effect could have been described by the program fragment

a := A.f(r); b := B.g(a)

where a is an intermediate variable of type t2, and b, of type t1, contains the final result of B.g(A.f(r)). The rationale for function composition is to avoid the definition of intermediate variables, which often are an unnecessary overspecification.

Analogous compositions can be done with **ofun,** which return parameters. In this case we will use a colon instead of a period to apply the function to a particular object name. For example, if h is an **ofun** of type t, then B:h indicates that B is changed according to h's specifications.

Note, however, that the meaning of an assignment of a value returned by an **ofun** to an appropriate variable is not the one given by the axiom of assignment, as defined in Chapter 6. In fact, if h is an **ofun** applied to an object X, which returns a value of the same type as another object Z, the execution of h and the assignment of its returned value to Z changes *both* the state of X and the state of Z. The weakest precondition of this assignment for a postcondition R is equal to the weakest precondition of h for the required postcondition R, in which for all occurrences of the symbol indicating the output parameter the symbol Z has been substituted.

The ofun's have side effects

For example, if the weakest precondition of h is (p is a symbol standing for h's output parameter)

$$wp(h, R) = (X)\ is\_0k\ \textbf{and}\ p \geq 0$$

then the weakest precondition of the assignment

$$Z := X{:}h$$

is

$$wp(Z := X{:}h, R) = (X)\ is\_0k\ \textbf{and}\ Z \geq 0$$

We now have a set of concepts about abstract date types. We also have a notation that permits us to examine the construction of a hierarchy of abstract data objects. Together, the concepts and notation mean that we can reduce the intellectual gap between the user-visible and the hardware data types. In the next chapter we will see that data abstraction permits a partition of the system design problem. Furthermore, the problem can be broken not only into smaller portions of a program text, as in procedural abstraction, but also into pre- and postconditions of more manageable proportions.

HIGHLIGHTS

Program specifications are expressed in a precise manner as relationships between data values. These relationships become very complicated when the only data types available are those existing in the hardware.

In this chapter we saw that we can avoid the details of the representation in the hardware. That is, we can define the meaning of abstract data type operations without being required to enumerate the type's values. We do so by introducing operators to construct statements, which may be evaluated as true or false, about relationships between data objects of abstract data types. To this end, a notation and a syntax to describe abstract data types was introduced.

REFERENCES

Boyd, D. L., and Pizzarello, A. 1978. Introduction to the WELLMADE design methodology. *IEEE Transactions on Software Engineering* SE–4 (no. 4):276–282.

Boyd, D. L.; Pizzarello, A.; and Wood, W. T. 1979. Abstraction and refinement in RDM. Honeywell Corporate Computer Science Center Report, Bloomington, Minn.

Dahl, O. J.; Dijkstra, E. W.; and Hoare, C. A. R. 1972. *Structured programming.* New York: Academic Press.

Dijkstra, E. W. 1970. Structured programming. In *Report on a conference sponsored by the NATO Science Committee: Software engineering techniques, Rome, Italy,* edited by J. N. Buxton and B. Randell, pp. 84–88.

Hofstadter, D. R. 1980. *Gödel, Escher, and Bach.* New York: Basic Books.

Parnas, D. L. 1972. A technique for software module specifications with examples. *Communications of ACM* 15 (no. 5):330–336.

CHAPTER TWELVE

Hierarchy of Abstract Machines, Part 1

INTRODUCTION

This chapter presents a technique for dividing a large system's design into small steps organized as a hierarchy. This technique uses the idea of abstract data type introduced earlier.

We have seen that real computer hardware capabilities can be defined as data types. Then appropriate machine instructions are the functions of various data types, such as memory locations, registers, segments, and disk spindles. All these entities put together form a hardware machine, which runs programs to manipulate permanently stored information, to receive information as input, and to produce information as output.

As mentioned previously, we can construct abstract machines that essentially look like hardware machines. Actually, all programming languages permit the creation of abstract machines. In the abstract machines defined by programming languages, there are global data declarations, each and every object of which is of a particular data type, whose functions are available to the user. Also, a procedure part specifies the flow of control of the program. Within this part, data type functions are applied to the declared data objects, and the sequencing of their execution is controlled by the appropriate control constructs.

In a programming language, however, there is no mechanism to express the meaning of the data type functions. That is, the purpose of the programming language is to specify computations to a hardware machine. So the meaning of the type functions is implicit in the language's code generator. Also, the programmer is going to use the language for many different programs. Since there is no difference of type function meaning from one program to the next, the user simply consults the user's manual to obtain information relative to the language data types. In a similar manner, we want to have a user's manual for our abstract machine language. However, we use abstract machines to verify program correctness without executing the program. Thus the user's manual will be different from the usual one.

ABSTRACT MACHINES

Let us consider the possibility of defining machines that include abstract data types. Because each machine may be different, i.e., may contain completely different abstract data types, we clearly need to attach a user's manual to each machine. The discussion in the preceding chapter gave us the necessary notational tools to express the meaning of abstract data types. We can therefore define an abstract machine as a machine that can perform operations on data objects of various abstract data types, according to the flow of control prescribed by "abstract" programs. These abstract programs, in turn, transform states defined by some precondition into states defined by some postcondition, both written in terms of abstract predicates whose meaning is defined by properties expressed by their characterization. Furthermore, if we can express enough properties of the abstract predicates, we may even be able to rigorously prove the correctness of these abstract programs (or use Dijkstra calculus).

Abstract machines are informally defined and used in current practice

The above presentation is not preposterous. Actually, this form of organization is used by software system designers when they define layers of system architecture. Their process, however, is currently not rigorously organized and hence produces rather imprecise specifications. But the informal use of abstraction is a common practice; designers often make decisions in terms of abstract entities such as databases, files, and buffers, and operations that are to be performed on these entities. What we are attempting to do here is to give rigorous bases and precise rules to these informal discussions.

THE ORGANIZATION OF ABSTRACT MACHINES

Let us organize the content of an abstract machine in such a way that it can be used as a guideline for the expression of software design ideas. In this organization we want to use, as a method for validating design correctness, a proof-based method such as Dijkstra's calculus. That is, we will not use an operational verification such as code testing or mental simulation of the testing process.

Most real-world computing systems have a repository of permanent information, the system's database. A database, once it is created by some set of programs, is accessed (read and modified) by several programs at different times. A database exists before and after any program execution and represents an essential element of the information-processing system. This database is the global set of data objects for all programs in the machine. Some relation for the values of the global data may exist and may have to be verified before and after every program's execution. This relation is called the *data invariant*. Each program may also operate on *local data*, which are created at the inception of each program's execution and annihilated at termination.

Formal structure of an abstract machine reflects design needs

We are now ready to define the various building blocks of an abstract machine, a design abstraction of a real information system expressing its functionalities in terms of powerful abstract data types instead of hardware data types. Note that with an appropriate choice of abstract data types, the description for an abstract machine can be much shorter than its actual realization expressed in a programming language and all the additional primitive commands for linker/binder, loader, operating system's directives, etc.

If we enumerate all the elements we have discussed above for the abstract machine, we create the following list:

1. type declarations
   a. type composition
   b. type invariant
   c. function list
2. predicate declarations
   a. definition (<predicate> **means** <expression>)
   b. characterization
3. permanent data objects
   a. object list
   b. invariant
4. abstract programs
   a. program 1 local data
   b. program 1 precondition
   c. program 1 postcondition
   d. program 1 procedural text

   ⋮

   a. program n local data
   b. program n precondition
   c. program n postcondition
   d. program n procedural text

These entities are all necessary to specify the design of an abstract machine.

The data invariant is a predicate defining the only correct states of the system database, which we have called permanent data to indicate that they survive program executions. A program executing transformation of states for these data must find only states respecting the invariant, and when it terminates, it must leave the permanent data in states respecting the invariant. Thus the permanent data invariant corresponds to the concept of the type invariant.

The purpose of an abstract machine is to facilitate the expression of complicated system functionalities by relatively short (and consequently intellectually manageable) programs, which become possible by the use of suitably powerful data types. These programs are associated with short (and also intellectually manageable) pre- and postconditions, short because of the presence of abstract predicates. However, abstract machines are not real ones. To close the conceptual gap between the abstract machine, the real machine (which may be described by the same template), and the user-visible functionalities (described by a set of abstract data types), we must decompose the design problem in steps.

HIERARCHICAL DECOMPOSITION OF SYSTEM DESIGN

The decomposition of design presented here is the one introduced and refined by Boyd and Pizzarello (1978; Boyd, Pizzarello, and Vestal, 1978). The original idea, however, goes back to Dijkstra (1970) and has been precisely formalized by Hoare (1972). A similar approach was also suggested by Parnas (1972) and in several subsequent papers.

Decomposition is based on the idea that the structure of an abstract data type and the structure of an abstract machine are very similar. That is, an abstract data type definition contains a set of components (possibly only one) of information and a set of functions with their own pre- and postconditions. Similarly, an abstract machine contains the definition of a set of data objects and of a set of programs with their own pre- and postconditions.

An abstract data type function differs from a program because it does not show any control flow. But control flow is needed only to coordinate the sequence of execution of data type functions. It is thus attractive to imagine that for an abstract data type the execution of a function is a single step indicating a change of state in the state space defined by the abstract data type. Only two states per function execution are thus visible. On the other hand, a program execution involves a sequence of state changes in the program state space, the first and the last defined by the program's pre- and postconditions. Thus a hierarchy can be imagined for which an abstract data type function at one level becomes a program at a lower one by the conceptual device of adding details to the data. In this process components are added to the state space at a higher level in the hierarchy, and the single-step state transformation indicated by the type functions becomes a sequence of steps defined by the execution of lower-level data type function. Consequently, a data type is the higher-level view of an abstract machine. Note that the type functions at a particular level are determined in order to supply the necessary commands to write a program, which, in turn, is the realization of a higher-level type function.

Abstract machines are refinements of data types

Adding details to the components of abstract data types means that abstract predicates must also be expressed in more detail. These predicates define the intermediate states of the abstract program execution, which is now done by using the functions of the lower-level data types. In other words, any abstract machine at any level in this hierarchy "refines" some abstract data type defined in some other abstract machine at a higher level by adding details to the type's state space.

These ideas are illustrated in Figure 9. At the level called layer 1 the user is observing (or commanding) the execution of a program as a sequence of state transformations performed by functions of the data types available (as defined in the machine of layer 1). These functions are indicated by F1, F2, etc. No intermediate details about their execution are visible in layer 1. However, each of these functions is, in turn, a program executed at the level of layer 2, where functions on more elementary data types are available. These functions are indicated by f1, f2, etc., in Figure 9. The essential requirement for correctness is that all the initial states and all the final states of any functions Fi at layer 1 must also be the initial states and the final states of the "refining" program at layer 2. In other words, the pre- and postconditions of functions and programs must describe the same states, but these states are defined in terms of different visions of data in different state spaces.

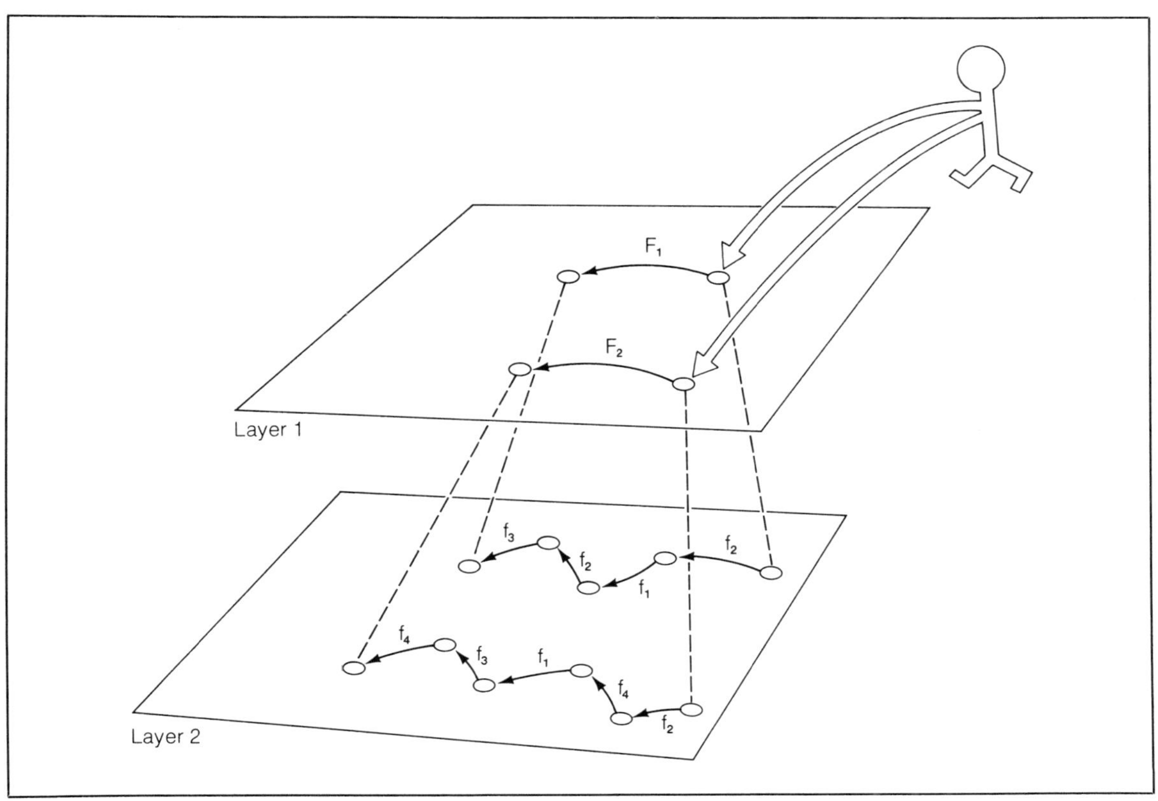

FIGURE 9 HIERARCHY OF ABSTRACT MACHINES

The problem now is to show how these states, defined in terms of types at different levels of details, are consistent throughout the hierarchy. Note that we are looking for a solution sufficiently rigorous to permit the use of design techniques such as Dijkstra's approach. We must keep in mind that the effectiveness of a design method resides in its ability to verify the correctness of design decisions. If we were to use the currently common approach, this verification would have to be delayed until the system is coded and tested. The use of a rigorous verification approach, *applicable at each step* of the hierarchical development, is therefore a necessary requirement for a design method.

You may be wondering whether a hierarchy of machines containing programs that can be tested on real hardware with the help of *stubs* (i.e., throwaway code that supplies the results of the invocation of abstract data type functions) could be used for design verification at each step of the hierarchical development. This procedure is quite feasible for the implementation of a design already fully developed. But the stubs approach is not suggested for the design stage for many reasons. One is the advantage of a design that relies on the concept of state transformations rather than enumeration of computations. A second is the intrinsic unreliability of testing. But a more important reason is that the creation of stubs may be impossible without defying the purpose of data abstraction, i.e., hiding representation details. It is impossible to write a real program dealing with abstract values of an abstract data type without in some way supplying an acceptable representation of these values.

We present two methods of hierarchical decomposition, i.e., of adding details to abstract data types. The first one (much simpler and of broader application than the second) is called data expansion; it is discussed in the following sections. The second method is called data representation; it is discussed in the next chapter. Both methods are necessary for the hierarchical design of software systems.

DATA EXPANSION

Data expansion mapping expresses the correspondence between data object properties between levels

The fundamental idea of *data expansion* is to hide all the unnecessary representation details of a component's type at one level and, *without modifying the structure of the type,* to add more details to the components in the next level of the machine hierarchy. An example, shown in Figure 10, may be a data type "archive" defined as an array of objects of the type "file," which in turn is defined as abstract. No further details are visible at this level. In the machine where "archive" is defined, state transformations for objects of the type "file" are performed by the use of this type's functions. Therefore only the initial and final states for each function execution need to be considered at the level.

The type "file" is then refined in another machine where "file" is described as an array of records. The functions performing state trans-

Archive:			
file:	file:		file:
abstract	**abstract**	...	**abstract**
File:			
record:	record:		record:
abstract	**abstract**	...	**abstract**

FIGURE 10 EXAMPLE OF DATA EXPANSION

formations on "file" are now programs realizing those state transformations in terms of state changes of objects of the type "record."

In terms of the state space model, data expansion boils down to substituting for a component (dimension) of the higher-level state space a new multidimensional subspace. This substitution is done in such a way that exactly one state of the new subspace represents one of the postulated states (one point) of the upper-level state space. In the example of Figure 10 each single state of all files in the archive is realized by one distinct configuration of records in the lower-level array.

The hierarchy is built by having one lower-level machine refining one (or more) type of the higher level. But at the higher level more than one object of that type may have been defined. The hierarchy indicates how all these objects are to be realized by presenting only one document (the lower-level machine design) specifying this realization.

For a correct refinement of the abstract types of a machine at one level by a machine at a lower level, some rules must be respected. Essentially, these rules state that we must show that for each function of a type its requirements (its pre- and postconditions) are rewritten, in terms of the lower-level machine types, as program specifications, and that this rewriting operation has been done consistently.

AN EXAMPLE OF HIERARCHICAL DESIGN

The best way to show how to rewrite consistent specifications is by an example (see Figure 11). Let us suppose that at a certain level we have to deal with a type "library," which is made up by a number of things of the type "book." Let us suppose that at this level we are concerned only with the operation of grouping the books by "subject"; within a subject we will batch them together if there are duplicates.

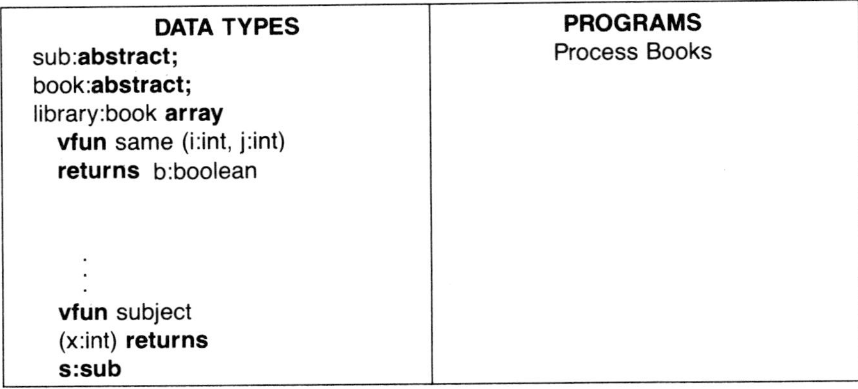

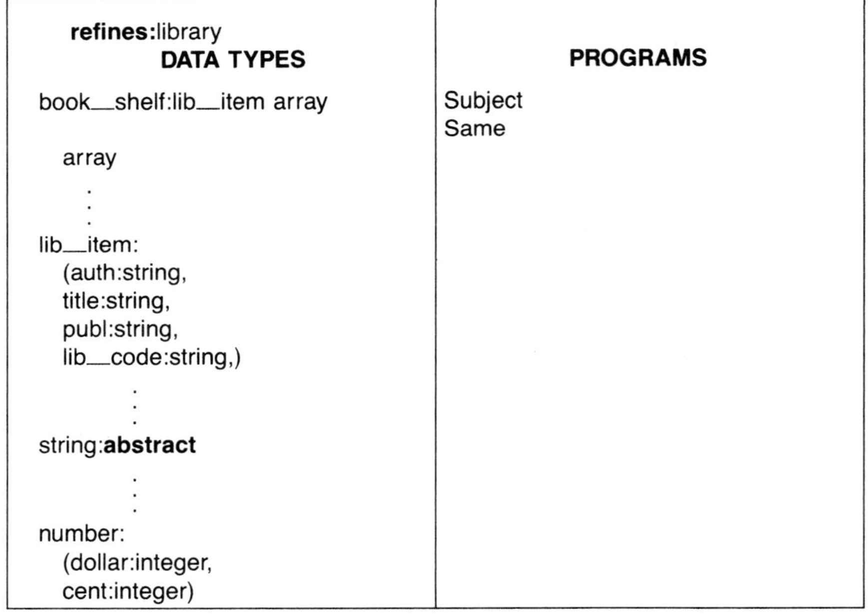

FIGURE 11 AN EXAMPLE OF MACHINE HIERARCHY

What we have said above is an informal description of a machine (which is called UPPER__LIB in Figure 11). Because it is informal, it is imprecise and therefore confusing, so we cannot consider it a satisfactory specification.

On the basis of our knowledge of the application world, we can immediately identify types like

library:book **array**
book:**abstract**

Although we do not want to define excessive data details, objects of the type "book" need to be manipulated by whatever program we are currently writing for execution in this machine. So we have to actually design the machine while we are designing the program. Furthermore, the whole design problem and its rigorous description must be reasonably defined and intellectually manageable. We will not consider here the details of the program development because we want to concentrate on the process of data type development. A full example of hierarchical development of program and machines is given in chapter 14.

Let us imagine that we want to write a program for some library with the purpose of performing the work informally described above. We need at least two operations on objects of the type "book": one to recognize if two books of the library are the same and another to identify which subject the book is treating. By using these two functions, we can group books by subject and can batch together all duplicates, as required. Thus the above type declarations are as follows:

```
sub:abstract
book:abstract
library:book array
   vfun same (i:integer, j:integer)
      returns b:boolean
         .
         .
         .
   vfun subject (i:integer)returns s:sub
```

Note that since we are interested in knowing something about two books in the same library, the functions are defined as being operations on the type "library," which is an array of books. Thus an index value is sufficient to identify a book. Note also that we have created a new type "sub," which is needed to qualify the returning value of the function "subject."

Next, we express the pre- and postconditions for the two type functions:

```
let L:library
vfun same (i:integer, j:integer)returns(b:boolean)
      pre: L.lob ≤ i, j ≤ L.hib
      post: EQ(L(i), L(j)) ⇔ b = true

vfun subject (i:integer)returns(s:sub)
      pre: L.lob ≤ i ≤ L.hib
      post: SBJ(L(i),s)
```

With the meager knowledge of the properties of books that we have at this level, we are forced to invent two abstract predicates. The first is EQ(a, b), which operates on two objects a and b of the type "book" and will be true when a and b are the same. The second predicate is SBJ (a, s), which is true when s is the subject of the book a.

The meaning of "book" is still abstract, but we also know a few additional properties that are useful to declare. (The declaration of these properties is mandated by the need to show at this level that any abstract program designed for this machine is correct before we proceed to add details.) One known property is that two equal books have the same subject. We can express this fact with a simple formula in the syntax we introduced earlier:

```
PREDICATES
let x, y, z:book, s:sub;
EQ(x, Y) means abstract
SBJ(x, s) means abstract
{s is the subject of the book x.};

characterized by
[EQ(x, y) ⇒ [SBJ(y, s) ⇔ SBJ(x, s)]],
[SBJ(x, s) and not SBJ(y, s)] ⇒ not EQ(x, y)
```

We now must define another level of machine, namely, a machine that will realize a generic object of the type "library." To this end, we define a machine LOWER_LIB. To show that this machine is the refinement of the type "library," we write the statement

refines:Library

We have thus introduced another key word: **refines.**

The purpose of this machine is to make the representation of "book" more detailed so that programs realizing the functions "same" and "subject" can be written. This example is a typical case of data expansion, where details are added to an abstract data type.

Mapping is the precise description of the connections between levels

The details to be added are mandated by two sets of requirements, one for "same" and another for "subject." These two sets of requirements must coexist in the definition of the refining machine. The purpose of the programs that use the functions "same" and "subject" is now irrelevant and can be completely ignored. But we still need more knowledge about the problem as presented in the real world (the presence of abstract predicates is a sure symptom that we still need real-world knowledge).

MAPPING BETWEEN LEVELS

The problem of *mapping* (in data expansion) is the problem of explaining what role these added details are to play in the realization of the upper-level properties of the abstract data types. The solution to this problem is usually (in practical cases) rather simple. That is, we must merely define the abstract predicates in terms of the new data details. To show how the mapping of states is defined, we will concentrate here on the simpler of the two predicates, EQ, and we will specify the program that implements "same." Under these conditions the mapping is a simple task.

The process of refining a design by levels of abstraction means that the data objects of the lower-level machine are the realization of one generic object of the type refined in the machine. Therefore in the machine LOWER_LIB we will declare the data object

K:book_shelf

This data object is an array according to the type definition. Every object of the data type "library" that we are refining here is an array.

A very simple mapping of these two data structures is needed to tell us what is what. For example, the low bound and the high bound of K represent the low bound and the high bound of any object of the type "library." Thus we write the following as the **mapping** (note the use of another new key word, **represents**):

```
MAPPING
   let L:library; n:integer;
   K.lob represents L.lob;
   K.hib represents L.hib;
   for all n[0 ≤ n ≤ K.dom] ⇒
   K(K.lob + n) represents L(L.lob + n)
```

In this example the mapping occurs between the permanent data of this machine and generic objects of the type the machine is refining from the machine above it in the hierarchy. These generic objects must be declared as objects whose meaning is limited to their use for the mapping (in the example this declaration is done by using the key word **let**).

The above mapping says that the correspondence between the two arrays is from one element to one element in the same order. However, it does not say that the actual values of "lob" and "hib" are the same. This kind of trivial mapping, whereby one element corresponds to one element and the order is preserved, is the usual mapping in data expansion. It can be abbreviated as

```
let L:library;
   K represents L
```

We showed additional details above to introduce the concept of mapping. More intricate cases of data representation, in which such detail is actually needed, are presented in the next chapter.

Hierarchical development attempts to break the correctness demonstration into simpler pieces, each one contained in a level

In the case of mapping in data expansion, we are simply showing that the lower-level array K is the same size as the upper-level array L, and there is a one-to-one correspondence between all the elements of K and L. In this way we ensure the one-to-one correspondence of the two state spaces.

Note, however, that the whole state space here has been redefined with additional details. This technique is not the only one possible. We could have created a new machine that refines only the type "book." In this case the upper-level state space would be augmented by the details defined for "book" at the lower level, but the structure in which book is imbedded would not be visible at the lower level. In this second way the one-to-one correspondence of state space points is obtained by construction.

We are not yet finished with the mapping of UPPER_LIB on the objects of the type "library." We must also map the abstract predicates. Let us consider EQ(a, b). We may decide, after examining the problem requirements, that two books are the same when they have the same author and title (but they can be from different publishers and a different library code). Then the abstract predicate EQ(a, b) will be represented as follows:

```
for all i, j in K.dom
[[i, j represents m, n] ⇒

[K(i).auth = K(j).auth
and K(i).title = K(j).title]
represents EQ(L(m), l(n))]
```

Representation details are added during the hierarchical development with data expansion.

For the sake of illustration, let us write the above mapping in English, remembering only the following rules:

- The objects of the low-level machine should represent generic objects of the upper-level data type.
- We use the conjunction *and* and the phrase *if-then* in the precise sense of logic.
- Every object name of LOWER_LIB must be one of the names defined in LOWER_LIB as the machine's data objects, and every object name representing an UPPER_LIB object must be declared locally.

In English the mapping can be interpreted as follows:

If two books in K have the same title and author, then this fact represents the equality of two books in any generic object of the type "library," which we are refining.

This statement can be made more precise by avoiding the use of the ambiguous words *book* (used to identify elements of K as well as elements of a generic library), *equality,* and *same* (whose meaning depends on the context of the problem). A more precise statement, then, is as follows:

If any two generic indices i and j of the array K, not necessarily different from each other, represent two generic indices m and n of any object L of the type "library," then the fact that the two strings K(i).auth, K(j).auth and K(i).title, K(j).title are equal represents the fact that the upper-level abstract predicate EQ(L(m), L(n)) is true.

This statement is easily translated in the more concise formal expression used above.

The mapping is shown graphically in Figure 12.

At this point you may wonder why all this work is necessary. It is needed in order to write the specifications (and therefore the program) for "same" (additional work is needed for "subject"). The requirements

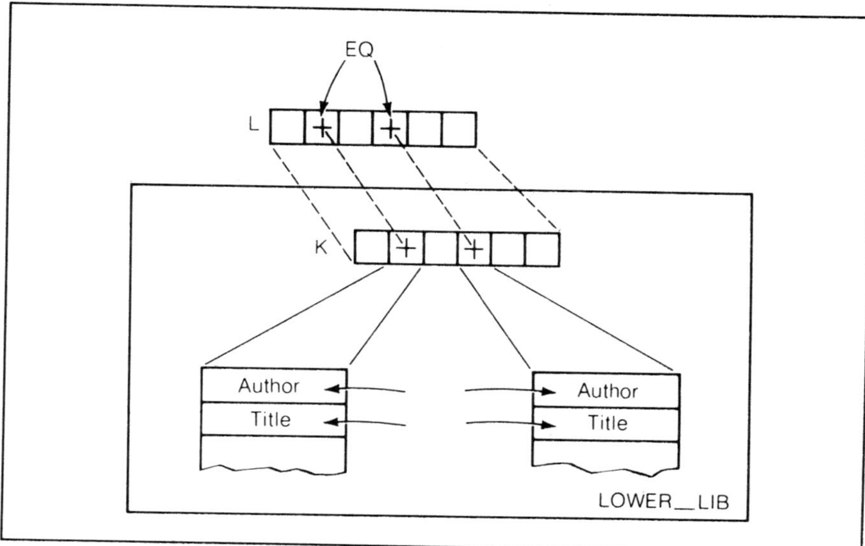

FIGURE 12 MAPPING EXAMPLE

of the function "same" and the specifications of the program "same" are shown next, side by side:

UPPER__LIB	LOWER__LIB
library . . .	⋮
let L:library	
	K:book__shelf
vfun same(i:int,j:int)	**Program:**same(i:int, j:int)
returns b:boolean	**returns** b:boolean
pre	precondition
L.lob ≤ i, j ≤ L.hib	K.lob ≤ i, j ≤ K.hib
post	**postcondition**
EQ(L(i), L(j)) ⇔ b	[K(i).auth = K(j).auth **and** K(i).title = K(j).title] ⇔ b

Note that if the specifications for the program "same" are all expressed in concrete terms, the program may be written in a programming language. Note also that the correctness of the program "same" together with the correctness of the mapping assures us that the correctness of the upper-level program that uses the function "same" is fully determined by consideration of things known at the upper level only. It is this fact that permits the orderly decomposition of large programs into smaller ones.

Lower-level details are created to realize the requirements from the upper level

In data expansion the mapping must show the correspondence of the data objects of the (lower-level) machine with generic objects of the refined type, when needed. In addition (and more importantly), all the abstract predicates of the refined type(s) must be mapped by the more detailed formulas used in this machine.

In the next chapter we discuss a detailed example that sets the technique of data expansion. That example puts the loose ends of the current (preliminary) discussion together.

NOTATION FOR MAPPING

In the preceding section we introduced the mapping concept, and we used the verb **represents** in an example of mapping. More intricate cases of mappings require additional syntax. The following notation is used in these more complicated mappings:

```
<local object declaration>;
<representation__clause 1>;
   .
   .
   .
<representation__clause n>
```

The first line is the declaration of local objects used in the mapping section. The scope of this declaration is limited to the mapping section. As in the local object declaration for predicates, this declaration may be written by using the key word **let,** or it may be written for each data object name. In this latter case the <local object declaration> need not be present.

The form of a <representation__clause__> is as follows:

<predicate__expression> **represents** <expression>

or

<predicate__expression> **represents** <predicate__expression>

or

<predicate__expression> <implying__op>
[<representation__clause>]

or

if <predicate__expression> **then** [<representation__clause>]

Also, the representation clause may have the form of an English text included in braces { } whenever we think we can do without the intricacies of predicate calculus formulas.

The following examples present notation used for mappings:

A(i).K ≤ A(i + 1).K **represents**
(X:record)precedes(Y:record)
(K) is_a_word_in (T) ⇒ [K **represents** R:block]

let K:small_set; H:large_set;
R ≥ G.lob ⇒ [**for all** i [G.lob ≤ i ≤ R] ⇒ [(G(i)) are_members_of (Q)]]
represents [(K) is_included_in (H)]

In a <representation clause> all objects to the left of the key word **represents** must be objects of a type declared in the machine where the mapping is declared (the lower level).

HIGHLIGHTS

Abstract machines are perfect analogs of real machines, but they use abstract data types. The abstract data types in a machine are defined in such a way that programs can be written and specified in a form that permits the application of a rigorous design method such as Dijkstra calculus.

The use of abstract data types allows us to create rather short programs, even for the solution of complex problems. To complete the design problem, however, we must refine abstract data types down to real-machine data types. To this end, abstract machines can be organized in a hierarchy. In this hierarchy each abstract data type at the higher level corresponds to an abstract machine at a lower level that refines its representation. When this hierarchy is constructed by expressing representation details at the lower level in such a way that a one-to-one correspondence exists between the state spaces of levels, the hierarchical development is called data expansion. In this case the mapping of the entities of machines in two levels is a straightforward operation that establishes the correspondence between data objects and their set of states defined by abstract predicates.

The hierarchical development can be seen as a way to break down the complexity of the correctness proof of a large program (or system) into many steps, with one design decision at each hierarchy level. The use of mapping allows us to preserve the coherence of the whole design.

REFERENCES

Boyd, D. L., and Pizzarello, A. 1978. Introduction to the WELLMADE design methodology. *IEEE Transactions on Software Engineering* SE–4 (no. 4):276–282.

Boyd, D. L.; Pizzarello, A.; and Vestal, S. C. 1978. Rational design methodology. Report RADC–TR–78–208, Rome Air Development Center, Griffiss Air Force Base, N.Y.

Boyd, D. L.; Pizzarello, A.; and Wood, W. T. 1979. Abstraction and refinement in RDM. Honeywell Corporate Computer Science Center Report, Bloomington, Minn.

Dijkstra, E. W. 1970. Structured programming. In *Report on a conference sponsored by the NATO Science Committee: Software engineering techniques, Rome, Italy,* edited by J. N. Buxton and B. Randell, pp. 84–88.

Hoare, C. A. R. 1972. Proof of correctness of data representation. *Acta Informatica* 1 (no. 4): 271–281.

Parnas, D. L. 1972. A technique for software module specification with examples. *Communications of ACM* 15 (no. 5): 330–336.

CHAPTER THIRTEEN

Hierarchy of Abstract Machines, Part 2

INTRODUCTION

In this chapter we continue the presentation of the design method based on a hierarchy of abstract machines. In the previous chapter we studied the technique of data expansion. A more complex method of hierarchical design decomposition is called data representation. It is described in this chapter. Data representation is used whenever the particular characteristics of a programming problem do not permit the use of the simpler approach of data expansion.

DATA REPRESENTATION

In the preceding chapter we examined the refinement of an abstract data type by a lower-level machine. In the lower-level machine a data structure containing elements of an abstract type was represented again as a structure so similar to the one to be refined that a one-to-one correspondence existed between the points of the newly enlarged state space and the original one. Actually, in that example all addition of details was done inside the components (elements of an array in the "book" example), which were declared abstract at the upper level. The representation of the containing structure was done more for the convenience of naming the component objects than for real needs of the development process. In our previous example the representation of "library" as an array permitted us to address books in the library by using indices, as was done at the upper level.

Data representation, in contrast, applies to cases where the correspondence between state spaces at two levels is not one-to-one. For example, suppose we have developed a data type having the structure of a Dijkstra array, and we have defined programs by using the simple operations of extension and removal. Unfortunately, in our object machine (as in most programming languages), these operations are not available. What *is* available is a file of fixed size. The mapping now must indicate the fact that the domain of the array must not be greater than the size of the file. It also must show which objects of the lower level represent

Data representation is a many-to-one correspondence between the lower and the upper levels

lob, hib, and all the elements of the array. This situation is depicted in Figure 13, where the upper-level array is called U and the lower-level file is called L.

Note that an additional variable R has been introduced in the lower machine to represent the high bound of the upper-level array. In Table 3 we present the description of a situation like the one shown in Figure 13.

By using the representation described in the section called "mapping" of the machine LOWER, we can substitute objects of the lower level for the objects they represent in the formula describing the type data invariant in UPPER. In this way the data invariant of LOWER implies the type invariant of the type "blob," once the substitutions are performed. Actually, the definition of the representation comes as the first step in design. That is, the permanent data at the lower level (including the data object invariant) is designed with the representation of the properties at the higher level in mind. The specifications of the programs in the machine LOWER are built up in a manner analogous to the method used for the data invariant. The example in the next section will clarify this process.

TABLE 3 REPRESENTATION OF DATA TYPES

Machine UPPER **Types** blob:things **array** **let** B:blob; . . . **permanent data** . . . **inv** B.dom ≤ Z	**Machine** LOWER **refines** blob **Types** permfile:things **array** . . . **permanent data** L:permfile; R,size:integer **inv** L.dom = size **and** L.lob ≤ R ≤ L.hib **mapping** let U:blob n:integer s:integer; L.lob **represents** U.lob; R **represents** U.hib; for all n[0 ≤ n ≤ (R − L.lob)] ⇒ L(L.lob + n) **represents** U(U.lob + n); S **represents** Z; R ≤ size **represents** U.dom ≤ S;

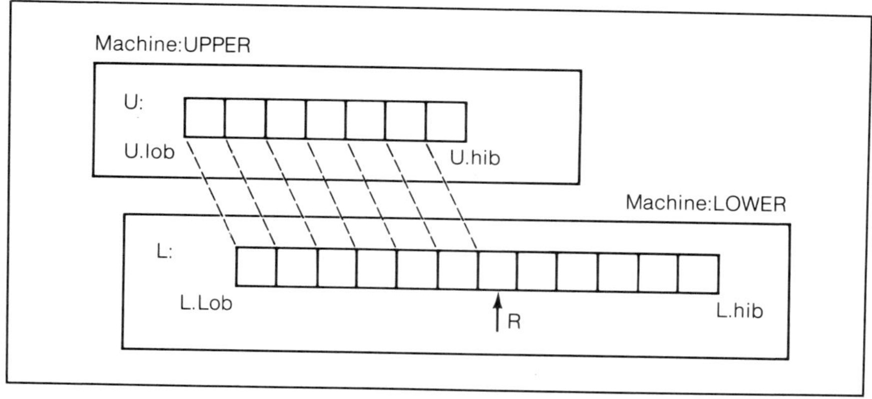

FIGURE 13 EXAMPLE OF REPRESENTATION OF DATA TYPES

It should be clear from this example that for the new representation several values of the permfile L may represent only one value of an object of the type "blob." Thus, suppose we examine a generic case where the pointer R in L divides L into two regions. For the correctness of the development the values in the region (L.lob . . . R) must be mapped to all the values of a "blob." But L may contain a lot of additional values in the region (R + 1 . . . L.hib) that are irrelevant for the correctness of the higher level. That is, any combination of values in this latter region together with the properly mapped values of the rest of L is a correct representation of the upper-level design.

This situation is typical of cases where an idealized expandable-storage machine is to be realized in a constant-size storage machine. To appreciate the amount of information needed to ensure the correctness of this design decomposition, consider an array represented as a linked list stored in a constant-size chunk of memory. Only a few pieces of this chunk of memory are actually mapping elements of the ideal array. The pointers needed to represent the order of the idealized array are additional elements of the state space, and they have no direct correspondence to any object at the higher level.

The situation of data expansion described in the preceding chapter—a one-to-one correspondence from one point to one point—is quite different from the examples here. That is, in data representation *a set* of points of the state space of the refining machine maps onto *one point* of the state space of the upper-level machine. So several states of the lower level are a correct representation of one state of the upper level.

AN EXAMPLE OF DATA REPRESENTATION

Let us assume that we have defined a family of integer stacks (as objects of a data type), which we are going to represent in a constant-size list. The following discussion describes the necessary documentation of the definition of the data type "integer stack" and its representation in the

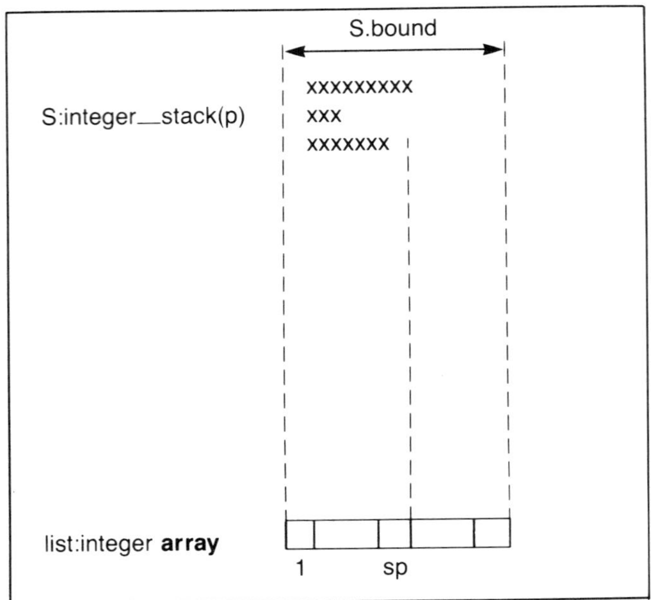

FIGURE 14 INTEGER STACK AND ITS REPRESENTATION

machine "array_and_pointers." The word *necessary* here means what is needed to ensure that correctness of the decomposition can be demonstrated by a rigorous process.

The representation problem is shown in Figure 14. The upper-level definition of the stack is documented in Figure 15.

Note that "integer_stack" is defined as a parameterized type. In this definition the type name (integer_stack) is followed by a parameter in parentheses, which is called p in Figure 15 and is of the type pos_int (also defined in Figure 15). A number of types of different-sized stacks can be defined from this declaration and their size can be set up at object declaration time by giving a specific value to the parameter p. To do so, we put the stack parameter in parentheses as part of the type name. Thus we can declare data objects of type integer_stack (1024), integer_stack (2048), or any other convenient number, expressing in this way the size limitation of the stack. So by using type parameters, we can define a whole class of similar types in only one declaration.

The representation of "integer_stack" and the implementation of its functions in terms of the new representation is shown in Figure 16.

The following list shows all the programs of the machine "array_and_pointer" realizing the functions of the type "integer_stack":

```
Program empty
Specifications
   precondition
      true
   postcondition
      sp' = 0
```

```
Types
  pos__int: integer
    let p:pos__int
    inv p ≥ 0
  end pos__int;

  integer__stack (p:pos__int):(seq:integer array;
    bound:pos__int)
    let s:integer__stack(n)
    inv 0 ≤ s.seq.dom ≤ s.bound and s.bound = n
    ofun push (x:integer)
      pre  s.seq.dom < s.bound
      post s'.seq.lob = s.seq.lob and
        s'.seq.hib = s.seq.hib + 1 and
        for all i [[s.seq.pob≤i≤s,seq.,hib] ⇒ [s'.seq(i)
          = s.seq(i)]
        and s'.seq.high = x
    ofun pop returns (x: integer)
      pre  s'.seq.dom > 0
      post s.seq.lob = s.seq.lob and
        s'.seq.hib = s.seq.hib − 1 and
        for all i [[s.seq.pob≤i≤s,seq,hib] ⇒ [s'.seq(i)
          = s.seq(i)]
        and x = s.seq.high
    ofun empty
      pre  true
      post s'.seq.dom = 0
    vfun is__full returns (b: boolean)
      pre  true
      post [b = true and s.seq.dom = s.bound] or
        [b = false and s.seq.dom < s.bound]
    vfun is__empty returns (b: boolean)
      pre  true
      post [b = true and s.seq.dom = 0] or
        [b = false and s.seq.dom > 0]
    init open
      pre  true
      post s'.seq.dom = 0
  end integer__stack;
```

FIGURE 15 INTEGER__STACK

```
Program text
  sp := 0
end empty;

Program push (x: integer)
Specifications
  precondition
    sp < list.hib
  postcondition
    sp' = sp + 1 and
```

```
Machine array__and__pointer
              .
              .
              .
refines integer__stack (p: pos__int)
Types
   pos__int: integer
      let p:pos__int
      inv p ≥ 0
   end pos__int;
Permanent data
   list: integer array;
   sp: integer;
   inv: list.lob = 1 and list.hib = 0 and
      0 ≤ sp ≤ n
mapping
   let s: integer__stack(n);
      list.hib represents s.bound;
      1 represents s.seq.lob;
      sp represents s.seq.hib;
      sp represents s.seq.dom;
      for all i [1 ≤ i ≤ sp ⇒ list(i) represents
         s.seq(i - 1 + s.seq.lob)]

Program list
   empty,
   push (x:integer),
   pop returns (x:integer),
   is__full returns (b:boolean),
   is__empty returns (c:boolean),
   init open
```

FIGURE 16 REPRESENTATION OF INTEGER__STACK IN THE MACHINE ARRAY__AND__POINTER

```
      postcondition
         for all i [1 ≤ i ≤ sp ⇒ list'(i) = list(i)]
            and
         list'(sp') = x
      Program text
         sp := sp + 1; list (sp) := x
      end push;

   Program pop returns x: integer
   Specifications
      precondition
         sp > 0
      postcondition
         sp' = sp - 1 and
```

```
        for all i [1 ≤ i ≤ sp ⇒ list'(i) = list(i)]
          and
        x = list(sp)
      Program text
        x := list(sp); sp := sp − 1
  end pop;

  Program is_full returns b: boolean
  Specifications
    precondition
      true
    postcondition
      [b = true and sp = list.hib] or [b = false
        and sp < list.hib]
    Program text
      if sp = list.hib → b := true
      □ sp < list.hib → b := false
      fi
  end is_full;

  Program is_empty returns c: boolean
  Specifications
    precondition
      true
    postcondition
      [c = true and sp = 0]
        or [c = false and sp > 0]
    Program text
      c := (sp = 0)
  end is_empty;

  Program open
  Specifications
    precondition
      true
    postcondition
      sp' = 0 and for all i [list'.lsb ≤ i ≤ list'.hib
        ⇒ list'(i) = 0]
      and list'.lob = 1
    Program text
      sp := 1;
      list := (1);
      do list.hib ≤ n →
        list.hiext (0)
      od
```

Data representation usually applies to lower levels of the hierarchy

Notice that there is very little abstraction in the level of definition of integer_stack. Actually, the representation is a way to show the implementation of a rather low-level definition of integer_stack in a language that does not have Dijkstra's array. Low-level implementation problems are generated by differences in the data types of the available hardware and the lower-level abstractions created by the designer.

RECAPITULATION

At this point it may be helpful to recapitulate the concept of hierarchies of abstract data types. There is a precise correspondence between abstract machines and abstract data types. For a given abstract machine whose state space is made up of n objects of m ($m \leq n$) different types, programs can be specified in terms of the properties of the types. Programs can be written—i.e., classes of computations can be specified—by using the control constructs and the type functions. Appropriate selection of types ensures that these programs and their specifications will be of manageable size. Thus with this device of abstract machines we can verify the correctness of the programs or, by using Dijkstra's calculus approach, derive a correct program from specifications. The only requirement is that the effects of the abstract type functions be sufficiently characterized to permit the validation of program correctness.

Any abstract machine behaves like a real one. It can (in an abstract sense) run its abstract programs (probably generating abstract results). More importantly for our purposes, it permits us to describe program specifications. If all data types in a machine are concrete—i.e., if there is some hardware or software that executes all data type functions according to requirements—the design problem is completed when all programs for that machine are written. If one (or more) data type in the machine is abstract, or if some of its components are abstract, then a new machine has to be created to refine this data type in terms of concrete or less abstract types. Each of the functions of the upper level becomes a program in this lower-level machine, and the type invariant of the upper level is reformulated as a data invariant at the lower level.

The hierarchy is thus defined: Abstract data types become an abstract machine, which in turn needs the definition of new and more detailed data types. Some of these detailed data types may still be abstract and so will be refined in lower-level machines in the hierarchy.

Machines refine data types, not objects

This idea of implementing types by a new abstract machine—i.e., by a set of permanent data and programs—implies that for each occurrence of the type at the upper level, there is a copy of the data objects at the lower level. In other words, the lower-level machine shows the refinement of a generic object of the type. The way this design is packaged to realize a number of objects of that type is a decision left to the implementor.

Note that in such a hierarchy types must be defined only once. Thus each type name must be unique throughout the entire design.

To make a correct refinement from one level of machine to a lower one, we must follow two rules. First, we must show that for all functions of the types the requirements are rewritten in terms of the lower-level machine types as program specifications. Second, we must show that this rewriting operation has been done consistently with the function requirements of the higher-level machine.

The construction of the hierarchy of machines is more precisely described by using the state space model. When objects of an abstract type are used in a machine, no precise values are associated with them. However, a characterization of these values has been given by defining subsets of the state space (by using predicates for function requirements). In the new-level machine, in general, each object at the upper level will be implemented by one (or more) object at the lower level.

To interpret this technique in state space terms, we imagine that each level is a state space. The act of adding details transforms the state space of one level into one closer to the final state space of the whole system. This final state space is described by the hierarchy of abstract machines.

Hierarchical development as a step-by-step transformation of the state space

In state space terms, a point P at the upper level will be made up of a set of values, some of them (possibly) of a concrete type X, others of an abstract type Y_i:

$$P = X_1, \ldots, X_n, Y_1, \ldots, Y_m$$

The lower-level machine, if it implements the type of the object whose values are Y_1, will, in general, create a set of values. For the purpose of this explanation, we will assume that these values are all concrete; i.e., they are known in terms of some familiar representation, such as a programming language:

$$u_1, \ldots, u_n$$

These values, when substituted for Y_i at the upper level, together with all the other necessary substitutions for the other Y's, will make all the abstract predicates about P valid. Thus program specifications, invariants, and program text respect all the arguments used to show correctness.

Let us now define a mapping REP(X) between the set of points of the lower-level machine's state space X and the upper-level state space. This mapping establishes the correspondence between one or more points of the lower-level state space and one point of the upper-level state space. If REP(X) establishes a one-to-one correspondence, then the lower-level machine is the data expansion of the upper level. If the correspondence is many-to-one, it is a data representation.

The mapping idea is clarified by considering the similarity of a point of the state space with the more familiar concept of core dumps. Suppose that a core dump of an abstract machine is taken. Blurred areas will appear in correspondence with abstract object values. However, enough information about less blurred areas is supplied to allow us to judge whether or not that core dump (a point in the state space) is a "good" one. By creating a lower-level machine, we can envision a whole new set of core dumps, the ones generated for all points of the lower machine's state space. The mapping REP(X) (where X is the set of all data of the lower-level machine) establishes which of these less blurred core dumps can be "copied" into the blurred spots of every possible core dump of the higher-level machine, maintaining the "goodness" (or perhaps the badness) of the higher-level machine's core dumps.

It is conceivable that in some cases the implementation is such that more than one core dump satisfies the requirements of the abstract type. For example, if a real number value, say 1.75, is represented by six numerical digits, three for the integer part and three for the decimals, either 001750 or 001754 or 001753 is an acceptable representation. It is also possible that additional variables can be defined at the lower level to represent an object of an abstract data type, as we have seen in all the examples above.

The mapping concept can be summarized in a more formal manner, as follows. We make the following definitions:

X:	The set of data objects at the low level.
$PRE(X)_i$:	The postcondition of the *i*th program at the low level.
$POST(X, X')_i$:	The postcondition of the *i*th program at the low level.
$IN(Y)_i$:	The required precondition for the *i*th function of the refined type (at the higher level).
$OUT(Y, Y')_i$:	The required postcondition for the *i*th function of the refined type (at the higher level).
DATA_I(X):	The data invariant (at the low level).
TYPE_I(Y):	The refined type invariant (at the higher level).
REP(X):	The mapping that transforms any nonempty appropriate set of data in X into the corresponding datum in Y.

The rules for a correct refinement of an abstract data type are as follows:

1. DATA_I(X) ⇒ TYPE_I(REP(X))
2. For all programs P_i refining functions F_i:
   a. DATA_I(X) **and** PRE(X) ⇒ TYPE_I(REP(X)) **and** IN(REP(X))
   b. DATA_I(X) **and** POST(X, X') ⇒ TYPE_I(REP(X)) **and** OUT(REP(X), REP(X'))

Note that a program correctly designed (or verified) for a top-level machine need not be verified again. Only the type function requirements and type invariant representation have to be verified.

HIGHLIGHTS

Sometimes, it is impossible to construct a hierarchy of abstract machines by using the rather simple techniques of data expansion. For example, data expansion cannot be used when a structure at a higher level, say an array, must be represented by another structure at a lower level such as a linked list. In these cases there is no one-to-one correspondence between state spaces at the two levels. Instead, a set of states at the lower level corresponds to a single state at the higher level. An example illustrating how this situation can be handled was discussed in this chapter. The technique used is called data representation.

The two techniques of hierarchy—data expansion and data representation—are both necessary to cover all possible cases in practice.

The technique of hierarchical construction was also formally described in this chapter in terms of the state space model.

CHAPTER FOURTEEN

An Example of Hierarchical Development

INTRODUCTION

As described in Chapter 12, in data expansion we add details to data types in their development in a lower-level abstract machine. This chapter shows how this technique works in practice by presenting an example. The example is not a large and complex development, but it is sufficiently detailed to show the characteristics of the technique.

In this example we use the notational and conceptual machinery presented in the preceding chapters. Reading a program design example is never a pleasant activity, particularly if the development does not involve challenging requirements that may produce elegant ideas. The example presented here is rather unattractive in this sense, but it is an appropriate one for showing the conceptual difficulty of software development even in what could have been judged as a rather banal case. We emphasize again that conceptual difficulty is usually not apparent when designs are expressed informally. However, it is still there, and it pops up at a later time as testing, integration, and maintenance difficulties.

THE PROBLEM

A text file is given. This text is made up of ASCII characters, and it is organized into lines. Each line is a sequence of zero or more characters terminating with a character denoted by CR (carriage return). The whole text terminates with the character EOF (end of file). We are required to design a program that counts (1) the number of lines in the text; (2) the number of words (a word is defined as a sequence of printable ASCII characters delimited by blanks or by CR and EOF, which are not printable) in the whole text; (3) the number of characters (printable and non-printable) in the text, including CR and EOF.

The hardware is assumed to recognize both characters and integers as types. Also, an instruction (a type function) that permits determination of the printability/nonprintability of an ASCII character is assumed to exist in the given hardware.

The above description of the problem is the typical form of the requirements for a problem like this one. It might be, in practical cases, the result of numerous discussions between the developer and the originator of the requirements.

HIGHER-LEVEL DESIGN

Identifying Components

Definition of the problem state space is the first step

As with the program in Chapter 7, the first mental step is to recognize the data objects we have to deal with. In other words, we begin our definition of the state space by identifying its most evident components. One of these components is the text file itself, which we decide to call T. Also, three integers—lc, the line count, wc, the word count, and cc, the character count—are clearly needed. We consider T a data object of an abstract machine (for the purpose of this example we ignore how T has been put in the machine, i.e., its initialization), and lc, wc, and cc are the output parameters of the program. We also decide to call our program "text_count," and we decide that it will reside in an abstract machine called "m_text." The only program in m_text is

```
Text_count returns (lc: integer, wc:integer, cc:integer)
{This program counts the lines, the words, and the characters in T.}
```

The next mental step is to decide on the amount of detail we want to show in the machine m_text for T. We make this decision by considering the type of T. A quite plausible choice is to define T as an array of lines. That is, the details of the representation of T by words and characters are not visible in m_text.

The documentation of the design of m_text at this point appears as follows:

```
m_text
    .
    .
  Types
    line: abstract;
    text_file: line array
  permanent data
    T: text_file
  Program text
    text_count returns (lc:integer, wc:integer, cc:integer)
```

Precondition and Postcondition

The next step should be the definition of the program specifications. We will do this step informally first, and then we will formalize the result, defining appropriate predicates.

The precondition should state that at least one line (perhaps an empty one) is going to be in T. This result follows from the fact that T containing only EOF is a one-element (one-line) array. Also, the fact that the last line ends with EOF is to be stated in the precondition.

The postcondition must state that the content of lc, wc, and cc will be the number of lines, words, and characters, respectively. The number of lines is completely definable at this level of detail. For the expression of the number of words and characters, we have to define abstract predicates, since at this level we are not aware of the representation details.

```
precondition
   T.dom > 0 and
   (T(T.hib)) contains_eof
   {There is at least one line, and the last line
      of the text T must contain eof.}

postcondition
   T = T' and
   lc = T.dom and
   (wc) word_count_of (T) up_to (T.hib + 1) and
   (cc) char_count_of (T) up_to (T.hib + 1)
```

Note that we have expressed the fact that T cannot be changed by this program by writing T = T′.

Abstract Predicates

Three abstract predicates are used to define the pre- and postconditions. Their meaning can be expressed in English in their definition in the predicate declaration:

```
Predicates
   let P:text_file; c:line; m, n, r, s, i,
      j:integer;
   (c) contains_eof means abstract {the line c
      ends with EOF};
   (n) word_count_of (P) up_to (i) means
      {the number n is the total number of words
         in P up to, but not including, the ith line};
   (m) char_count_of (P) up_to (j) means
      {the number m is the total number of characters
         in P up to, but not including, the jth line}
```

The last two predicates express a property of the cumulative number of words and characters. Since we have defined a text_file as an array of lines, it is useful to define two predicates that designate whether an integer is the number of words or characters in a specific single line. That is:

```
(r)word_in (c) means abstract
    {r is the number of words in the line c};
(s)char_in (c) means abstract
    {s is the number of characters in the line c}
```

Note that some additional detailed description of the predicates

```
(n) word_count_of (P) up_to (i)
```

and

```
(m) char_count_of (P) up_to (j)
```

can be supplied at this level. They can be defined in terms of, say, the number of words in c, which we can define by using the predicate "words _in."

This statement simply says that these two predicates are not abstract; i.e., they may be defined in terms of more elementary statements on the basis of things known at this level. In this particular case we define the two predicates

```
(r)word_in (c)     and     (s)char_in (c)
```

which we must declare as abstract.

The fact that (so far) we have used a rather informal definition of

```
(n) word_count_of (P) up_to (i)
  (m) char_count_of (P) up_to (j)
```

does not mean that this is the only way to do it. In fact, there is no difficulty in making the above definitions more precise.

To define the two symbolic predicates that state that two numbers are the sum of a sequence of numbers, we need to define this sequence. To do so, we define an array of integers as a dummy variable whose scope is the predicate declaration only. This array will give us the necessary elements to talk about the integers m and n as the sum of other integers of the kind used for the predicates (r) word_in (c) and (s) char_in (c).

This object declaration becomes

```
let P:text_file; c:line; m, n, r, s, h, k, i,
    j:integer;
    N:integer array;
```

The two symbolic predicate declarations are thus rewritten as follows:

```
(n) word_count_of (P) up_to (i) means
P.lob = N.lob
and for all h in (P.lob . . . i − 1), k in (N.lob . . . i − 1)
[k = h and (N(k)) word_in (P(h))] ⇒
n = N(N.lob) + N(N.lob + 1) + · · · + N(i − 1);
```

(m) char_count_of (P) up_to (j) **means**
P.lob = N.lob
and for all h **in** (P.lob . . . j − 1), k **in** (N.lob . . . j − 1)
[k = h **and** (N(k) char_in (P(h))] ⇒
m = N(N.lob) + N(N.lob + 1) + · · · + N(j − 1)

We use notation such as: h **in** (P.lob · · · i − 1) to indicate that the values for h range from P.lob to i − 1, at steps of 1, including the two extremes (P.lob and i − 1).

Characterizing the Predicates

Characterization is done by expressing all known properties of the states defined by the abstract predicates

The two predicates are now expressed in terms of known entities and of the two abstract predicates already invented. We may now attempt to characterize these abstract predicates. Some properties already known from the problem requirements can be expressed at this time. We write these properties first in English, and then we put them in characterizing formulas. In English the properties are as follows:

- Only the last line in P contains EOF.
- The number of characters increases with the number of lines, but this result is not necessarily true for the number of words, since a line may contain only blanks.
- The only value the integers m and n can assume, if they are to satisfy the predicates

(n) word_count_of (P) up_to (i) **and** (m) char_count_of (P) up_to (j)
when i and j are equal to P.lob, is zero.

- For any index i greater than or equal to P.lob, the predicate

  (m) char_count_of (P) up_to (j)

  must be false for m = 0.

The above properties can be formally expressed as follows:

characterized by

not (P(i)) contains_eof ⇔ i ≠ P.hib;
[i > P.lob **and** h > P.lob **and** h ≤ P.hib
and h > i **and** (m) char_count_of (P) up_to (i)
and (s) char_count_of (P) up_to (h)] ⇒ m < s],

i = P.lob **and** (n) word_count_of (P) up_to (i) ⇔
n= 0,
j = P.lob **and** (m) char_count_of (P) up_to (j) ⇔
m = 0,
i > P.lob **and** m = 0 ⇔ **not** (m) char_count_of (P)
up_to (i);

Algorithm

It is now possible to design the program text from the specifications. It is during this stage that the necessary functions of the type "line" and of text_file can be precisely determined.

Before we proceed further, we note that the development order presented is not the only possible one. An alternative would be to derive a sketch of the algorithm from the informal program pre- and postconditions and then define and specify the type functions. We chose to formalize the predicates on the basis of the real-world knowledge before we attempted any algorithm derivation.

Top-level algorithm is designed by using Dijkstra calculus

We want to apply Dijkstra calculus as described in Chapter 7. The only difference between this example and the ones presented in Chapter 7 is that here we are deriving an abstract program (one that uses abstract data types) from specifications containing abstract predicates.

The presence of an array suggests that the algorithm requires a loop. Therefore we must define the loop invariant and the termination function. By examining the postcondition and keeping in mind the predicate properties, we determine the following loop invariant:

```
(wc) word_count_of (T) up_to (i) and
(cc) char_count_of (T) up_to (i) and
i ≥ T.lob
```

We also choose, as the termination function, the integer value of T.hib − i + 1, which is the count of the number of lines to be processed.

At this point we derive the following algorithm. Note that we are inventing functions while we write this algorithm.

```
i := T.lob;
wc, cc, lc := 0, 0, 1;
wc := wc + T(i).countword;
cc := cc + T(i).countchar;
do not T(i).eof →
   i := i + 1;
   lc := lc + 1;
   wc := wc + T(i).countword;
   cc := cc + T(i).countchar
od
```

Functions

The above algorithm specifies the existence of three functions: countword, countchar, and eof. These functions are the only operations that can be performed on an object of the abstract data type "line." It is thus possible to write the definition of this abstract data type:

```
line:abstract
   let:l:line
```

```
vfun eof returns (b:boolean)
   pre T
   post (l) contains_eof <=> b

vfun countword returns (c:integer)
   pre T
   post (c) words_in (l)

vfun countchar returns (a:integer)
   pre T
   post (a) char_in (l)
end line
```

These function postconditions are such that they respect the loop invariant (they are written for this purpose).

Critical examination of the algorithm shows performance problems

The above choice for the algorithm and the "line" functions can be shown to be a poor one, however, even though a correct design can be developed along these lines. It is hard to justify the above choice on the basis of our knowledge of the problem requirements. In fact, we know that words are sets of characters and that EOF is a character. On the basis of this knowledge the specifications of sequential execution in the above abstract program of the functions "countword" and "countchar" do not make any sense, because they would probably make the program scan a line once to count words and then again to count characters. We clearly want to count words and characters while we scan the line only once. A similar problem is encountered for the detection of EOF.

We have shown the above choice because it is a rather common pitfall in using hierarchical development. In a hierarchical development we cannot hide details indiscriminately. In this example, for instance, the existence of words and characters and some expression of their relationship cannot be hidden.

Alternative Method

The appropriate way to develop this program is to not specify any sequence of calculation for the parameters b (for eof), c (for countword), and a (for countchar). That is, we specify only one function for the type "line," which returns the composite of three values a, b, c as a parameter. These values are, respectively (the same symbols were used above), the number of characters, a Boolean to signal the presence of eof, and the number of words.

The declaration of the type "line" thus becomes the following:

```
lines:abstract
let l:line

vfun process line returns (Q:counts)
   pre T
   post (l) contains_eof <=> Q. b = true and
```

```
        (Q.c) word_in (l) and
        (Q.a) char_in (l)
    end line;

    counts:(a:integer, b:boolean, c:integer)
```

A new algorithm is designed

For the above data type the following algorithm can be derived from the pre- and postconditions, the loop invariant, and the termination function determined previously:

```
Local objects
   i:integer;
   wc, cc, lc:integer;
   g:boolean;
   H:counts

Program text
   i := T.lob;
   wc, cc, lc := 0, 0, 1;
   H := T(i).process_line;
   wc, cc := wc + H.c, cc + H.a;
   do not H.b →
      i := i + 1
      H := T(i).process_line;
      wc, cc, lc := wc + h.c, cc + H.a, lc + 1
   od
```

In this new version of the algorithm we make no commitment about the order of computation of wc, cc, and b.

DESIGN OF LOWER LEVELS

Refinement

We are now ready to move to the design of the next level of the hierarchy. The only abstract type we have in m_text is "line."

The refinement process is the same as the design process for the first machine. We merely consider the type function specifications and the abstract predicates and their characterization as requirements for a new problem. We define a new machine "m_line," which refines the type "line." We can thus immediately state, as the first piece of information for the description of the new machine m_line, that

refines line

In the machine m_line the following program must be envisioned as the implementation of the sole function of the abstract data type "line" in terms of the entities in the machine m_line:

process_line **returns** (Q:vals)

We have defined the type of the returned parameter as "vals," which is a different name from "counts" used in the upper-level machine function. We used a different name because we may change some representation details of this parameter.

Data Types and Data Objects

The next step is to determine the data objects and their types. This step implies a decision about the level of detail to be shown in this machine for all the objects of the type "line." From the problem requirements we see that we have two choices. One is to represent a line as a character array, thus ending the hierarchical development. The second choice is to represent a line as an array of "blocks," which may be either words or sequences of nonprintable characters. We choose the second alternative because of the knowledge that lines are made up of words, which in turn are made up of characters.

This representation requires definition of an object L, which, according to the above decision, is of a type

phrase:blocks **array**

Blocks, in turn, are not further detailed; therefore

blocks:**abstract**

We also need the type "vals," defined as

```
vals:(c:integer,
      w:integer,
      e:boolean)
```

Note that instead of adding details to "counts," we defined "vals" as a combination of the same elementary types but in different order. We chose this definition merely to demonstrate that it could be done. However, this technique is not recommended in practice.

As a permanent data object of m_line we can declare

L:phrase

The pre- and postconditions of the one program of m_line are already expressed in m_text as function pre- and postconditions.

Precondition and Postcondition

The next step in the design is to express the pre- and postconditions of this function in terms of "blocks." To do so, we have to reexpress the abstract predicates used in m_text, showing any additional detail we are now aware of about the representation of the data object L.

The abstract predicate "contains_eof" defined at the upper level is characterized by (P is a text_file, i is an integer)

not (P(i)) contains_eof $\Leftrightarrow$ i $\neq$ P.hib

However, this characterization has no impact on the design of m_line. The above property was already used to design the algorithm for the program text_count in the machine m_text. By proceeding in the hierarchy by data expansion, we have neither a way nor a need to distinguish among various objects of the type "line." If we have this need, we cannot use the technique of data expansion.

One more property about eof, which comes from the problem requirements, must be expressed here. It is that the character EOF is not a character that may be part of a word. If EOF exists in a line, it must be in the last (as the last character) of the "blocks" of that line. This property allows us to write the postcondition for the program process_line" in m_line:

```
for all i in (L.lob . . . L.hib − 1) [not (L(i)) is_eof]
and (L(L.hib)) is_eof ⇔ Q.e
```

Mappings

In this partial rewriting of the process_line postcondition, we used our understanding that the object L is the representation of any generic object of the type "line." As a consequence, we have a new expression for the predicate "contains_eof" of m_text.

All these facts may now be expressed in the mapping of m_line:

```
mapping
   let li:line; i:integer; H:counts;
      Q.w represents H.c;
      Q.c represents H.a;
      Q.e represents H.b;
      L represents li;
      for all i in (L.lob . . . L.hib − 1)
      [not (L(i)) is_eof] and [(L(L.hib)) is_eof
      represents (li) contains_eof]
```

In the process of rewriting the postcondition, we introduced a new abstract predicate, "is_eof," which should now be declared:

```
Predicates
   let B:block; P:phrase; j:integer;
      (B) is_eof means abstract;
      characterized by
      j ≠ P.hib ⇒ not (P(j)) is_eof;
```

We can now proceed to determine the representation of the two other predicates: words_in and char_in. Predicate words_in can be rewritten as follows:

```
mapping
   .
   .
   .
   for all h in L.dom [Q.w = #(L|L(h)) is_ printable)]
```

```
        represents (H.c)words_in (li);
        .
        .
        .
    Predicates
      (B) is_printable means abstract;
        characterized by
        (B) is_eof ⇒ not (B) is_printable
```

Here we indicate, with "#(L|((L(h)) is_printable)," the integer counting the number of elements in the array L that satisfy the predicate "((L(h)) is_printable)."

The characterization of is_printable states the obvious fact (deduced from the problem requirements) that a block containing EOF cannot be a word of printable characters.

Analogously, for the predicate count_char used in m_text, we can write the following representation:

```
mapping
   .
   .
   .
   (Q,c) character_count_of (L) up_to (L.hib)
     represents (H.a) char_in (li)
Predicates
   .
   .
   .
   let D:integer array; l, m, n, r, s:integer;
   (r) character_count_of (P) up_to (m) means
   D.lob = P.lob and for all l in (P.lob . . . m),
   n in (D.lob . . . m) [count_char_of (P(l))is(D(n))
   and l = n] and
   r = D(D.lob) + D(D.lob + 1) + · · · + D(m)
     {r is the character count of the first m
       blocks of P};
     count_char_of (B) is (s) means abstract;
   {s is the number of characters in the block B}
   characterized by
   count_char_of (B) is (s) ⇒ s ≥ 1
```

The last part of our development is to define the last block of a "line." We have already said that it may contain an eof, but that is not enough. We now define a predicate as follows:

```
(B)is_end_of_line means abstract;
characterized by
if (B)is_printable then
not (B)is_end_of_line,
if (B)is_eof then (B)is_end_of_line;
```

The mapping is not affected by this definition. However, we must state the fact that the last block of L is an end of a line. We do so by using the clause **inv** (defining a type invariant) for all the data objects of the type "phrase":

Types
phrase:block **array**
let B:phrase
inv (B.high) is_end_of_line

This fact will be kept in mind when we derive the program text. In fact, a test of whether a block is the high element of L is equivalent to a check of the truth of the predicate "is_end_of_line." Since we still have to reach the "given" hardware, the definition of a function to detect this end-of-line situation is suggested.

The Program Process_Line

We are now in a position to write the program process_line. The pre- and postconditions are as follows:

precondition T
postcondition
for all h **in** L.dom [Q.w = #((L|L(h))is_printable)]
and
(Q.c) character_count_of (L) up_to (L.hib)
and
[(L(L.hib))is_end_of_line **or** (L(L.hib)) is_eof ⇔ Q.e]

A loop invariant is derived by dropping the term after the last **and** and by changing the high-bound-related symbols to symbols related to a generic index j:

Loop invariant
[**for all** h **in** (L.lob . . . j)
[Q.w = #((L.lob. . .j)|((L(h)) is_printable)]]
and
(Q.c)character_count_of(L)up_to (j)

At termination the final block L(L.hib) must be an end of file or an end of line. Therefore, the loop invariant will become the postcondition.

To write the program text, we will follow a reasoning analogous to that used for the program text_count in m_text. Four pieces of information are still needed, and they are related to the still-hidden character representation. Namely: Does the block contain EOF? Does a block contain end of line? Are the characters of the block printable? And how many characters are in the block? We choose a unique function for the type "block," which returns as a parameter the composition of four objects containing this information. The type of this returning parameter is called "buffer." To express the information about the characters of a block as being printable, we define a component of the type "buffer," x, which may assume only two values, the literals "printable" and "nonprintable." We indicate this condition by listing these two values separated by a bar (|):

```
buffer:(x:("printable"|"nonprintable"),
        y: boolean, z:boolean, n:integer;
block:abstract
   let B:block
   vfun process block returns (A:buffer)
      pre T
      post
         [(B) is_printable ⇒ A.x = "printable"
            and
         not (B) is_printable ⇒ A.x = "nonprintable"]
            and
            (B)is_eof ⇔ A.y and A.z
            and
            (B)is_end_of_line ⇔ A.z
            and
            count_char_of(B)is(A.n)
end block
```

Note that if B is an end of file, the Boolean indicators both for end of file (A.y) and for end of line (A.z) are true.

The program can now be written as follows:

```
process_line returns (Q:vals)

Local objects
   R:buffer;
   j:integer

Program text
   j := l.lob;
   Q.c, Q.w, Q.e := 0, 0, false;
   R := L(j).process block;
   if R.y → Q.e := true
      not R.y and R.x = "printable" →
               Qw := Q.w + 1
   □ not R.y and R.x – "nonprintable" →
               skip
   fi;
   Q.c := Q.c + R.n;
   do not R.z →
      j := j + 1;
      R := L(j).process_block;
      if r.y → Q.e := true
         not r.y and R.x = "printable" →
            Q.w := Q.w + 1
      □ not R.y and R.x = "nonprintable" →
               skip
      fi;
      Q.c := Q.c + R.n
   od
```

Design of the Lowest Level

We are now ready to move to the design of the last element of the hierarchy. We define a new machine, which we call "m_block," that is the description of our ideal hardware machine.

At this point you should understand the development process. Thus we present only the design documentation of this machine and a few comments:

```
Machine m_block refines block

Types
   word:character array;
   character:given
   {The ASCII character set. In this development we use the name CR
      for the carriage return, which is the end-of-line delimiter, and the
      name EOF as the end of file. Both of these characters are not
      printable. We will indicate with ␢ all the other nonprintable characters
      of the set.}

Permanent data
   p:word

Program list
   process block returns (m:("printable"|"nonprintable"),
                          b1:boolean, b2:boolean,
                          ch:integer)

mapping
   let B:blocks; C:buffer;
      m represents C.x {the message part of C};
      b1 represents C.y {when true it is end of file};
      b2 represents C.z {when true it is only CR};
      p represents B;
   for all i in (p.lob . . . p.hib)
      [p(i) ≠ ␢ {blank} and p(i) ≠ EOF and p(i) ≠ CR]
      represents (B) is_printable;
      p(p.hib) = CR and
      for all i in (p.lob . . . p.hib − 1) [p(i) = ␢
          represents (B) is_end_of_line;
          p(p.hib) = EOF and
          for all i in (p.lob . . . p.hib − 1) [p(i) = ␢]
            represents (B) is_eof
```

The program documentation contains the following:

```
precondition T

postcondition
[[for all i in p.dom [p(i) ≠ ␢ and p(i) ≠ EOF
 and p(i) ≠ CR] and m = "printable" and not b1 and not b2]
or
[for all i in (p.lob . . . p.hib − 1) [p(i) = ␢] and not b1 and not b2]
```

```
or
[for all i in (p.lob . . . p.hib − 1) [p(i) = ƀ] and
p(p.hib) = EOF and m = "nonprintable" and b1 and b2]
or
[for all i in (p.lob . . . p.hib − 1) [p(i) = ƀ]
and p(p.hib) = CR ⇒ m = "nonprintable" and b2 and not b1]]
and ch = p.dom
  {The number of characters in block is the number of elements in p,
  regardless of their nature}
```

Program text

```
  j := p.lob; ch := 0;
  b1, b2 := false, false;
  m := "nonprintable";
  do j ≤ p.hib cand p(j) = ƀ →
     j := j + 1;
     ch := ch + 1
  od;
  if j > p.hib → skip
  □ j = p.hib and p(j) = EOF →
     b1, b2 := true, true;
     ch := ch + 1
  □ j = p.hib and p(j) = CR →
     b2 := true;
     ch := ch + 1
  □ j = p.lob → m := "printable";
  do j ≤ p.hib cand p(j) ≠ ƀ →
        ch := ch + 1;
        j := j + 1
     od
  fi
```

OBSERVATIONS ABOUT THE DATA EXPANSION EXAMPLE

Even a cursory examination of the program text of the example shows that each program in each machine is actually rather short. But the resulting program that must include the text of the programs in three machines is of respectable length. And each level is intellectually more manageable than the overall text considered in one lump.

Another immediate observation is that we succeeded rather easily in applying Dijkstra calculus to the programs at all levels. Even though we have not shown formal correctness proofs, we were able to organize the whole development along the lines of the technique we introduced in Chapter 7.

Representation details were hidden as much as possible

The key to the successful hierarchical development was the ability to hide representation details of the abstract data types. This technique is not an easy one to master, particularly for designers who are used to exploiting representation details at all levels. The difficulty is not that the representation is not known but that it may already be known (albeit not precisely) and therefore may influence the justification of design decisions at higher levels.

On the other hand, it is impossible not to exploit some of the representation knowledge. In fact, in the example the representation of a line was evident from the problem requirements. The success of the technique results from showing only what is needed for the derivation of a correct abstract program at each level. So the process boils down to making the informal knowledge obtained from problem requirements precise enough that a correct abstract program can be designed. To proceed in this way, we must fully define all the necessary abstract data types, including the necessary abstract predicates and their characterization. However, only the type functions necessary for writing the correct abstract program need be defined, and therefore only these functions have to be refined as programs at lower levels.

OTHER TECHNIQUES OF HIERARCHICAL ORGANIZATION

Data abstraction specifications can be written without deriving abstract programs

The technique used for the example presented above was developed by Boyd and Pizzarello (1978) from ideas of Dijkstra (1970) as formalized by Hoare (1972). This technique, however, is not the only one available. Several other techniques for hierarchical specification of large software systems were developed on similar principles. Berg et al. (1982) give an excellent presentation of these techniques. Most of these techniques (but not all) do not explicitly use the derivation of a correct abstract program for the determination of the abstract type functions. Instead of abstract predicates being introduced, some relevant relations between the type functions and their parameters are created to specify the meaning of these functions. The rationale is to make the specifications completely implementation-independent.

There are a few drawbacks in this latter approach to the specification of data types. One is that in some cases it is impossible to find relations among the type functions that are sufficient to describe the meaning of the type. For the solution of this problem additional functions actually representing intermediate states for some potential implementation of the type functions must be defined. These functions, called *hidden functions,* are indications about a specific implementation more or less at the same level as an abstract program.

The technique expounded above, as well as the very similar one presented by Mills et al. (1980), seems to present considerable practical advantages with respect to other specification techniques. The principal advantage is that the abstract program, once correctly derived, is a model implementation that supplies an existence proof that a solution has been found. Also, everything needed for the correct implementation of that program at lower levels has been defined.

On the other hand, the abstract program is actually only one possible implementation. It conditions the lower-level details because it dictates which types and programs must be developed. Consider in the above example the first design of the data type "line." We had to stop the development at that point and change the design decision, because a simple argument showed that the decision was not a wise one. But we could have kept this decision, producing a hierarchy of specifications conditioned by the original design of the program text_count. So the method does not guarantee that wrong decisions at one level are not generating poor lower-level design.

HIERARCHICAL SPECIFICATIONS IN PRACTICE

The effectiveness of the technique presented above is, thus far, based exclusively on purely theoretical considerations. Practical design of large systems involves several factors that were not considered in the analysis shown above. We will discuss the practical uses and experiences with this approach in the next two chapters.

However, one consideration can be discussed at this point in order to show the importance of data abstraction to the practitioner. Data abstraction can be considered a pure scientific theory. It is an attempt to describe, with precision, an observed phenomenon. Such scientific descriptions usually help, for example, the engineering community explain and predict the behavior of phenomena in a safer way than by mere reliance on intuition and experience. The observed phenomenon here is the current design practice of dividing a system design into a hierarchy. The hierarchy is expressed through the creation of abstractions both for data and programs in an intuitive and informal way. But current practice does not give us full control of the complexity of the design problem, as shown by the considerable number of design errors discovered at the integration phase and even later when the system is put into practical use.

Data abstraction as a scientific theory helps us to understand the origin of errors

The theory presented here helps us to understand why errors occur. One of the features of the development in the example in this chapter is that the properties of some abstraction, say "line," actually depend on our knowledge of things not yet defined, such as the structure of a word. These items are types to be defined at lower levels, and the description of these properties is connected by mappings. In data expansion, mappings are exclusively used to express the relationships between these properties at various levels, as described in our formalism by abstract predicates. The need for this mapping shows us that the partition into subproblems does not allow us to ignore the global view of the system at each level of design. This is a difficulty we have to live with because it is intrinsic to the solution of large programming problems. The theory and the derived technique are only means to indicate this difficulty and to control it.

It appears safe to say that whenever the requirements are established with a relatively high level of certainty, the hierarchy of abstract machines is an effective way to show an architectural organization of the system that should minimize design errors. Note that design errors do not necessarily include misinterpreted requirements. This is not to say that a formal design technique is of no help for reducing the potential for error in requirements interpretation. In fact, in the next chapter we will see that in a practical case a design hierarchy was of considerable help in clarifying the requirements. The point, again, is that external requirements are not confined to the top level of the abstract machines' hierarchy, and they cannot be. Thus in the example of this chapter the type "character" is as user-visible as words and lines, and yet it does not appear explicitly until the bottom-level abstract machine is designed.

HIGHLIGHTS

We have discussed an example of hierarchical development through data expansion. The system in the example, though not of large size, presents features typical of any system development. The example shows how the intrinsic difficulty of software development can be controlled by the use of data abstraction. We do not claim, however, that the difficulties of large-system development disappear once the problem is subjected to the discipline of hierarchical development. What the hierarchy technique does is control the difficulty through the application of rigorous formalism.

The example showed how a problem can be broken down into steps that can be attacked separately. The only connections between these steps are the rather simple consistency checks, expressed by mappings. Also, we saw how design decisions at one level may be changed because of performance problems detected at that level.

REFERENCES

Berg, H. K.; Boebert, W. E.; Franta, W. R.; and Moher, T. G. 1982. *Formal methods of program verification and specification.* Englewood Cliffs, N.J.: Prentice-Hall.

Boyd, D. L., and Pizzarello, A. 1978. Introduction to the WELLMADE design methodology. *IEEE Transactions on Software Engineering* SE–4 (no. 4):276–282.

Dijkstra, E. W. 1970. Structured programming. In *Report on a conference sponsored by the NATO Science Committee: Software engineering techniques, Rome, Italy,* edited by J. N. Buxton and B. Randell, pp. 84–88.

Hoare, C. A. R. 1972. Proof of correctness of data representation. *Acta Informatica* 1 (no. 4):271–281.

Mills, H. D.; O'Neill, D.; Linger, R. C.; and Dyer, M. 1980. The management of software engineering. Parts I–IV: Principles of software engineering. *IBM Systems Journal* 19 (no. 4):415–420, 421–431, 432–450, 451–476.

CHAPTER FIFTEEN

Experiences with Hierarchical Design

INTRODUCTION

In this chapter we examine experiences with the use of a rigorous design approach for the development of software systems.

From theory it is difficult to judge how factors such as entrenched habits and social trends affect the practical use of any new development method. Also, a large proportion of software development is not new development but rather is work to modify and to add functionalities to existing systems. Theoretical examination of techniques is of little help in appraising these effects.

Another consideration in analysis is that the existence of experimental success is not a proof of the goodness of a software development technique. The computer literature shows an abundance of papers demonstrating total or partial success in the application of some particular technique, but very few describe failures. This lack is a natural phenomenon: Nobody likes to talk about failures. There are, however, some exceptions. Hoare (1981) in his 1980 ACM Turing Award Lecture described his failure to realize an ambitious software project. Also, Brooks (1975) in his *Mythical Man-Month* was not shy about describing several wrong decisions he made while he was managing the development of a large operating system.

A lot can be learned from failures, particularly with regard to the applicability of techniques that are used by humans. Therefore in this chapter we will examine a few applications of the technique of hierarchical development of software with the specific intent of pointing out its weakness for practical application.

Another problem with the analysis of experiences with techniques is that the effect of a technique is not necessarily visible in the short term. It is quite possible that a particular project benefits by the use of some technique in the sense that the first release is delivered on time and under budget with fewer errors than usual. But in the long run the practical use of the system may show undesired features such as lack of modifiability and reliability. Unfortunately, papers are published after the success (or the failure) of the first attempt, and no follow-up indicating later problems is ever published. Therefore we must consider all published results with caution.

SOME EXPERIENCES WITH DATA ABSTRACTION

A series of articles by Mills et al. (1980) describes the overall organization of the software development process at IBM–FSD. The technical core of the process is a rigorous approach to design based on the same principles and on techniques very similar to the ones described previously in this book. These techniques (according to the Mills articles) are supported by a rigorous educational program for both developers and managers, an impressive array of tools, and the enforcement of a design-first discipline.

Impressive results

The results of this approach are not presented quantitatively, probably (and understandably) because such figures are considered company data. However, an overall qualitative judgment is given, presenting the system LAMPS as an example, citing the fact that this system was developed on schedule and below budget with a total effort producing over 7 million lines of code in 45 releases. This effort required 200 man-years for its completion. If the lines of code cited in the article are counted in the same way we discussed in Chapter 2, these figures bring out the impressive result of 2900 lines per man-month for overall productivity. That result amounts to an increase in average productivity of over seven times the average reported in Chapter 2 by RADC.

Even though the productivity gain may have not been this high, the feeling Mills et al. convey to the reader is one of a smashing success. On the other hand, the application of technique (according to Mills et al.) was not without difficulties. We have no details about these difficulties, but the article indicates that they were mostly relative to a resistance to the introduction of the technique on the part of the development personnel.

AN EXPERIMENTAL APPLICATION OF DATA ABSTRACTION

Details of a controlled experiment shed light on advantages and difficulties of the approach

The experimental evidence that we are going to examine in detail is reported by Foreman (1979). Since I was involved in that experimental development as a consultant, some of Foreman's observations are integrated with my direct experience. Of course, my involvement may bias the analysis of the results of this project. However, most reports about software project success (or failure) are written by persons directly involved and interested in describing the positive aspects of the experiment. So the material here really has no more bias than is usually found in published articles.

The project we are going to describe and analyze is named SWISP. Its objective is to furnish a database administrator (DBA) with the ability to control access to information stored on a number of databases, all part of a very large (preexisting) command and control system. The purpose of SWISP is to enhance the security control of the system by supplying the DBA with appropriate verification tools. These tools allow the DBA to do the following:

- Create an entry in a particular database called the security database (SDB), which specifies the acceptable space for the parameters of a user-written procedure (these entries are called procedure profiles).
- Enter a user's identification number (USERID) into the SDB along with the name of the procedures to which the user is given access (these entries are called user profiles).

In this manner the DBA may specify security policy. The project, however, was not attempting to create an absolutely secure system. For example, one problem that SWISP was attempting to solve was to prevent a program from producing an unclassified report if this program read a classified database. However, since the DBA is a trusted officer, he or she might authorize such a report on a case-by-case basis.

The organization of SWISP's operations is to permit the DBA to use an administrative process to update the security policies in SDB. Other system users have their access to various system databases checked and authorized by the DBA.

REQUIREMENT ANALYSIS

A very exhaustive analysis of the requirements was planned and attempted before any design work was initiated. No prototyping was used, but the behavior of similar system functionalities was discussed with the representative of the user community.

For the purpose of studying the set of user-visible commands to the system, a finite state machine model was constructed. This model was a graph in which each node represented the external manifestation of a state of the system. This state showed how the system manifested itself to the user at a terminal by printing some form of message. From each node (a state) several edges may exit, each representing a user-introduced command, which may bring the system to another state or possibly back to the same one. That is, in this latter case the user command prompts the system to repeat the same message.

Note that these states are not necessarily in direct correspondence with the set of states defined during design by abstract predicates. The purpose of this analysis was only to identify the various interactions between the user and the system so that the user could judge if the requirements were correctly interpreted by the designers.

Strangely enough, it was not possible to ensure correct interpretation of requirements without discussing some details of the design with the user. The novelty here, compared with a traditional approach, is that instead of discussing implementation details, the designer and user discussed the SDB, which is an abstract data type. In other words, the finite state machine model, as described above, did not supply sufficient information about the effect of the commands on the database (SDB). Since the purpose of the system use was to manipulate the SDB, it was impossible to discuss the correctness of the requirements interpretation without supplying information about the SDB itself.

Data abstraction helped designers define problem requirements

Thus this example illustrates the presence of fuzzy boundaries between system design decisions and requirements analysis. An interesting result of the SWISP experience, then, is that a design technique affected the process of interpreting the user's requirements.

THE DESIGN OF SWISP

The design of SWISP centers around the design of the SDB. The information to be stored in SDB is of two general types: procedure profiles and user profiles. These profiles must be related to each other to describe which users have access to which procedures. Also, procedure policies must be able to describe what space is acceptable (for security reasons) for the storage of parameters and for the location (during its use) of the text of procedure.

These relations convinced the designers that SDB had to be organized as a labeled tree. This labeled tree is the view of SDB to the outside world. In other words, the DBA can think of the SDB as though it were organized in the way shown in Figure 17. The SDB is treated as an abstract data type whose representation is not made available to the user, and it can be accessed exclusively by a prescribed set of operations. The meaning of these operations, however, is expressed in a way that implies the tree model shown in Figure 17.

The overall structure of the system in terms of abstract machines is shown in Figure 18. The highest-level machine, M_SWISP, presents the functionalities needed to access the abstract data type SDB. This type, in turn, is refined in another machine, M_SDB, where the representation of the database becomes manifest in terms of the labeled tree's nodes and edges.

The top-level machine showed 50 type functions for SDB. Each function is one of the commands available to the DBA for manipulating SDB. This number is much higher than anything we have seen so far in the textbook examples about data abstraction, and its magnitude deserves more detailed discussion, which will be presented below.

Large number of type functions reflects the user-visible functionalities

The 50 SDB functions, in turn, become programs manipulating the tree in M_SDB. For example, if a parameter P is to be added to a procedure profile X, the external interface (as expressed by the abstract data type SDB in M_SWISP) requires the following steps:

1. The function IS PROC(X) must be executed to determine whether X is an existing procedure.
2. The function IS_PARAM(P, X) must be executed to find out whether P is already a parameter of X.

3. The function CREATE_PARA(P) must be executed to create a new parameter in the database.

The level below M_SDB is the machine M_LIST, where nodes are collected into logical records and where the Dijkstra's arrays used to represent information at the level above are now detailed as linked lists. At this level the abstract data type logical_record_store presents only eight functions.

In the next level of machine, M_LOGICAL_RECORD_STORE, the linked list pointers and their manipulation mechanisms in M_LIST are transformed into addresses of storages represented as arrays. The need for this level is not readily apparent. However, it was too cumbersome

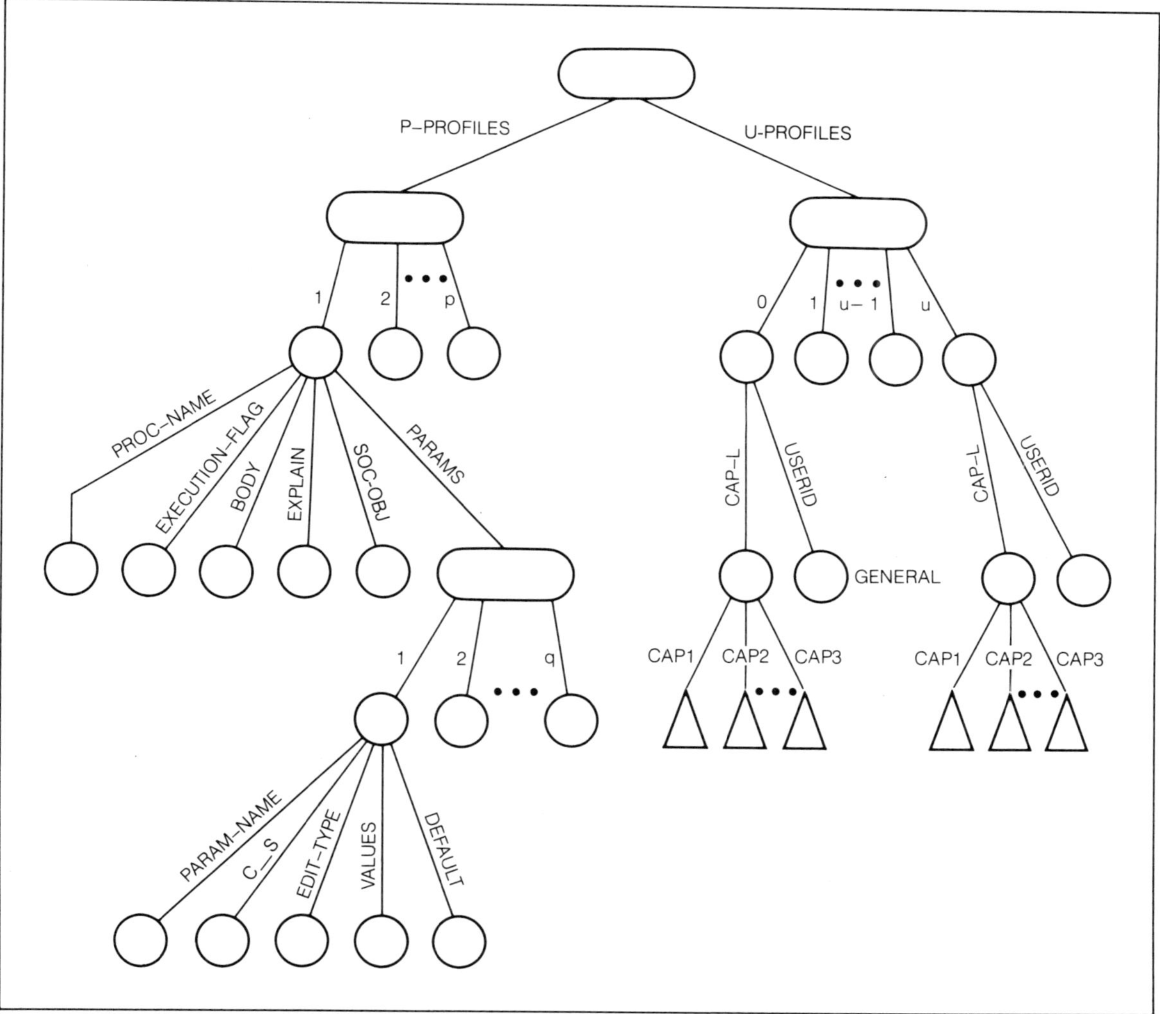

FIGURE 17 MODEL OF THE SECURITY DATABASE

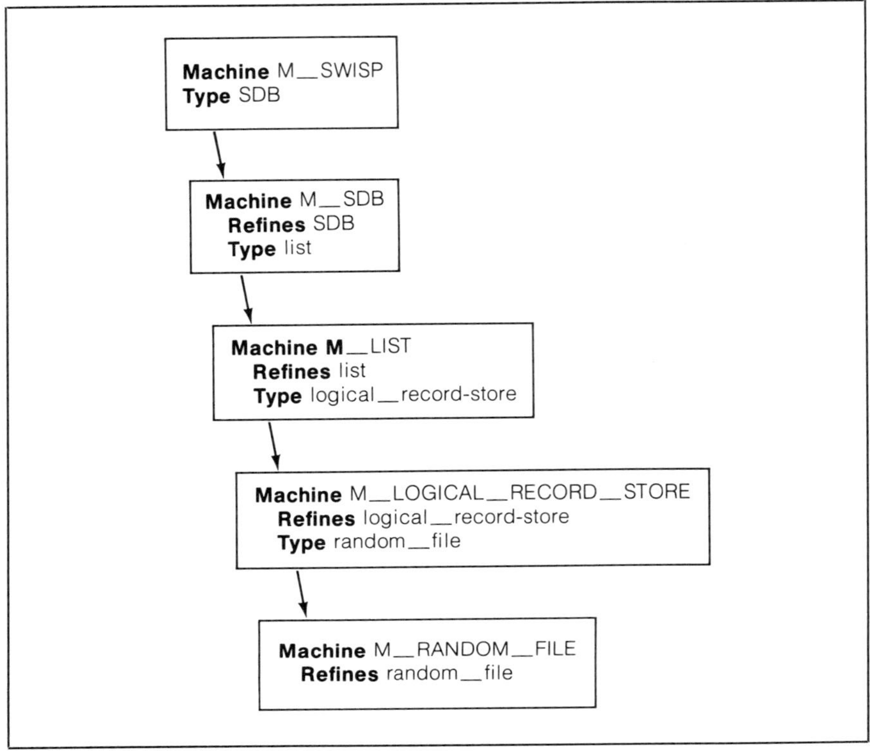

FIGURE 18 HIERARCHICAL ORGANIZATION OF THE SWISP DEVELOPMENT

to pass from the linked list to the available features of the random storage available in the supporting operating system without this intermediate step.

The next level, M_RANDOM_FILE, refines the database represented as a series of arrays in an array of blocks of records to which storage templates in terms of bits and words are assigned. At this level two functions only are usable, to read and to write a block.

EVALUATION OF THE DESIGN EXPERIENCE

The following observations come from the participants in the SWISP project. These observations are divided in two parts: The first part (described in this section) is about design. The second part (described in the next section) considers implementation issues.

First, the DBA has the power to create undesirable security policies through a misunderstanding of the semantics of the human-machine interface. Therefore it was very important that the DBA have a simple, understandable model of the SDB and not be burdened with any extraneous representation information. This observation is the basis for the decision to make the labeled tree model of SDB visible to the DBA. The

Top-level description facilitates the understanding of the system for the user

data abstraction approach did facilitate the creation of a system that could be fully understood by its users, because the user's world was modeled at the top level of the design. Thus the initial effort serves two purposes. The first is a detailed specification for further refinements. The second is a semantic model with which to explain the workings of the system to the user. The use of this model for the DBA was indispensable for clarifying the user's requirements in such a way that the subsequent design could proceed without major requirements interpretation problems. This observation matches the contention repeated several times in this book: that an abstract data type is a natural form to present the user-visible functionalities of a software system.

Second, the specification of the database was done almost entirely in predicate calculus. (Programs that output formatted reports were specified in English.) The designers found this fact surprising, because they were not convinced of its feasibility.

Third, one of the most surprising results of the project was that predicate calculus was an effective tool. It was effective for two reasons:

1. Data abstraction allows one to write abstract predicates in terms of high-level data objects in a form close to English sentences, although more precise.
2. Characterization is a powerful tool both for making properties of the interface clear to designers and for expressing those properties precisely.

The specification of the SDB data type in M_SWISP required 700 lines (300 lines of predicates and 400 lines of type specification). However, these specifications suffered from a bit of sloppiness because there were no automatic tools to enforce syntax conventions. No formal verification of the design was performed, but most abstract programs were derived from specifications according to the technique described in this book.

The size of the specifications is equal to procedural code

Fourth, four abstract machines were produced from the 700 lines of the abstract database specifications in M_SWISP. These four abstract machines contained 5000 lines of specification, procedural text of abstract programs, and explanatory comments. Of these lines 700 lines were procedural code and 1500 lines were explanatory comments. These 700 lines of procedural code were distributed over 75 abstract programs. One might ask whether 700 lines of specification to generate 700 lines of procedural code indicates a weakness in the methodology. While this statement might be true, the result is probably more indicative of a process refinement through the hierarchy that is as simple as possible.

Fifth, the question that overshadowed the whole design effort was, "How close should the design be to the implementation and how much latitude should the implementors have?" It was decided that the implementor should have little freedom. This decision leads directly to the need for 50 functions in the specification of the SDB data type. The alternative was to break the 50 functions into several types that represent subtrees of the SDB. The problem with this alternative is that it might imply the transfer of a large amount of information via parameter passing. So that any decisions at implementation time would be avoided, the whole database was specified as a single data object as it was envisioned it should have been implemented. This question of freedom given to implementors is discussed further in the next section.

Sixth, the design of the 50 functions for the SDB data type shows another interesting element. Earlier, the sequence for adding a parameter to a procedure profile was described. Notice that the function IS_PARAM(P) has no parameter to indicate to which procedure profile the parameter belongs. The procedure profile is indicated by the previous call to IS_PROC. In this way the user of the data type SDB is constrained to make function calls in an efficient order. This decision requires the designer both to exploit some data component at a higher level and to use careful characterization of the abstract predicates specifying pre- and postconditions and the type invariant of the SDB functions. Otherwise, this side effect could not be specified. These data components were eventually refined into the buffers of the database.

OBSERVATIONS ABOUT THE IMPLEMENTATION OF SWISP

SWISP was implemented in assembly language by a team different from the design team. The implementation raised a number of interesting questions that could not be discovered by just doing a paper design.

First, the implementation team built a runtime support package (RSP) to aid their efforts. This package is the analog of a compiler runtime support. The RSP was not designed by using the same technique the designers used; it was a "traditional" development. Thus a controversy arose over whether or not the experiment with data abstraction was completed properly. One camp argued that design is the process of building an abstract machine and implementation is the process of simulating the abstract machine on a general-purpose computer. In this case the RSP is needed for simulation and therefore is not part of SWISP; so the design was properly completed. The second camp argued that all software built for SWISP should be designed according to the hierarchical technique; thus the project was not completed properly. This controversy was somewhat academic because of the experimental nature of the project and the fact that the implementation was nearly complete when the argument arose. However, it does point out the potential ambiguity of statements that indicate that a whole project has been realized according to some methodology.

Operating system interfaces were the major problem

Second, the aspect of the SWISP design that caused the most debate among the design team was the definition of the interface with the available operating system. One reason for this debate is that the software design method used gives plenty of detail about how to build new software, but it is much less extensive in its description of how to interface with old software.

In retrospect, the two poles of this debate are quite clear. They are characterized as follows:

1. Use of the real supervisor calls in the text of the abstract programs expressed in the design language.
2. Use of type functions that look like supervisor calls but, in fact, may require several real supervisor calls.

The problem with the first approach is that it tends to propagate too much information into higher levels of the design. The problem with the second is that it does not give adequate direction to the implementors.

Let us consider an illustrative example of this difficulty from the SWISP design. At one point an abstract program needs to know the USERID of the job that it has just spawned. A supervisor call that will return the content of a control block, called the UST, contains all sorts of information, including the required USERID. But the design principles require that all this other information be hidden since it is useless for the particular design decision. Therefore the SWISP design contains an abstract supervisor call that returns only the required USERID. As it turns out, the real UST contains two fields, both with a USERID, and, of course, the first implementation chose the wrong one. This result indicates a flaw in the design: not using the real supervisor calls and the exact representation of all data made available by those calls.

The way to resolve these two opposing points of view is to use two abstract data types that represent the operating system. Let us call these types T_AOS and T_ROS, where AOS stands for "abstract operating systems" and ROS stands for "real operating system." The functions of the T_ROS are the real supervisor calls, while the functions of the T_AOS represent supervisor calls to some ideal operating system for the application. The abstract machine that refines T_AOS is the only one that declares a data object of type T_ROS. This approach should be obvious to anyone who is familiar with the design of the "THE" operating system. However, in the top-down approach to the problem, this technique was missed.

Error rate was very low

A third observation is that although no formal verification of the implementation was performed, the SWISP implementation was "thoroughly" tested before its shipment to the customer. (The approach used for testing is described in the next chapter.) During coding and testing the implementation team wrote 32 error reports. Of these errors, 27 were hard errors (i.e., a real bug as opposed to a disagreement about the format of an output). Of these 27 errors, 10 dealt with the handling of files via operating system calls. This result again may be a consequence of the difficulties encountered in interfacing with the real operating system.

The final size of SWISP was 13,000 DSLOC. Then from the number of error reports (32) we have 2.4 errors per thousand DSLOC for SWISP. Compared with the average for this type of project (see Chapter 2), this result is a considerable improvement (more than ten times better than the 26.6 errors per thousand DSLOC reported in Chapter 2). No productivity data for the whole project were gathered. However, the project was concluded within schedule and budget constraints, which were established on the basis of past experiences with projects of similar size and complexity.

The system, once delivered, was subjected to very severe acceptance tests by the customer. No error was reported during these tests. The SWISP system was then declared defect-free. For nontechnical reasons SWISP was never put into practical use. Therefore no follow-up experience about its maintainability is available.

THE EXPERIENCE IN PERSPECTIVE

All the SWISP team members were not experienced in the hierarchical technique, and no one was part of the study group that was responsible for the definition of the notation and of the design methods. All the team members were subject to training in hierarchical development. The success of the training program (mostly informal) was not outstanding. A large percentage of the people who attended were not able to produce a design according to the dictates of the technique. Even those who became the designers of SWISP were not convinced of the usefulness and viability of the technique at the beginning of the project. The implementation team members also showed skepticism, if not hostility, for a considerable length of time.

Under these circumstances the very fact the project was completed (and successfully) seems to be a miracle. The reason it was completed may be due to the insistence on the part of the customer (who funded the project as a research work) to proceed until data relative to the practicality of the technique could be collected.

An interesting result of the project was the positive effect of the abstract model for correct interpretation of the requirements. Whether this result has general validity remains to be seen. However, the resistance of the software developers to the introduction of this development discipline [also hinted at by Mills (1980)] is a factor I have observed in several other cases. And developer resistance was the cause of failure in these cases.

Besides resistance to the technique, there is another source of practical difficulty in the SWISP experience, namely, the difficulty in interfacing existing software. In the case of SWISP the amount of this interaction, because of the problem's nature (very little use of operating system features, no interaction with operating system data), was minimal. And yet according to the judgment of the implementors, 10 out of 27 reported errors were related to operating system interfacing. Both designers and implementors were very experienced in the use of the operating system supporting SWISP, thus excluding the possibility that the errors were caused by inexperience.

Interaction with existing software was the largest source of errors

OTHER EXPERIENCES WITH THE USE OF HIERARCHICAL DEVELOPMENT

In this section we will examine briefly three experimental applications of the technique of data abstraction that I observed in three different organizations. These experiences were not as carefully controlled as SWISP. However, they add insight to the problems of applying the technique in the real world.

Note that all experiences depend strongly on the background of the developers. The approach reported by Mills (1980) relies heavily on an education program created specifically to prepare the developers for using the technique. Nothing of this sort was done in the cases discussed below. Only informal training was supplied, and there was no company policy to encourage the introduction of the technique.

One experience with the technique is the creation of a system for the control of the concurrent access to a database. The system included extended capabilities for recovery/restart, deadlock detection, and i/o buffering for improving performance. The technique was applied diligently in the first version developed. The results were described by the project leader in a company internal paper as very satisfactory. The most astonishing result was the extremely short time and the minimal effort required in the phase of integration and system tests, which was accomplished in about two weeks. For a system of that level of complexity it would be reasonable to expect at least four months for that phase.

After this first success, however, the development team was enlarged, the requirements were widely changed, and the supporting operating system was changed. The follow-up development did not use the hierarchical technique but relied on the usual approach of direct modification of the executable code. This change was sufficient to revert the process to the traditional pattern. In subsequent versions the system did not show that exceptional characteristic of a smooth integration phase it had shown for the first version.

The second experience is rather unusual because it did not involve a real design activity but rather a development of a paper prototype to study the requirements for a sophisticated end-user facility for database manipulation. The hierarchical development was used by only one individual to demonstrate, via the use of a few levels of abstract machines, the possible variation of capabilities in the end-user facility. This individual found the technique very useful because it allowed him to maintain an intellectual grasp on the problem throughout the analysis of several variations of end-user interfaces and functionalities. The actual system was implemented in a fully traditional manner. The interesting result of this experience is that hierarchical development is an effective way to produce paper prototypes for the study of complex requirements. In fact, this experience confirms the similar result discussed in the description of SWISP, where a level of hierarchical design was instrumental in the correct interpretation of the requirements.

Sloppy design verification was the cause of project failure

The third experience relates to the development of a part of an operating system that was to monitor the system resource utilization and to display the level of use on a screen. This development required a rather intimate interface with the operating system because it needed to access several system resource tables in order to monitor their levels of utilization.

This project initiated very well. The designers were delighted with the mental grasp on the problem they could maintain throughout the design phase. However, the formal design process was stopped too early. Because of this decision, only a very ineffective review of the rather incomplete design was performed. Consequently, several design errors were discovered at implementation time. The hierarchy was not extended, as in the case of SWISP, down to the actual operating system interface, but the design was stopped at some arbitrarily chosen level of abstraction. The idea was to leave some freedom for the implementation because of the well-justified concern of the possibility of changes in the interfaces with the operating system, which was undergoing considerable modification work at the same time.

Despite the initial enthusiasm of the designers, the project can only be described as a failure. The design was drastically changed during implementation by direct modifications of the implementing code. These changes were necessary both because of design errors and because of changes in the interfaces with the operating system.

Two lessons can be drawn from this experience. One is that a formal design must be complete; i.e., it must extend to the actual interface with the supporting software (or hardware). If these interfaces change, the whole design process must be repeated to accommodate these changes. If the design is not redone, any advantage of the technique disappears completely.

The second lesson is that any design process is useless if it does not provide confidence in its correctness through a reliable process of verification. The technique presented in the previous chapters relies on formal verifications of the programs and of the mappings between levels. This validation is done by humans, and therefore the only way to make it reliable is to subject it to reviews. And once again, the design process must be repeated in order to assess all the effects of any errors on the whole design. As before, if the design is not redone, all advantages of the technique are lost.

The novelty of the approach is one reason it is not accepted

The problems identified in this experience arose from the developers' halfhearted acceptance of the hierarchical development technique. The organization was implementation-oriented. The developers, while they were willing to try a new technique, were not really comfortable with a process that relied so heavily on design. The occurrence of a problem is always a cause for concern about the effectiveness of a new approach. It was therefore very difficult for the developers not to return to the familiar traditional approach when problems were identified. Unfortunately, the two approaches are so intrinsically different that it is impossible to use both for the same project. Since the implementation approach is more familiar, it was natural that the whole process rapidly became dominated by implementation.

CONCLUDING REMARKS

These experiences indicate that two problem categories—resistance in accepting the technique and difficulties in interfacing with the supporting system—have a serious impact on the practical applicability of the data abstraction method. This impact cannot be dismissed by arguing that training and improved implementation techniques will solve these problems. Much deeper organizational and managerial changes are required, since these problems are essentially nontechnical, a consequence of tradition and a reluctance to change.

We note, too, that this new technique is not a panacea but only a more rational way of developing software. Consequently, major advantages may be obtained by the mere education of developers in the theory behind the technique.

As mentioned above, acceptance problems may be overcome by directing organizational and managerial philosophy away from its current approach of observing computer runs to verify design ideas. The problems relative to interfacing existing software may then disappear since development will no longer be implementation-driven. We conclude that a design method based on data abstraction can be a very effective one. All the developers involved in the experiences described above who overcame the method's difficulties were impressed with the intellectual grasp it gave them of the design process.

HIGHLIGHTS

Publication detailing experiences with the rigorous design method of data abstraction are rather limited. Most of the existing descriptions, however, point out that the method can be very effective. On the other hand, its application will not necessarily be successful. The difficulties of introducing what amounts to a completely new paradigm for the software community are enormous and not all solved by any means. Also, interfacing new development with existing software is a major source of problems, and these problems too are not yet solved.

Nevertheless, when properly applied, the method is very effective in controlling the complexity of large-system development. In particular, the integration phase of software development is greatly facilitated by the correct use of the approach. Since integration is the major problem in developing large systems, this finding allows us to conclude that the data abstraction technique is a very effective tool in software development.

REFERENCES

Brooks, F. P. 1975. *The mythical man-month.* Reading, Mass.: Addison-Wesley.

Foreman, I. 1979. Data abstraction in the design of SWISP. Paper presented at the 19th annual NBS/ACM Technical Symposium, Washington, D.C.

Hoare, C. A. R. 1981. The emperor's old clothes. 1980 ACM Turing Award Lecture. *Communications of ACM* 24 (no. 2):75–83.

Mills, H. D.; O'Neill, D.; Linger, R. C.; and Dyer, M. 1980. The management of software engineering. Parts I–IV: Principles of software engineering. *IBM Systems Journal* 19 (no. 4):415–420, 421–431, 432–450, 451–476.

CHAPTER SIXTEEN

Analysis of Implementation and Maintenance

INTRODUCTION

In this chapter we examine current system development in terms of the new concepts we have studied thus far. We have explored in previous chapters some of the techniques available for the design of new software. We have also examined the problems and the payoff of the application of these techniques in practice. In the process of this study we have found that a program and a system can be thought of as intellectual objects subject to rational analysis. The purpose of this chapter is to use the insights we have gained about programs and systems to study the problem of the maintenance (extensions as well as error corrections) of large systems without assuming that any particular design technique was used. Because the systems to be maintained must have been implemented, the analysis of the maintenance process necessarily entails implementation considerations.

The purpose of this exploration of current systems is twofold. First, we want to obtain a rational picture of the reasons behind the phenomena of high maintenance cost (Chapter 1) and of limitations on maintenance work in a large system, as indicated by the Belady-Lehman study (see Chapter 2). Second, we want to verify whether the data abstraction technique is of any help in understanding the maintenance problem.

Software is actually much more involved than most engineering products. For instance, most of the life cycle work for a software product occurs after the first shipment (the original design). Considerable design work goes on in adding and/or modifying existing software. So the applicability of our design technique must be demonstrated for modification work as well.

A CONCEPTUAL MODEL FOR LARGE-SYSTEM SOFTWARE ERRORS

It is useful to build a model of the software system in order to put the data about errors (Chapter 2) in perspective. The term *model* is used here in the sense of physics, i.e., as a description of a phenomenon that presents the essential properties of reality and yet is simple enough to be intellectually manageable. With the help of a realistic model we can create a theory that may, in turn, be confirmed by the existing (or future) experimental data. The model consists of classification of errors, errors in the data-addressing mechanism, and parameter passing. In the succeeding subsections we will consider each of these elements in turn.

The following discussion is a recapitulation of concepts introduced in this book. Its purpose is to put appropriate emphasis on the concepts needed for the creation of a realistic software error model.

The meaning of a program (i.e., one of the system's modules) can be precisely established in terms of data value transformations. A program can be associated with a particular data set (in core variables, files, input/output lines of information) that is accessed and manipulated by only that program. Then any error can be defined as a transformation of the data set values that does not satisfy some indisputable outside requirement.

Scope of variables is a tool for limiting error propagation

In a program of some size the text is usually split into subprograms (procedures), and each of these procedures may contain data that are accessible only to the procedure. Also, the procedure has access to some data in other procedures (perhaps the main program), which are made available to the procedure at invocation time. These data are called parameters. An error for a program or a subprogram now must be defined as a violation of some condition expressed not only in terms of the local data values but also in terms of the parameters. For example, if the procedure is supposed to retrieve an element in an array that contains a particular key, this particular key is passed as a parameter at procedure invocation. The output of the execution (a return parameter) will be the element of the array containing that key. In this example both local data (the array) and input and output parameters can be identified. All these data were needed to express (even in a very formal way) the meaning of the program.

Note that high-order programming language scope rules limit the visibility of variables to the procedure where they are declared. This concept is important in programming language design because of the resulting localization of the effect of errors in the procedure to the erroneous procedure itself.

In any large software system several program modules invoke each other, and the communication is affected by parameter passing. We have also discussed another element in the communication between modules in a system: a set of global data that can be accessed and manipulated by all modules of a certain level.

Our question now is, Is there a meaning that can be defined for the system as a whole? A system is supposed to supply certain functionalities to its users. This requirement can be translated into a relation over global data or relating local data from different programs that represent the legitimate system states corresponding to the desired functionalities. At any time during system execution an appropriate set of data values defines whether or not the system is correctly performing its services. Therefore a system error is a violation of the relations describing the desired functionalities. In terms of the concepts we have learned in the preceding chapters, this type of error is a violation of the system's data invariant.

The correctness of individual modules must be determined also by considering values of global data. We know that the pre- and postconditions are expressed in terms of the system's permanent data. But the actual values of these global data are manipulated by various system modules, whose correctness depends on the appropriate use of parameters and local data. Consequently, an erroneous module affects the outcome of a correct one, since it may produce data values that do not correspond to legitimate system states (the data invariant), which are the only states a correct module may accept for its correct execution.

System global data are created by permitting a program to declare external data and to refer to these data. External data are made global by the use of the linker/binder. Because of the use of this technique, any beneficial effect of high-order language scope rules on error rates disappears.

Classification of Errors

As a consequence of the above discussion, three forms of errors can be detected in a large software system:

1. Errors caused by wrong manipulations and manifested by unacceptable values of data local to an individual module.
2. Errors caused by wrong manipulations and manifested by unacceptable values of local data and parameters.
3. Errors caused by wrong manipulations and manifested by unacceptable values of local data, parameters, and global data.

Errors are classified according to the scope of the data where they are manifested

Errors are deviations from the desired behavior that may be caused both by inconsistency of the program with its specification (Hoare-Floyd correctness) and by specifications that do not reflect the desired function of the program (as detectable by some infallible oracle used to judge testing results). The reduction of this latter type of error is the purpose of hierarchical development by data abstraction.

Errors of the first type are (in principle) detectable by testing an individual module in a simulated environment. Their effect is usually minor, and their impact is largely irrelevant in a large system, assuming that the simulated environment is a faithful reproduction of the interface of the individual module with the rest of the software. Examples of these errors are inappropriate printing of correct information by a printing module, erroneous calculations of values for output, etc.

Errors of the second type are (in principle) detectable by testing two modules, provided all calling sequences can be identified. Their effect is always relevant in a large system because it may trigger incorrect elaboration of correct data with far-reaching effects.

Errors of the third type are (again, in principle) detectable only by testing the set M of all the modules accessing these shared data directly and testing the set N of all those modules that can be invoked directly by the modules in M, and by all the modules that access the same data of the modules N, etc. Large software systems are commonly built in such a way that once this criterion is applied for some crucial piece of data, all the modules are interconnected.

Note that the definition above does not say that the effect of errors due to the violation of a type invariant of an object may propagate to other objects. This result is likely only in the case of the parameter-passing mechanism we have assumed for our formalism of data abstraction. As we will see later in this chapter, this is not true for most current programming language implementations. Also, if a design is split into several abstract machines within the same level of hierarchical development and these machines' programs communicate with each other via parameter passing, the interconnection described above does not exist because there are no data objects accessible to programs of different machines. This decoupling, however, may be impossible because of the problem's requirements or performance conditions.

A further note is that errors of type 3 propagate within an abstract machine. If the system at some level (or all levels) of the hierarchy is designed as a single machine, this potential propagation will extend to the entire system.

The essential difference between the three types of errors is the degree of isolation obtainable in principle. Clearly, type 3 error effects are not isolatable even in principle. To clarify this point, let us assume that the module-testing process is such that at the termination of each and every module execution the infallible oracle can be invoked to judge the correctness of the just-performed computation. Under these circumstances, it would be possible to exclude errors of type 1 and type 2 but not of type 3. In fact, the purpose of the simulated environment is to test the features of that module, and the oracle is infallible about judging the correctness of these features in terms of the particular module's functions in the whole system context. However, undesired side effects on the global data (i.e., violation of the data invariant) are not necessarily tested because they may be not relevant for this module's purpose. Consequently, the effect of erroneous manipulation of global data may reach an unknown number of modules in a manner fully unpredictable from a local point of view, even though the effect of a single module may be assessed as completely correct. In other words, it does not suffice to ensure the correctness of each module with respect to its pre- and postconditions. It is also necessary to ensure the correctness of the global data with respect to their invariant.

Errors in the Data-Addressing Mechanisms

Errors in the addressing mechanisms are the most insidious

It is useful for an understanding of the practical impact of the analysis above to consider data-addressing mechanism errors separate from the data content manipulation errors. Errors in the addressing mechanism are much more subtle because they affect unsuspected modules when applied to global data.

To illustrate the difference between these two types of errors, let us consider the data-addressing mechanism in more detail. At one level of discourse a piece of data is identified by a name. All programming languages (including the lowest-level assembler) permit identification of all the pertinent variables symbolically. However, these names refer to data values only after they have become correspondent to some "location" (central memory, virtual memory, disk space, etc.). A logical problem arises when a location may be referred to symbolically also. In this way a location is treated as any other data made available to the programmer through a name.

As an example, consider the names (as seen by the programmer) of two elements of an array A: A(i) and A(j). These names are different because the qualifying index names i and j are different. However, if the content of i (which actually indicates a location) is equal to the content of j, these two names are two different names for the same data object. Since i and j may be data manipulated by other modules in a system, the programmer of an individual module cannot tell whether these two different names are addressing the same piece of data by merely examining information available locally. The creation of different names referring to the same object is called *aliasing*. The multiple names are "aliases" for the data object.

Much more intricate cases of the above problem are caused by the use of pointers, which are made available to programmers in almost all programming languages.

The possibility of treating the location as a datum and therefore subject to manipulation by another program is a frequent cause of serious errors. Unfortunately, problems of this kind are not conveniently treated by the Hoare proof technique, which is the one we have used to develop a rigorous design method.

But before you jump to the conclusion that all the preceding chapters of this book describe techniques and programs of very limited practical application, let us clarify this point with an example. Let us consider the assignment

$$A(i) := 5$$

According to the axiom of assignment introduced in Chapter 6, if we want to verify the above assignment for a postcondition

$$A(i) \geq 5$$

the weakest precondition would be

$$wp(A(i) := 5, A(i) \geq 5) = 5 \geq 5 = true$$

This formula indicates that the correct working of the program does not require any restriction on the state space before its execution. However, if i = j (as in the example above), the value of A(j) (a different name for the same object) is also such as to verify A(j) ≥ 5 after the assignment.

This fact is not visible in any of the formulas needed to show the correctness of the statement above. Therefore such a side effect may not be detected by the "proof."

It should be obvious that as long as the whole system is designed constructively, following the process we have shown in the preceding chapters, such side effects can be kept under control. That is, all the pre- and postconditions are hierarchically constructed to satisfy some abstract external properties expressed by their characterization formulas. The abstract programs are then constructed as correct transformations of states, as defined by the pre- and postconditions. Thus in the example above it is unlikely that a programmer would arrive at a situation whereby i = j without having a postcondition for the assignment explicitly stating this fact (i.e., i = j **and** A(i) ⩾ 5). However, it is not obvious that implementations of these designs may not be incorrect even though they appear, on a superficial examination, to be faithful realizations of the design. Also, it is not obvious at all that these side effects are controllable when a new piece of software is added to a previously existing system.

Data-addressing errors are thus difficult to detect when they involve different modules through some mechanism of intermodule communication. We have already indicated that the use of global data is a dangerous mechanism for intermodule communication. The purpose of data abstraction design is to control this mechanism by explicitly specifying all the possible side effects when abstract data types are defined. But there is another method of intermodule communication that is permitted by most currently available implementation tools, and this method too may have dangerous effects. This method is the mechanism used for the passage of parameters.

Parameter-Passing Mechanisms

Different mechanisms used for parameter passing produce different results

A subroutine invocation (or the invocation of an operating system service) may furnish different results depending on the type of parameter-passing mechanism used (e.g., see Wirth, 1973). Currently, three types of mechanisms are used to pass parameters: by *name*, by *reference*, and by *value*.

Passing parameters by name means that the data are made fully available to the called procedure. Passing parameters by reference means that a mechanism to locate the data (usually a pointer) is given to the invoked procedure. Passing parameters by value means that the current values of the data at invocation time are copied in the invoked procedure space.

Often some parameters are locations of data inside other data objects, which may also be among those passed as parameters (a typical example is the index of an array, which is also a parameter). In passing by name the invoked procedure can modify the addressing parameter to obtain some information in the addressed parameter, as though these items were data existing in its private space. In parameters passed by reference a modification of the addressing parameter made by the invoked procedure has no effect on the addressing of the data, but the invoked procedure may use any other location mechanism to peruse the passed data object. In parameters passed by value no change to the original data can be effected by the invoked procedure.

Even though the whole program is supposed to execute in a unique state space, its partitioning into procedures attempts to minimize the overlapping of states between the subspaces of the various procedures. The parameter-passing operation is considered a substitution of the names, locations, and values of the parameters from the subspace of the caller into the subspace of the called procedure. It is needed because these two spaces are considered to be disjoint, but they should be allowed, at least temporarily, to share one or more of these three attributes (name, location, value) of some of the data objects in their state spaces. This substitution in currently implemented programming languages is done by making the formal parameters (the objects in the called procedure) match some of these attributes of the actual parameters (the corresponding objects in the calling procedure).

Assume that A(i) is an actual parameter (of the type "integer") and X is the corresponding formal parameter for the invocation of a procedure P. Assume also that the only thing P does is modify first i (i.e., by adding 1) and then X (i.e., by assigning 15 to it). In parameter-passing by name P owns both name and location of A(i) (in other words, A is global). Therefore upon completion of P, A(i + 1) is made equal to 15. In passage by reference the location of X is the same as the location of A(i). Adding 1 to i increases i only. When X is made equal to 15, the original location of A(i) will contain 15. In passing by value X contains 15, but A(i) is inaccessible to P and therefore will remain unchanged. Upon return, the calling procedure has to decide what to do with this returned value.

Parameter passing by name and by reference do not stop error propagation

In both by-name and by-reference passing the actual locations of the data selected as parameters by the caller are accessed and modified. Different names—A(i) and X in the example—i.e., aliases, are created. In parameter passing by value the data in the caller's area are unknown and untouchable by the invoked procedure. In this case there are actually two data with two different names and two different locations. Their value is made equal at procedure invocation time.

The mechanisms of parameter passing by name and by reference are ways to create global data. In fact, a procedure may pass the received parameters to another one, etc. In passing by reference this process also produces additional aliases.

Now we can explain why these mechanisms produce different final states for a procedure. In passage by name the two subspaces of the caller and the called procedure are considered as only one space. Some of these components may represent the locations of components of some complex object. The resulting addressing mechanisms are unique for all subspaces.

This case, in current practice, is almost never associated with a mechanism for procedure invocation in a programming language. It is, however, a frequently used mechanism for intermodule communication in a large system. And it may be implemented in different ways. One is used in the context of a single program written in a block-structured language to permit access to outer-block declared variables by inner-block procedures. In another technique several different programs (modules), perhaps written in different languages, are put together to build a system. The modules are combined with the linkage editor, a system program that links these different programs by allocating the separately declared data (by different system modules) to a unique location accessible by the linked modules.

In passage by reference two distinct subspaces are considered, but the components relative to the parameters are made the same at invocation time. Since the two spaces are not the same, a data object used to locate a component of one space is not a locator for the matched component in the other space. This mechanism is used in many procedure-calling mechanisms of most current programming languages and also is realized by some hardware architectures and operating systems.

Parameter passing by value is the technique we have chosen for communication between abstract data types in our data abstraction formalism. In terms of the state space model it is equivalent to saying that a relation exists only over fully separated subspaces; this relation describes the status of these parameters as being equal after the parameter substitution has been performed. The function composition semantics described in Chapter 11 are an application of this concept.

EFFECTS OF INTERMODULE COMMUNICATION

The mechanisms of intermodule communication—global data and parameter passing—have far-reaching effects on software system quality. We will examine these effects by first pointing out a commonly observed phenomenon in large-system maintenance. Then we will give a plausible explanation of the causes of the phenomenon in terms of the conceptual model we have discussed.

Integration cost is a consequence of the intermodule communication mechanism

We have already pointed out the high percentage of development cost for integration-related activities. As mentioned earlier, the use of mental simulation of program executions during design (which neglects the interaction of the various sequences of computations via global data) is a probable cause of this cost for the first release of a system. Normally, integration cost for subsequent releases is as high (or higher) as the first release's.

The most plausible explanation for this high cost is the existence of mechanisms of intermodule communication, which are imperfectly known to the maintenance personnel, just as they were to the developers of the first release. During the modification work typical of the maintenance phase, a programmer may develop a new module or modify an existing one on the basis of an imperfect knowledge of the ways the new module will affect the work of others via the manipulation of global data. And interactions may often be quite subtle, especially when the manipulated data are the locations of other data objects. Unfortunately, reading module code does not give an overall picture of these interactions. Even if the global data representation is documented someplace and to a satisfactory extent, the actions of all system modules on these data are not easy to determine unless the system global properties (data invariants) precisely documented.

At integration time any deviation of the programmer's interpretation of the system's global properties from reality will manifest itself and will require correction of the modified module. It is likely that the second time around knowledge of global properties is improved. But clearly, the process of discovering errors by testing computations does not provide any assurance to the programmer of converging toward a correct solution. Indeed, frequently the particular faulty computation suggests a module correction that, in turn, generates another error in some other module in the system.

The process, however, may eventually converge toward a tolerable level of system reliability, even though several residual errors are in the system and may manifest themselves later. The high cost of integration is a consequence of this trial-and-error process the programmer is forced to use because of imperfect knowledge of the interaction between modules.

ERROR-PRONE MODULES

Error-prone modules refer to global data more often than the other modules

In Chapter 2 we indicated a frequently observed phenomenon during large-system maintenance activities: A relatively small number of modules are responsible for a large percentage of system errors, i.e., errors discovered at system integration time or during the regular use after shipment. For one of the sets of data (Zaharchuck, 1980), relative to different releases of a large operating system, I made an additional investigation. I determined that these error-prone modules are also the ones presenting the largest number of references to global data objects in their code. A large number of references to global data objects means the module has the potential of communicating with a very large number of other modules, namely, all those accessing even only one of these data objects.

The great impact of intermodule communication is probably the reason that different programming languages have no effect on the error-proneness of these modules (see Chapter 2). All features of programming languages are conceived to simplify the process of constructing algorithms that manipulate a specific set of data. How the state of these data may be changed by some other algorithms cannot be expressed in a programming language. And understanding the intermodule communication is not made easier by the clearly more readable HOL text, for the simple reason that the relevant information is not expressed at all in that language. The beneficial presence of scope rules is defeated by the need to use external data declaration for the construction of a large system.

MODULE CLEANUP

Restructuring module code helps the developer understand the system, but it does not impede further structure deterioration

The Belady-Lehman studies (1979) have shown that during the life cycle of a large system, ambitious releases (more work than the system can accept) are followed by releases containing very few new system functionalities. Consequently, in the long run an invariant average amount of changes per unit of time is applied to the system.

For less ambitious releases, personnel power is applied to some form of restructuring work, i.e., reorganizing the software without adding new functionalities. Usually this restructuring work is done by conscientious developers in conjunction with the discovery of some problem. Because ambitious releases that add a large number of new features have a higher probability of showing problems in practical use than the less ambitious ones, it is probable that more restructuring work is done after ambitious releases. This restructuring work is often called, in the developer's jargon, cleanup of a module.

Cleanup, however, is generally limited in scope, since very few developers dare to modify the structure of the global data of an existing system because of the high risk of affecting the correctness of other modules. However, some improvement in the error rate of the modified system may be obtained by cleanup activity, even though global data structures are essentially unaltered. The reason is that the developer is likely to obtain a better understanding of the interaction of the module with the rest of the system during cleanup work. Consequently, the module algorithm, which may have been originally incorrect in some cases, can be modified to avoid those errors. On the other hand, it is unlikely that the overall ability of the system to accept modification work is significantly affected by the cleanup.

Controlled experiments supporting this conjecture are not available. However, through a series of interviews with a group of large-system developers, I found very strong indications that this conjecture is true. These interviews were constructed so as not to reveal their measuring purpose; they were disguised as normal work conversations. A definite picture emerged showing that the conscientious developer is unsatisfied about his or her understanding of the functions of a module as it relates with the other modules in the system.

This concern cannot be attributed to difficulty in understanding the meaning of the programming language or of the hardware and supporting software commands. Knowledge of the effect of hardware instructions, of the implementation language used, and of the supporting system's capabilities is generally satisfactory. It is the effect of these commands on data objects (and consequently on modules), which are often not even explicitly named among the data manipulated by the module, that is the cause of concern. And this problem is solved only through painful experimentation and a considerable amount of conversation with other developers.

Thus it seems reasonable to conclude that the peculiar behavior of an individual system in accepting a constant quantity of work per unit of time depends on the structure of the system's global properties, which are realized by state changes of the system's data. In other words, the productivity of maintenance personnel as well as error rate may primarily depend on the software system's architecture.

SYSTEM CULTURE

Difficulty in obtaining information about the system design rationale causes the creation of a rigid culture

Because no precise and written source of information about intermodule communication exists, empirical knowledge about it is an essential prerequisite for the success of any system developer involved in maintenance and modification work. This knowledge, both because of its intrinsically high value and because of its formulation as unwritten rules, is the basis of a true system culture. According to Sowell (1979), a culture is a set of acquired concepts and beliefs that are used to reduce the cost of direct gathering of the knowledge needed to support decision processes within the group of individuals who are part of this culture.

The reliance on a culture is a mechanism typical of human societies to speed up and facilitate decision processes that would otherwise be cumbersome because of the high cost in time and labor needed to gather essential knowledge. However, a high level of rigidity is exhibited in all decision processes that rely on a culture. For example, in software development changes in the outside environment, such as changes in the hardware architecture or in the programming language used, are a major shock for the culture. The cost of accommodating those changes to the system culture is very high, and it is manifested by a considerable inertia in accepting these outside environmental changes. This cost, in fact, may be the reason for the reluctance of most developers to accept or even to consider the idea of a new development technique (such as data abstraction). That is, it is difficult to relate this technique to the existing culture.

The rigidity of the culture also generates considerable reluctance to change the system's architectural concepts, even when they are recognized as inadequate. The knowledge surfacing in a culture is of a very practical type. Also, the decisions people involved in modification work have to make are usually of a practical nature, such as putting a new functionality into the system in time for a particular release. These decisions have a vital impact on the individual's welfare. It is thus natural that little attention is paid to any fundamental architectural concept that may help future work, if this knowledge is contrary to the accepted beliefs of the culture. This is because the culture is the essential support for the developer's activity.

SYSTEM DETERIORATION

Culture-dependent maintenance is done with little understanding of the original design rationale

All systems are originally designed with some architectural concept in mind. Gradually, however, changes and modifications to the system, which are done by developers dependent on a culture and who thus may not understand the original architectural ideas but are reluctant to change them, cause a deterioration of the system structure. Deterioration of system structure means that needless computational and data representation complexity is added to the system to circumvent potentially dangerous interactions (as a protection against the ill effects of lack of knowledge) and to accommodate changes (which obfuscate the original intent of the code). This deterioration makes any further modification work difficult.

As a generalized example of this deteriorating effect of the culture-based decision process, consider the case of a module M1 that currently invokes another module M2 for the execution of some service. For some reason M2 is changed and the service M2 used to supply to M1 is now obtained through the invocation of another module, say M3. It is very likely that the calling sequence of the modified system will still show M1 calling M2 (and passing reference to the necessary parameters), which in turn will call M3 (also passing reference to these parameters). Thus the only role M2 may have is merely to avoid not changing the calling code and the parameter representation in M1.

The culture-based knowledge does not include the explanation of the rationale for the coding in M1. Therefore knowledge about the effects of any change is not available to the person performing the modification. The cost of gathering the necessary knowledge for a more rational modification is so high that the developer can rely only on the culture-based knowledge, which says: M1 calls M2 for that service in that particular manner.

Another and perhaps more important source of deterioration is related to the reluctance to change data representation. New information, even if it should logically be represented within an existing data structure, is put in a separate structure. Because data representation is the most important element of a system's culture, the developer does not dare to modify existing data representation.

It is usual to blame lack of professionalism among maintenance personnel for the type of modification work exemplified above. However, such phenomena are too frequent to be dismissed on the grounds of sloppiness of some workers. There is a threshold in the cost any person is willing to pay for the acquisition of the knowledge needed to support a decision process. Note here that the decision is not whether a change has to be made but whether the change can be made in such a way as to preserve some intellectual simplicity in the system. Actions toward this goal are usually judged as aesthetically pleasing but not important, because the less elegant solution will also work. Unless the culture's paradigm attaches high value to aesthetically appealing solutions, it is quite natural for the developer to choose the decision involving minimum effort.

The point above has two aspects. A culture is a repository of useful knowledge. The usefulness of elegant solutions to modification work is often not recognized. Therefore individuals in the culture do not seek knowledge that supports aesthetic solutions.

But even if the value of an elegant solution were recognized, it is often too expensive to obtain knowledge of the software system's interactions, knowledge that is necessary to support an elegant solution. To pay this high cost, the average developer would be required to produce an effort much above the acceptable threshold. Consequently, even though the danger of inelegant modification work is recognized, it is considered the only viable solution. Obviously, as the deterioration proceeds, the difficulty of modification work increases, thus forcing some restructuring work to maintain the level of difficulty of the modification work at acceptable levels.

The system architecture is the framework of the system culture

The Belady-Lehman studies pointed out both the invariance of the capacity of a system to accept work and the dependence of this capacity on the intellectual structure of the system (its architecture). Thus it appears that the system's architecture represents the framework of a culture that both permits modification work to be performed at an acceptable cost and is responsible for the deterioration of the system's intellectual structure. In the long run, then, the culture increases the cost of the maintenance work.

MAINTENANCE OF DATA ABSTRACTION DESIGNS

Let us now return to the idea of a system as a hierarchy of data types/abstract machines. We have few observations about the behavior during maintenance of systems designed according to this technique. So we have to rely mostly on educated guesses about the impact of this technique on system maintainability.

Design documentation should help maintenance work

Documents describing the design process rationale either formally or semiformally, should be of great help to the maintenance people. However, the value of these documents is related to a faithful reproduction of the design decision in the code. Faithful reproduction is not easy to accomplish in many cases for several reasons, such as subtle differences between the semantics of design and implementation languages, the uncertainty and the consequent misinterpretation of some interfaces with the hardware or the supporting software, and the existence of some previous system culture.

Let us now examine these difficulties case by case. The difference in semantics between the design formalism and current programming languages that has the greatest impact is the mechanism of parameter passing. It is possible to faithfully implement designs described in a formalism that implies value-passing parameters with programming languages that use reference-passing mechanisms. But as we have seen above, this implementation may be difficult, and subtle deviations of meaning may occur. The description given in this chapter of different results produced by the different mechanisms gives an idea of the potential problems.

An assembler implementation may be less dangerous than the use of high-order languages if the value-passing mechanism can be implemented faithfully by the mechanisms of the hardware, typically by moving information. The increased difficulty of coding, however, and the total loss of the scope rule discipline have the potential for more intricate implementation solutions.

In the preceding chapter in the discussion of SWISP, we examined the problem of interfacing with existing system functionalities. A potential danger is that an interface whose meaning was incorrectly known at design time may be corrected by an implementation that does not faithfully follow the design prescriptions. Therefore the value of the design documentation to a future maintenance worker may be considerably reduced.

The last point is relative to a previous system culture. Culture-based knowledge may suggest, to the implementor and to the maintainer, solutions to some of the design problems that are not the solutions prescribed by the designer. The designers are part of a culture that may rely on a different paradigm, one based on the principles supporting the design formalism. So the difference in paradigms may make the communication of design rationale to the implementors uncertain (and of course very difficult, as we have seen in Chapter 15). The point here is that the implementors may use different design decisions because they interpret the design specifications in terms of their culture's paradigm.

If the deviations from design specifications indicated above are allowed, the value of the design documentation for the maintainer, becomes practically nil. And in practice this result is often observed. The currently used informal design specifications are rarely updated to reflect drastic design changes introduced during the implementation and maintenance phase.

In contrast, in the development process described by Mills et al. (1980), great attention was paid to the creation of a uniform culture throughout all phases of the development process. The underlying idea in that project was that the development process is design-driven. If this idea is accepted by an organization, a new type of culture could be created. This culture, instead of relying on knowledge about specific features of a system, would rely on mental tools and concepts (like the ones expressed in this book) to solve problems. This culture may be essential for any improvement in the maintainability of systems conceived according to techniques of data abstraction and realized by correctly designed programs.

Design documents must be maintained

The above discussion can be boiled down to one requirement: the necessity of keeping design specification documents and implementation from diverging. One possible solution to this problem is to rely on computer-based tools, which make it easier to modify design specifications before code is changed. If scrupulous updating of design documentation is enforced, the maintenance process will benefit. And the use of automatic tools like the one proposed by Knuth (1983) would be a great help in keeping the design documentation and the code from deviating.

MAINTAINABILITY OF ARCHITECTURES BASED ON DATA ABSTRACTION

Data abstraction may encourage the creation of sound system architecture

Another potential advantage of the use of data abstraction is that the technique may be conducive to the creation of a system architecture that supports better system maintainability. The basic element of the design by data abstraction is the data type/abstract machine hierarchy. On the basis of our previous discussion of software errors, a system that appears to the user as a single large data type may result in a low degree of maintainability if this data type is not broken down in several separate abstract machines in the design hierarchy. This breakdown must be a conscious concern of the designer; otherwise, the resulting architecture will present a very high level of coupling via global data. Also, the parameter-passing mechanism, which we have assumed to be by value, may create global data when implemented in any of the current programming languages. Thus the designers must be aware of the implementation language mechanism and design the system accordingly.

As pointed out by DeCindio, Pomello, and Tessarolo (1982), a data abstraction formalism used in the design phase supplies considerable guidance in avoiding design solutions that are conducive to errors. That is, architectures susceptible to errors are considerably cumbersome when expressed in this design formalism. However, I have no experience to support the conclusion that a good design suffices to overcome all the potential pitfalls of implementation. In the SWISP case (Chapter 15) very little decision was left to the implementor, and this feature was felt to be a key factor in success. In another experience presented in Chapter 15, excessive freedom of decision left to the implementors destroyed all the design methodology advantages, but this happened before shipment, not during maintenance of a well-designed system. The negative effect of modification decisions based only on code may be, after all, limited if few architectural changes are introduced during maintenance.

SYSTEM TESTS

Bottom-up integration testing is the usual procedure

The current approach for system tests reflects the architectural arrangement of the system. In practice, systems are integrated in stages corresponding to the various layers of functionalities. This integration is usually done from the bottom up, i.e., from the integration of functions close to the hardware up toward the modules supplying the user-visible interfaces. These layers are not levels of data; any module at any level may access the same global data.

The testing of a low-level function shows error in that layer by exercising the low-level interfaces. The test of another layer of software will show errors both in this newly integrated level and in the previously tested software. New errors show up because the tests performed at the lower level did not show the interaction between the new modules and the global data also used at the preceding level. And it does not matter how extensively the preceding level was tested; the likelihood of remaining errors is very high.

This testing process is very long and expensive. It is reasonable to ask whether data abstraction design techniques are of any help for this operation, particularly in view of the experience described in the preceding chapter. There a surprisingly easy and short integration phase for a system was realized by the use of data abstraction.

One obvious way any rigorous design method may help is by yielding fewer (an optimist could say zero) residual errors. But there is another way to improve the effectiveness of system tests in a hierarchically organized system, as we will discuss next.

Random selection of programs within an abstract machine for testing

Let us consider a generic abstract machine in the hierarchy. Let us assume that all data types in this machine, abstract or not, are working correctly. Let us use G to represent the set of machine-permanent data, and $P_1, \ldots, P_i, \ldots, P_m$ are the programs defined in this machine. Let us also assume that all P_i's were satisfactorily tested by using the technique of random sampling of test cases (see Chapter 8); i.e., we have a measurable level of confidence about the correctness of the individual modules.

We can develop a test plan that uses a random selection of one of the m programs and of the values of the input parameters for that program. Obviously, the values of G must have been initialized with values respecting the data invariant by the initialization program. We may also select the initial values of G at random, within the range permitted by the data invariant. By repeating this random selection of one program among the m programs of the machine, we obtain a random sampling of the correctness of the cooperation of these programs via permanent data.

The occurrence of a sequence of successful runs of sufficient length is an indication that a reasonable level of freedom from errors has been obtained. The length of this sequence can be determined as in Chapter 8 and by experimentation with similar test cases.

The first advantage of this approach is that the programs P_i are tested for their interaction via the global data G explicitly. That is, the permanent data states defined by the data invariant are checked by sampling possible program invocation sequences. The random selection of which one among the m modules is tested gives statistical confidence that these modules are tested for any possible order of invocation. Also, the use of randomly generated data values avoids the inevitable bias of human selection, which usually tends to use values that are significant for some particular sequence of invocation. Because errors are usually found in computation sequences that may not have been considered by the designer to begin with, it is likely that the random selection will pick one of them, thus indicating this form of logical design flaw.

Once the programs of one machine are tested, the higher-level data types realized by this machine can be considered correct within the assumed confidence level. Thus the process can be repeated for the next higher level and so on for all the machine/data types in the hierarchy.

One assumption of this approach is that the representation functions of the hierarchy (i.e., the mapping of the various levels) are correctly implemented. If this assumption is not ascertained, a higher-level function may detect errors in states of lower-level data. In this case the advantage of a step-by-step testing of the hierarchy from the bottom up is lost.

The only experience with this approach, minus the random selection, is its use in the SWISP project. In that project the separation in levels appeared to work very well. All the problems with supervisor calls mentioned in Chapter 15 were detected at their level of call by this level-by-level testing approach.

HIGHLIGHTS

In this chapter we have examined the currently used implementation and maintenance process in light of the data abstraction method. We have pointed out critical aspects of a system's errors. One is generated by the intermodule communication via global data, both when voluntarily created and when generated as side effect of the parameter-passing mechanism. Another critical aspect is the subtlety of errors in data reference, which are consequences of the basic architecture of all hardware and programming languages existing today.

The errors caused by global phenomena make it very difficult for a programmer to understand the effect of changes in the code of a single module and of changes in representation of data. This difficulty is the basis of the creation of system cultures, which make the current development and maintenance process very rigid and resistant to change.

The modification work performed on the basis of information obtained within the culture causes the deterioration of the system structure. The culture makes the programmer reluctant to change the original design, which is only imperfectly known, making it more difficult to perform further modification work.

A design technique based on data abstraction helps to mitigate these problems because it shows global interactions much more clearly than the current implementation-driven approach. Furthermore, a development based on rigorous design allows us to use random selection of test cases for system tests. These tests are an efficient way to determine a system's correctness.

REFERENCES

Belady, L. A., and Lehman, M. M. 1979. The characteristics of large systems. In *Research directions in software technology,* edited by P. Wegner. Cambridge, Mass.: MIT Press.

De Cindio, F.; Pomello, L.; and Tessarolo, S. 1982. WELLMADE per il Disegno di um Sistema Ben Fatto (WELLMADE for the design of a well-made system. In Italian. *Note di software,* 17/18.

Knuth, D. E. 1983. Literate programming. Stanford University Report no. STAN–CS–82–981, Stanford, Calif.

Mills, H. D.; O'Neill, D.; Linger, R. C.; and Dyer, M. 1980. The management of software engineering. Parts I–IV: Principles of software engineering. *IBM Systems Journal* 19 (no. 4):415–420, 421–431, 432–450, 451–476.

Sowell, T. 1979. *Knowledge and decisions.* New York: Basic Books.

Wirth, N. 1973. *Systematic programming: An introduction.* Englewood Cliffs, N.J.: Prentice-Hall.

Zaharachuck, A. 1980. Error prone modules. Honeywell Information Systems internal memo.

CHAPTER **SEVENTEEN**

Concurrent Processing

INTRODUCTION

In the preceding chapters we discussed theory and rigorous design methods for programs and systems as though only one processor could execute the code. In other words, only a single thread of execution is identified in the system's state space. In this chapter we will discuss theories and techniques proposed by the computer science community to support the design of *concurrent processing.*

The idea of concurrent execution is not new. Operating systems from the very beginning of their history have allowed concurrent execution of code while I/O was performed. This feature is called *multiprogramming,* and it has attracted considerable attention in the computer science community since the mid 1960s. More recently, experimenters observed that a large database may be accessed simultaneously by several users, since only occasionally do some users attempt to read or modify the same piece of information. This technique shortens the waiting time of any particular user, because, in general, a user does not have to wait until all other users are finished.

Both operating system control of concurrency and database access are well-studied problem areas, and a vast literature exists on both subjects. However, the problem area we will introduce here, although related to them, is different. The area we address in this chapter is the design of a *network of programs* that can contribute to a common goal by occasionally exchanging information with each other. These programs are to execute at all times, whenever they are not "waiting" for information supplied by other programs. Programs that can run concurrently are called *sequential processes,* or simply processes.

The exchange of information between processes may be accomplished by two different mechanisms. One method is to supply common storage for some shared data, which are accessed by all processes. The second method is to have the processes exchange messages when needed. Both architectures will be examined in this chapter.

NETWORK OF PROCESSES

Parallel execution processes may realize a system without any need for global data

One interesting feature of a network of processes is relevant to the subject of this book. We have seen in the preceding chapter that intermodule communication is a major cause of difficulties in the maintainability of a system. It is also the cause of the continuous deterioration of the system's structure. Furthermore, we have pointed out that among the various forms of intermodule communication the passage of parameters by value is the safest one. Message exchanges among processes can be seen as a form of parameter passing by value. No global data exist in a process network. Thus a network of sequential processes cooperating for some global goal is a form of system architecture that should minimize the negative effects of intermodule communication on system maintainability.

This advantage of network architecture at this time is only a conjecture, however. A network system is not necessarily easy to design. Its specifications—i.e., the precise description of its global goals—would be as complicated as any based on hardware data types. Thus data abstraction will again be useful if we are interested in the precise definition of specifications and in a rigorous design process. Therefore the role of a network is to put together a set of processes for a global goal, each process described by specifications written in terms of abstract data types.

The idea of a network of processes, communicating via message exchanges, presents additional practical problems. The performance of a system organized in such a way, unless a large number of processors are available, could be worse than the performance of other architectural arrangements. Nevertheless, systems have been designed and put into service successfully with network architecture.

Because our purpose is to show how large-system development and maintenance can be made intellectually controllable, we wish to see whether concurrency and network architecture are making this task harder or simpler. We will address this issue in this chapter.

SOME NOVEL PROPERTIES OF CONCURRENCY

The wait for a global state introduces many new problems

Systems that use the concept of concurrent execution of tasks (such as operating systems and database access control systems) supply insight into the difficulties inherent in their design. In this section we introduce some of the properties of concurrent execution in an intuitive form. A picture of the differences between sequentially executing software and concurrent systems is given; it provides a basis for understanding the computational model and the rules defining the correctness of concurrent systems.

The mechanism that permits parallel execution of computational tasks is the ability for a process to wait for some particular global state essential for the process's progress. This state is detectable by the process but not controlled by it.

When the communication is realized through shared data, the values of the data are the representations of the global states relevant to the interprocess communication. These shared data, which are accessible to several concurrently executing processes, must be protected against the danger of inconsistent modifications. For example, suppose that an invariant defining the only legitimate states of these shared data exists. A process modifying the data may temporarily violate this invariant. Thus a mechanism that ensures that all processes are allowed to access these data only when the invariant is respected and that enforces a condition that all processes leave the shared data in states respecting the invariant must be provided. Otherwise, incorrect interprocess communication will result.

In the world of concurrency this mechanism can be realized only by allowing exactly one process to access the shared data at the same time. This provision is called a *mutual-exclusion mechanism*. Clearly, if one process is accessing the shared data, any other process that wants to access the same data must wait until the first process completes its manipulation of the shared data.

A construct permitting the access to shared data only by predefined procedures associated with these data is called a *monitor* (Hoare, 1974). A monitor is an abstract machine, as defined in the preceding chapters. The addition of the mutual-exclusion mechanism permits its use in a concurrent-processing environment.

Global states in a network of processes are manifested by message values at inlets and outlets

In a network of processes without any global data, the relevant global states manifest themselves as particular values of messages when these values are detectable by the receiving process. A process may expect several different kinds of messages, which we may imagine as materializing at different *inlets*, i.e., specific instructions where the messages are received within the process. Therefore a process may wait at a particular inlet for the appearance of a message that will give it information about the current global state of the system. The validity of this waiting behavior depends on the existence of some other process that sends the message through the appropriate outlet.

However, erroneous global-system arrangements may exist such that a process is forced to wait forever. An infinite wait may occur in a concurrent system using shared data as well as in a system using message exchange.

An infinite wait has two distinct causes. One situation arises when the state (message) a process P is waiting for has to be set up (sent) by another process, say Q, which is waiting for another state (message), which must have been set up (sent) by P or by some other process depending on P. A situation like this one is called a *deadlock state*.

Another cause of an infinite wait is a situation in which the waiting process P depends on a state S for some shared data, which may be detected either by P or by another process Q′. It is possible that a scheduling algorithm in the system allows Q′ to consistently detect the occurrence of S, instead of P, and therefore produces infinite waiting for the latter. In terms of message exchange the above phenomenon happens whenever Q sends a message m, for which P is waiting, consistently to Q′, thus forcing P to wait for it forever. This case is called *individual starvation* of P.

The two cases are different: In one, several processes are waiting for each other; while in the other, one (or more) processes are deliberately or inadvertently excluded from an ongoing exchange of communication among a set of running processes. Note that both phenomena are global; i.e., they depend on the realization of the interprocess communication mechanism.

The two phenomena above are two of the potential dangers that must be considered when we are reasoning about concurrency. These phenomena have been observed quite often in existing concurrent systems, and their avoidance is not always easy. In some cases (usually for system performance reasons) programmers prefer to risk deadlock or starvation, and then some detection mechanism for these phenomena is used. For instance, in detection of deadlock, one of the involved processes is aborted and then recovered in a previous safe state. The system may then proceed, and deadlock is not likely to occur again immediately after resumption of the operations. In detection of starvation, the processes guilty of neglect for the starving processes may be forced to send the needed message.

TERMINATION OF A NETWORK OF PROCESSES

Other global phenomena are relevant to the design of concurrent systems. One we consider here is termination.

Termination in a network requires communication to notify all participant processes

If a network of processes is to produce a particular global state as one of the goals of the system, all processes may have to be told that this state has been reached. In a sequential execution of a program that invokes various procedures, it is implicitly known that the needed procedure is executed when needed. Once the final state of the whole program is reached, all procedures no longer execute. In the case of a network of processes a typical process is not aware of whether or not it may have to elaborate more messages for that particular global goal. This information becomes evident, perhaps to only one of the processes, only when the final state is reached. Several other processes in the network may be waiting for messages of various kinds, possibly for additional work. So one of the responsibilities of a process that detects termination is to send appropriate messages to the other processes notifying them that the global goal has been reached.

Consider the following simple example, a network of only two processes. One process R generates random numbers. Another process S screens these random numbers to find out whether they are between two given limits. The purpose of this elementary network is to produce one random value within the limits. Process R does not know, after it produces a random number, if it will be requested to produce a new one. Thus R must be designed with the condition that after one number is produced and sent to S, a message from S may be received that will determine whether another random number has to be produced. When S detects a random number within the given limits, the desired global state is reached, but the system has not yet terminated because R is waiting for a message. Clearly, if S sends a message to R that the desired global state has been reached, R can terminate. This form of termination is called *distributed termination,* and it is a requirement for concurrent systems but has no counterpart in sequential executions.

Note that all the global phenomena outlined above are a consequence of waiting for global states to be detected. In the cases of deadlock and starvation, erroneous design causes an undesired situation. In the case of termination an additional responsibility of the system designer is to make known to all waiting processes that a desired state has been reached.

DESIGN TECHNIQUES FOR CONCURRENCY

In the remainder of this chapter we will present an introduction to the problem of design methods for concurrent systems. We proceed as follows: First, we examine how the world of applications requires concurrency and the effects of this requirement from an external user's point of view. This approach is consistent with the approach we have used in the description of the design methods for sequential systems; i.e., we relate the design approach to the needs of the world of the applications. Next, we present a model for the design of a concurrent system built as a network of separate processes communicating via exchange of messages. And finally, in later sections of the chapter, we introduce a different view of concurrent systems that may be applied (at the current state of the art) to systems using shared data as the communication mechanism between processes. This view outlines what appears to be a powerful method for the design of systems with respect to such global properties as deadlock and starvation.

Concurrency in Real-World Applications

Intuitively, concurrency should improve system performance. But the same result can be obtained by the use of faster hardware (up to a point).

Concurrency is a requirement of the problem

Before we proceed to describe the design of concurrent systems, though, let us see whether the introduction of additional complexity caused by concurrency is justified by necessities of real application.

Toward this end, in this subsection we examine a few real-world general applications that must be supported by concurrent systems. In this way we hope to arrive at a reasonably complete picture of the type of requirements necessary for concurrent systems.

It is hard to consider any modern large software system without being involved in some form of concurrent execution. With the exception of batch processing, for which concurrent execution between processors and I/O channels is hidden inside the operating system, all modern multiuser computer applications show concurrent execution of tasks. An example is the collection of inputs from users, who are permitted to request system services at any time and possibly simultaneously. Thus concurrency is a requirement of the world of applications, not merely a technique to improve performance. However, we must understand its impact to analyze this requirement.

Users of a system typically want to shop for information. If this information is exclusively owned and usable by an individual user, there is a very economical way to obtain concurrency: Each user will access a process (a set of programs and data sequentially executable) that performs the required service. No communication between these processes is needed; therefore no waiting period and consequent global phenomena such as deadlock and starvation have to be feared. These processes can be designed by the technique of data abstraction and maintained (i.e., modified to satisfy the user's changing needs) at a relatively low cost if the appropriate development discipline (Chapter 16) can be enforced. The solutions for problems of this type are currently supplied by personal computers, minicomputers, and small individually used systems, which represent a large percentage of the computer and software industry.

But some applications must make information available to several users in a common pool. Typical examples are bank systems and corporate management systems. In these applications one user's need for information (e.g., a bank customer who is allowed to peruse and modify her own account) overlaps with another user's need for information (e.g., a bank manager who needs to know the total money flow for all customers). In these latter cases concurrency becomes part of the system's requirements and is therefore unavoidable.

Continuous Availability of Computation Services

Another requirement of these systems must be considered: The user may ask for a service at any time. Thus the system must be able to process information continuously, even *ad infinitum*. At all the system's access points available to the users, the system must present accessibility to its capabilities at any time (when it is working).

We now face the problem of dealing with nonterminating computations, at least in the sense that a set of capabilities realized by separate functions is always executable. A quick review of the concept of abstract machines shows that we have already considered this potential. All programs in an abstract machine are designed to be executed any number of times, provided that only one is executing in that machine at one time. This feature arises because of the need for mutual exclusion of access to the permanent data of the machine. We thus have a method to design potentially infinite computations that are made up of any number of executions of terminating programs.

Nondeterminism in Concurrent Processing

Another new aspect is shown by the observation of modern system applications: an intrinsic nondeterminism in both the requests for service and the judgments of the correctness of results. We have already discussed nondeterminism in programming (Chapter 6); it is a consequence of the fact that some rather different paths of computation may produce equally acceptable results.

Intrinsic nondeterminism

Typically, different results for the same computation in the execution of exactly the same user-visible service at different times are considered equally correct for most concurrent systems. An example (a rather trivial but a fundamental one) is the reading of a clock that shows time with a very high precision. If I read this clock and then I attempt to communicate the reading to you, I am communicating the value I read when I looked at the clock. The recording of this value on your part depends on the rapidity of my communicating it to you and your promptness in recording it. It is likely that if you were looking at the same clock, your reading at recording time would be different from the value you are recording. Also, if this experiment is repeated, the difference between your reading and recording will not be constant, because you may record the number before or after you read the clock. Even if we attempt to keep the time spent in our activity constant, the system itself has a built-in nondeterminism. Therefore the difference in these two values is not a repeatable outcome of the system composed of you, me, and the clock.

Any concurrent system shows some form of nondeterminism. Thus even if the implemented programs are strictly deterministic, the behavior of the whole system is not necessarily so.

Levels of Description of Concurrent Systems

We can identify three levels of description of the design of a concurrent system. These three levels can be defined for systems using either message exchange or shared data as means of interprocess communication.

The first level, which may be called the *network level,* is the level in which the coordination among the activities of the various processes is described. At this level we must be able to express all the global goals the system is supposed to reach with provision for the absence of undesirable global phenomena (such as deadlock). This description can be done only with knowledge of the topology of the network and the data type of the messages for the various processes' inlets and outlets or the states of globally shared data. Message and shared data types, of course,

Three levels: network level, local goals, and implementation level

may be abstractions, defined as needed for this level by appropriate characterizations.

The second level includes all the processes as separate entities. The global goals are now broken down into separate *local goals,* which are the requirements of a system that can be designed as a hierarchy of data types/abstract machines. Thus a process may be defined as an abstract data type whose functions represent the processing activated by the various inlet and outlets.

The third level is the *implementation level.* This level is realized in various languages. Programming languages are used for the coding of programs designed by the data abstraction hierarchy of each process. The linker and the operating system will provide the creation of global data whenever this communication mechanism is used. Other programming languages, and perhaps firmware, can be used for the implementation of the mechanisms of message exchanges. Operating systems usually support message exchange among user processes.

Concurrency is limited in scope to the first level. The other two levels, where the bulk of the software is defined, can be designed according to the techniques introduced in the preceding chapters of this book. Also, testing of the implementation may be separated by the individual processes, before the integrated, fully concurrent system is tested.

Because we have already addressed the problem of the development of the second and third levels, we discuss only the first level here. If we are to arrive at a rigorous design of networks at this level, we have to define some formalism and rules for the determination of the network correctness. Thus we must be able to define the following:

1. A formalism to express the interchange of messages between processes and/or to express relevant invariants on globally shared data.
2. A formalism to express global goals for this set of processes, which may be expressed in terms of message states or globally shared data states.
3. A formalism to express the local goal for each process to ensure that these local goals, taken together in the framework of the specifications supplied in the formalism of point 1, are global goals, that all global goals are reached (weak correctness), and that no undesired global effect is possible (strong correctness).

To define an adequate formalism for the global goals, we need a model for the concurrent system, the analog of the state space model for the behavior of a program and of an abstract machine. We discuss such a model next.

A Model for Concurrent Network Systems

The system is the union of all its processes' state spaces

A set of processes defines a set of state spaces, one per process in the system. We are only interested in the components of these state spaces visible at the network level, i.e., some abstraction describing the messages received at inlets and sent out at outlets or the states of the shared data. To describe a global goal over the set of all these spaces independently from any specific arrangement of the communication, we must consider the infinite sequences of states for each inlet and outlet (or of the shared data). These sequences are infinite because any possible arrangement in time of these states can be considered.

We discussed the specification of the postcondition of a nonconcurrent terminating program in Chapter 4. There we recognized the necessity of writing predicates over the set of the Cartesian product of the state space with itself, because the final state may depend on some initial state.

If we want to maintain the objective of specifying a system's goal in some execution-independent way, we now have to write conditions over infinite sequences of states, because any state may depend on any other state of any other sequence. This situation is clearly undesirable, since it may produce extremely complex specifications. The rest of this chapter presents solutions to this problem.

Temporal-Logic Specifications

Operators represent time-dependent situations

One technique that appears promising in facilitating the specifications of global goals is *temporal logic* (Pnueli, 1979). Temporal logic introduces a few new time-related operations: the *unary operators* (always, sometimes, next time) and the *binary operator* (until). The meaning of these operators is as follows (w and u are any state properties expressed as classical predicates):

$\Box$ w is verified if and only if w is true for all states (at all times); i.e., w is "always" true.

$\Diamond$ w is verified if and only if w is true for at least one state over the infinite sequence; i.e., w is "sometimes" true.

$\bigcirc$ w is verified if and only if w is true over the first state of a sequence of states truncated at a particular instant.

$u \mathcal{U} v$ is verified if and only if u is "sometimes" true and then v is "always" true.

By using these operators, we can express facts about interprocess communication. For example, the formula w may describe that a message is of a specific value at some inlet. Then the formula $\Diamond$w will specify the fact that a message of that value must appear at that inlet.

Previously we used as an example a simple system made up of two processes, one generating random numbers and another testing them to see whether a value fits in a given range of values. We can specify this behavior by using the above operators. If n is the generated number, min and max are the bounds of the desired range, and b is a Boolean indicating that a new number must be generated, we can write either

$$\Box\ [b \Leftrightarrow \textbf{not}[min \leq n \leq max]]$$

or

$$[min \leq n \leq max]\ \mathcal{U}\ [not\ b]$$

Note that the above specifications do not require n to fall within bounds in a finite time. The system may continue forever producing random numbers.

The specifications written in temporal-logic formulas do not assume a particular interprocess communication mechanism. Global goals may be specified in this formalism and then implemented by interprocess communication through shared data as well as message exchange. We may also define freedom from undesired global properties, such as deadlock freedom, in terms of temporal-logic formulas.

PROVING PROPERTIES OF CONCURRENT PROCESSES THAT EXCHANGE MESSAGES

Let us now limit our discussion to processes in a network that exchange messages. Assuming we have written the specifications for global goals, the next step for the design of a concurrent system is to specify the local goals for all processes. It would be undesirable for the subsequent development of the individual process if we were forced to write these local goals in temporal-logic formulas. We clearly want to develop the individual process as though it were isolated.

To accomplish this goal, we first have to prove that a particular set of transitions at each process actually satisfies the global goals. This proof requires an idealized language with which we can express an abstract program responsible for these state transitions. In this way we will be able to determine which inlets and outlets are needed in the processes to realize the global goal. This procedure is analogous to the use of guarded commands for expressing an algorithm as the model implementation of some specifications, which then allows us to determine the necessary type functions.

As with sequential programs, the choice of language for the description of the abstract programs depends on factors that will vary from one development environment to another. In the following subsections we briefly introduce an extension of the guarded command language that permits us to describe networks of processes. The extension, due to Hoare (1978), is called the *CSP language* (CSP stands for "cooperating sequential processes"). This language was changed after its first presentation by Hoare. The version we show here was presented by Manna and Pnueli (1982), who also supply a proof system. A different technique for proofs of CSP systems is given by Hoare (1981).

The CSP Language

CSP is an extension of the guarded commands

The detailed presentation of a proof technique for CSP and/or a technique for deriving CSP programs from specifications are beyond the scope of this book. We will limit the discussion to a presentation of the syntax and a semiformal definition of the semantics of CSP. We will also describe some of the peculiar issues of concurrent program proofs.

A CSP program has the form

$$[P_1 \| P_2 \| \ldots \| P_m]$$

where $P_1, P_2, \ldots, P_m$ are the sequential processes forming the system network. In other words, CSP language sees the entire concurrent system as a unique program. No global data exist; i.e., each P_i ($i = 1, 2, \ldots, m$) can access data declared within its text only. The syntax for writing P_i ($i = 1, 2, \ldots, m$) is exactly the same as the syntax of the guarded commands, with the few additions described below. Hoare (1978) in his original paper, however, modified the Dijkstra syntax (which is used in this book) by substituting the symbol [for the symbol **if,** substituting] for **fi,** substituting *[for **do,** and substituting] for **od.** To avoid confusion, we will continue to use the Dijkstra symbols we used earlier. But the reader who wants to consult the literature about CSP should be aware of this syntax change.

The main additions to the guarded command language are the input and output commands, which define the inlets and outlets of the processes:

input: P_i ? y
output: P_i ! f(y)

The input instruction is executable in conjunction with the process P_i. It means that a value for the datum y is expected to arrive from P_i. The output instruction means that the output value of f(y) is sent to P_i as a value to be received in some appropriate inlet where an input command containing the sender's name exists.

These communication commands can be used within the guards of **if** and **do** constructs:

if $B_1; K_1 \rightarrow S_1$	**if** $B_1; K_1 \rightarrow S_1$
□ $B_2; K_2 \rightarrow S_2$	□ $B_2; K_2 \rightarrow S_2$
.	.
.	.
.	.
□ $B_n; K_n \rightarrow S_n$	□ $B_n; K_n \rightarrow S_n$
fi	**fi**
do $B_1; K_1 \rightarrow S_1$	**do** $B_1; K_1 \rightarrow S_1$
□ $B_2; K_2 \rightarrow S_2$	□ $B_2; K_2 \rightarrow S_2$
.	.
.	.
.	.
□ $B_n; K_n \rightarrow S_n$	□ $B_n; K_n \rightarrow S_n$
od	**od**

Here K_i ($i = 1, 2, \ldots, n$) is any communication command (! or ?) or is empty. If it is empty, the constructs become the traditional guarded commands.

The Notions of Justice and Fairness

We illustrate now, with a few informal examples, a series of properties that need to be proven by using CSP programs and temporal-logic specification.

Coping with a very erratic scheduling mechanism

We have seen, in the section introducing global properties of concurrent systems, that the mechanism scheduling the activities of the concurrent processes can be a cause of undesirable effects such as starvation. In a CSP process, because of the intrinsic nondeterminism of the guarded command (which is a way of saying that the scheduling mechanism can be very erratic), it is possible that when more than one guard is true, one is never chosen. Similarly, in a set of parallel processes within a CSP program, one process may not be scheduled to proceed even though it could. Because of these conditions, the notions of justice and fairness have to be defined. Note that this nondeterminism is a fact observable in the real world. A single CSP program may represent a network of computers. The speed of communication and of processing is unpredictable, and no scheduling mechanism that is fully deterministic can be envisioned. Also, each computer presents internal nondeterminism, which in the CSP model corresponds to the nondeterminism of the **if** and **do** constructs.

The notions of justice and fairness relate to any underlying scheduling mechanism (unknown and unknowable at this level), which enables the "processors" in the system. This mechanism is, by definition, erratic. However, if it is fully unpredictable, proofs are impossible. Therefore some limitations on its impredictability are introduced. The *justice* criterion says that if a process executes once, it may execute as many times as needed in the future. The criterion of *fairness* says that within a guarded command set a command with a true guard sooner or later will execute.

Originally, Hoare required only the justice criterion that the whole system be able to proceed if at least one process is in a state to perform a computational step. No fairness requirement was put forth. Several other authors later added a few requirements of both justice and fairness that are considered necessary in practice. The specific justice and fairness requirements, however, depend on what we expect the overall behavior of the system to be.

Examples of Justice and Fairness for CSP

To give an idea of the kind of problems appearing in a concurrent system because of the erratic nature of the scheduling mechanism, let us consider a few examples (from Manna and Pnueli, 1982). If in the language of CSP we want to have finite computations—i.e., we want the whole system as represented by the CSP program to terminate in some desired global state—properties like the following ones are necessary:

- *Process justice*: This property of the scheduling mechanism ensures that a process that may proceed (i.e., one waiting for a message that has arrived) is eventually proceeding. Even if this property is assumed, however, the following CSP program (b is a Boolean variable) may run forever:

```
P:[P₁||P₂]

P₁: b := true; do b → skip □ b; P₂ ? b → skip od
P₂: P₁! false
```

By the property of process justice P_2 must execute sometimes, thus sending the value "false" into b. But because P_1 may choose the first guarded command list forever, a message b = false is never received by P_2.

- *Process fairness*: The enforcement of this property for the scheduling mechanism would not permit the program above to cycle forever. In fact, process fairness prescribes that if a communication guard is activated by receiving a message, sooner or later the corresponding guarded command is executed. In spite of this property, the following program cannot be guaranteed to terminate (b and c, are Boolean):

```
P: [P₁||P₂]

P₁: b := true do b; P₂? b → skip od
P₂: c := true do c; P₁ ! false → c := false
         □ c; P₁ ! true → skip od
```

The reason we cannot ensure termination is that P_2 may start and finish before P_1 initiates its first assignment. In that case the value of b = false sent by P_2 isn't received, b is set true, and P_1 will go ahead forever.

- *Channel fairness*: This property requires that each individual communication be treated fairly. That is, an initiated communication must be completed. Under this assumption the program above that does not terminate under process fairness will terminate, because P_2 cannot terminate if the communication initiated by P_2 is not completed by the reception of its value by P_1. Therefore this property ensures that b = false is an eventual state for P_1. However, the following program still may not terminate unless process fairness is also ensured (b and c are Boolean):

```
P:[P₁||P₂]

P₁: b := true; do b → P₂ ? b od
P₂: c := true; do c → P₁ ! true
           □ c → P₁ ! false; c := false do
```

The correctness of CSP programs can be shown by constructing proof diagrams, which are surprisingly simple to inspect. Examples are shown in Manna and Pnueli (1982) and in Owicky and Lamport (1982). However, you should not jump to the conclusion that designing correct concurrent programs is an easy task. We want only point out here that methods exist that could be applied by trained specialists.

Network Complexity

Global system properties as represented by a process network need not be complex

Note that if a large system has to be represented by a CSP program, this program need not be a complex program. Most of the internal processing is irrelevant for the type of properties we wish to design and verify at this level. This processing must be presented by the passing of some time. The command skip may be the representation of a very complex processing that is irrelevant at this level. What must appear in the CSP program is the communication network. Consequently, the trivial programs we have discussed above to illustrate fairness and justice are not as trivial as they may appear at a first glance.

The idea of nondeterminism is a sufficient tool to represent the differences in execution behavior of even complex systems. The proofs—i.e., the intellectual process used for design—may be fairly manageable even if the underlying software system is a very large and complex one. The CSP program (and its proof) shows only the complexity of the level of coordination of the various concurrent processes. However, this statement is true only if the partition of the design into the three levels of description defined earlier is done scrupulously and is religiously observed during the whole development process. It is all too easy to make a concurrency proof invalid by dealing with concurrency issues directly at implementation time.

ANOTHER MODEL OF CONCURRENT SYSTEMS

Parallel processing as a nondeterministic sequential program

In this chapter we have pointed out a few peculiar characteristics of concurrent processes. We have also indicated that there is encouraging research work published in the literature describing techniques that permit the verification as well as the comprehension of concurrently executing processes in a network. Now we ask whether a technique of deriving a concurrent program from its specifications is available. A technique of this type would be the perfect analog of Dijkstra's calculus.

The answer is positive, and we will briefly illustrate such a method, which uses a different model for concurrency. In this model a set of concurrent processes is represented by a single nondeterministic (possibly nonterminating) sequential program, similar to the ones we have written in this book, using the language of guarded commands. Our purpose in introducing this different model is (among other things) to emphasize the intimate relationship between concurrency and nondeterminism.

Let us suppose now that a set of sequential processes $P_1, \ldots, P_n$ can operate concurrently to obtain some predefined global goal J. Assume also that once the goal J is obtained, this set of processes is in a state that permits the realization of this goal again (of course, with different input values). If execution times are not considered, a nondeterministic program that can cyclically perform the computations it was designed for is an equivalent representation of the behavior of this set of sequential processes.

The above point is best illustrated by a few examples. Let us consider two processes:

$$P_1: (x := x + 1) \quad P_2: (y := y + 1)$$

Let us assume that both x and y are initialized with the null value. These two processes are supposed to continually add one to x and y, respectively. Since their operations do not interfere with each other (P_1 does not operate on y and P_2 does not operate on x), they can operate in complete concurrency without any form of communication between them. The nondeterministic program

cycle true → x := x + 1 □ true → y := y + 1 **end**

is equivalent to the parallel execution of P_1 and P_2, because both produce two identical infinite sequences of integers for the states of x and y. In fact, we may say that the program cyclically (at each activation) realizes the global goal

$$J: x \geqslant o \ \textbf{and} \ y \geqslant o$$

Guarded commands for representing infinite programs

The above nondeterministic program is written in a syntax similar to Dijkstra's guarded commands, but with slightly different semantics. In this syntax a cyclic nondeterministic program is represented as

cycle $B_1 \rightarrow S_1$ □ . . . □ $B_n \rightarrow S_n$ **end**

In the operation of a nondeterministic program like the one represented above, all the guards B_i ($i = 1, \ldots, n$) are tested. Among the guards that return the value "true," one (say B_j) is chosen (no particular rule for this choice is to be considered), and the computation commanded by the statements S_j (followed by B_j) is performed. This operation is then repeated cyclically forever. If at any time all the B_i's are false, the program stops.

Note that we are limiting our study of this model of concurrency to infinitely executing programs. In the discussion of the justice and fairness properties presented above, we used examples of terminating computations. Both are potentially useful situations that may occur in practice. The study of infinite computation, however, gives us a clearer view of those undesired global phenomena such as deadlock and starvation, as we will see in the rest of this chapter.

Let us now consider again the parallel execution of the two processes

$$P_1: (x := x + 1) \quad P_2: (y := y + 1)$$

For each execution of either P_1 or P_2 the relation $x \geqslant \emptyset$ **and** $y \geqslant \emptyset$ is satisfied. The same is true for each execution of the nondeterministic sequential program

```
cycle true → x := x + 1 □ true → y := y + 1 end
```

Let us now consider two processes

Q_1: (x := x + 1)
Q_2: (y := y + 1; z := z + x)

Both Q_1 and Q_2 share the variable x; therefore they should be synchronized in their access to x. A nondeterministic program representing the operations of Q_1 and Q_2 including the necessary synchronization, is (C is initialized as zero) as follows:

```
cycle C = O → x := x + 1
    □C = O → y := y + 1; C := 1
      C = 1 → z := z + x; C := O
end
```

Note that the second process Q_2 needed to be split into two guarded command lists. At each cycle completion the nondeterministic program (assuming x = y = C = 0 at initialization) will reach a state satisfying

$$x \geqslant 0 \textbf{ and } y \geqslant 0 \textbf{ and } z \geqslant 0$$

which can be considered also as the global goal cyclically reached by the concurrent execution of Q_1 and Q_2.

COMPUTATION TREE

Global properties of parallel computations defined in terms of a computation tree

Assuming that a concurrent system is represented by a nondeterministic program, we can precisely define its behavior by considering the tree of all its possible computational states after initialization. This tree is constructed as follows (Flon and Suzuki, 1978):

1. Each node represents a system state relative to the completion of a cycle. The root represents the state outcome of some appropriate initialization.
2. Edges outgoing from a node N represent all the transformations that can be performed from the state represented by N.
3. In this (possibly infinite) tree nodes may exist that have no outgoing edges. These nodes represent a termination of the nondeterministic cyclic program and therefore of the concurrent system. Since we are describing infinitely repeated computation, termination here is a nondesirable state. It may, in fact, represent internally nonterminating computations (loop nodes) or nodes for which no further progress

can be obtained because of global reasons (hung nodes) such as deadlock.

4. The paths in the computation tree are called *system histories*. The system histories are the infinite sequences of states over which we have to write specifications for the concurrent system.

The computation tree for the program

cycle true → x := x + 1 □ true → y := y + 1 **end**

is shown in Figure 19. Note that the global goal (an admittedly noninteresting one) for this program is actually a relation that is verified for all states of all histories in the computation tree. Thus it appears that we can define a predicate invariant over the computation tree that defines global phenomena of the concurrent systems when represented as nondeterministic programs.

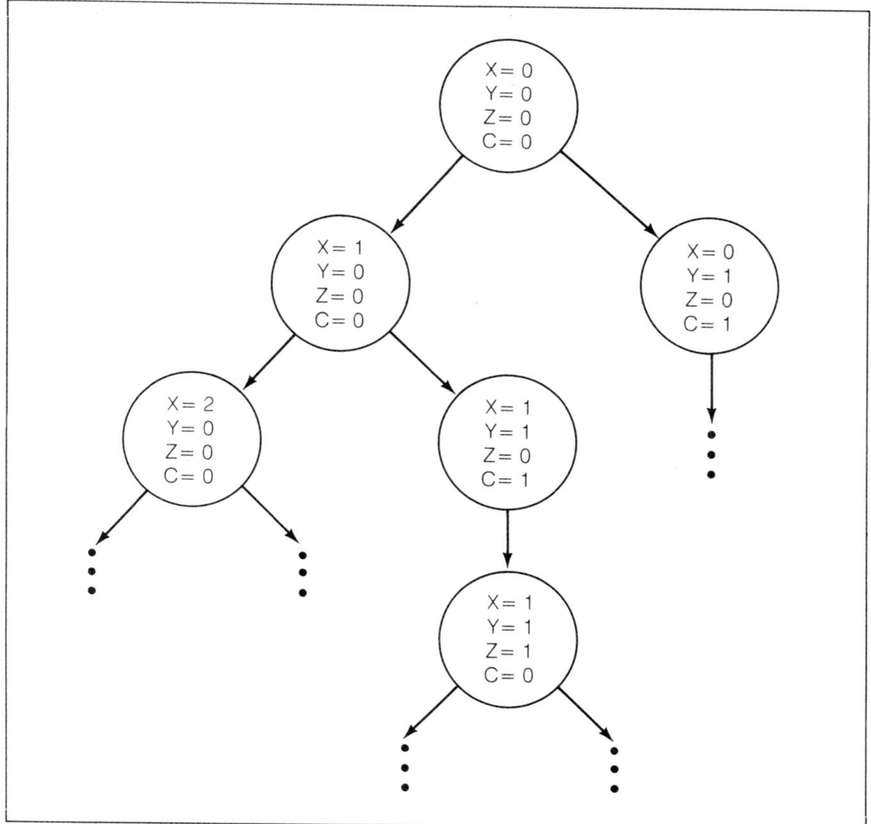

FIGURE 19 COMPUTATION TREE OF A SIMPLE PROGRAM

In these terms we will now discuss the definition of several global phenomena such as deadlock and starvation. Let S_i indicate the *i*th command list in the nondeterministic program that corresponds to a transition from one state to another (we will use the word *transmissions* to indicate the effect of S_i). Note that S_i *does not* necessarily correspond to a process of the concurrent system but only to a part of one. The global phenomena of this system are as follows:

1. *Invariance*: A predicate R defining some set of system states is invariant if and only if it is true at all nodes (except loop nodes) of the tree.
2. *Blocking* (or system deadlock): A system is blocking-free if its computation tree does not contain loop and hung nodes.
3. *Individual deadlock*: A system is deadlock-free for the execution of S_i if and only if from every node of the tree there is at least one path that leads to a node from which the execution of S_i is possible.
4. *Individual starvation*: A system is starvation-free for the execution of S_i if and only if for all nodes in the tree all outgoing paths lead to a node for which the execution of S_i is possible.
5. *Potentiality*: A system has the potential to reach a global state defined by a predicate P if and only if there is at least one path from the root to a node for which P is true.
6. *Inevitability*: A system will inevitably reach a global state defined by a predicate P if and only if all paths from the root lead to a node for which P is true.
7. *Global starvation*: A system is free from global starvation if and only if it is starvation-free for all transitions S_i ($i = 1, \ldots, n$).

To illustrate these phenomena with an example, let us consider the system represented by the program (with the initialization $x = y = z = C = 0$) whose computation tree is represented in Figure 19. The predicate

$$x \geqslant 0 \textbf{ and } y \geqslant 0$$

is kept invariant in this system; i.e., it is verified by all system histories. Also, the system has the potential to reach a global state for which

$$z = z + x$$

(some system histories contain states that verify it), but it will not inevitably reach a state for which this predicate is verified. In fact, the transition $x := x + 1$ may execute forever, leaving $y = z = 0$.

This program is clearly deadlock-free for all transitions, because for every node in the tree there is a path to a node for which all transitions are possible. However, it is not starvation-free for transitions

$$y := y + 1 \qquad z := z + x$$

because for the node $x = 1, y = 0, z = 0, C = 0$ it is possible to move along the path for which $x = 2, x = 3$, etc., while keeping $y = z = C = 0$, therefore impeding these transitions.

A design process for concurrent systems that guarantees the avoidance of undesired global phenomena is not that obvious. In fact, the very simple program examined above presents the possibility of starvation, which would probably be an undesired situation when we define what the program is supposed to do. We will now show that it is possible (at least in principle) to design methodically systems that are free of undesired properties while preserving desired behavior. To achieve this goal, we will use the concept of weakest precondition, which we introduced in Chapter 6.

The representation of a concurrent system by a nondeterministic cyclic program does not permit the definition of a weakest precondition for the whole program because it does not terminate. However, all the sequential command lists S_i must be terminating programs; otherwise, the computation tree would correspondingly present a loop node. Let us assume that we know how to calculate (or to postulate) the weakest precondition of any of these sequential command lists. This assumption is reasonable since in most cases that interest us here the evaluation of $wp(S_i, R)$ is not only possible but rather simple. These lists often represent only the passage of time for many complex computations that have no impact on the global properties of the network.

The global goal of a parallel-processing system is represented as an invariant for the nondeterministic program

After these preliminaries we are now ready to describe the design problem. A goal of an infinite (nonterminating) program that represents a concurrent system can be stated as a predicate to be maintained invariant. Examples are operating systems that are to supply an invariant environment and a set of services time after time to various users. Therefore as the first design step, we consider the derivation of the nondeterministic program from a given predicate that describes the legitimate system's states and that has to be kept invariant at every cycle of the program. More precisely, we are attempting to determine the conditions B_i that permit the needed synchronization (the sequencing of the execution of the guarded lists) to maintain this predicate invariant.

Let us call this given predicate P. From the structure of the nondeterministic program it follows that for some i

$$P \Rightarrow (B_i \Rightarrow wp(S_i, P))$$

This expression says that the condition described by the predicate P must be such that if P is true, then at least for one of the guards B_i, the truth of B_i implies that the program is in a state respecting the weakest precondition for S_i to terminate in a state satisfying P. Clearly, in this way and at each cycle we ensure the verification of P.

As a simple example, let us consider P as being the description of the state of an operating system in which a user's job can be executed. Guard B_i may then be interpreted as all the coded conditions for the execution of the user's job. State S_i is the execution of the user's job together with the necessary operating system services. At job termination a state satisfying P is then reassumed, permitting the execution of another job. If the job is not initiated in a state satisfying the condition B_i, there is no guarantee that S_i terminates correctly or at all (expressed by the fact that exactly the weakest precondition of S_i—the user's job execution—is implied by B_i). Therefore the operating system must not be permitted to do that.

The above expression, however, may define guards B_i that are unduly restrictive. To be sure that we are not imposing excessive restrictions on our design by the use of the relation

$$P \Rightarrow (B_i \Rightarrow wp(S_i, P))$$

we have to show that it is actually the weakest synchronizing condition for the guards B_i to maintain the predicate P invariant. The demonstration goes as follows:

By definition, P is an invariant of the program

$$S\text{: } \mathbf{cycle}\ B_i \rightarrow S_i \ \square \cdots \square \ B_i \rightarrow S_i \ \square \cdots B_n \rightarrow S_n\ \mathbf{end}$$

Let us assume that P is also invariant for another program identical to the one above but with different synchronizing conditions B'_i:

$$S'\text{: } \mathbf{cycle}\ B'_1 \rightarrow S_1 \ \square \cdots \square \ B'_i \rightarrow S_i \ \square \cdots \square \ B'_n \rightarrow S_n\ \mathbf{end}$$

Because the relation

$$P \Rightarrow (B_i \Rightarrow wp(S_i, P))$$

must apply to this program also, we have

$$P \Rightarrow (B'_i \Rightarrow wp(S_i, P))$$

for some i = 1, . . . , n. Therefore

$$P\ \mathbf{and}\ B'_i \Rightarrow P\ \mathbf{and}\ wp(S_i, P)$$

which gives

$$P\ \mathbf{and}\ B'_i \Rightarrow P\ \mathbf{and}\ B_i$$

Synchronizing condition in equation form

This latter relation shows that B'_i is stronger than (or the same as) B_i. Thus we know that a synchronizing condition satisfying

$$P \Rightarrow (B_i \Rightarrow wp(S_i, P))$$

is not unduly restrictive. This condition can also be written as

$$P \Rightarrow (B_i = wp(S_i, P))$$

which is equivalent to

$$P\ \mathbf{and}\ B_i = P\ \mathbf{and}\ wp(S_i, P)$$

This last expression defines the synchronizing conditions B_i in equation form. Since P and S_i—and therefore $wp(S_i, P)$—are known, its solution for B_i does not require any particular technique. A construction for B_i determination—i.e., for the design of a program that preserves the invariance of P—is given in Van Lamsweerde and Sintzoff (1979), together with some examples of its application.

Synchronizing condition representing a global goal can be strengthened to design blocking-free systems

Because we wish to give only a general introduction to the technique, we now show a case more significant from the point of view of the technique, the case of blocking.

Let us suppose that a program S has been shown to preserve the invariance of a predicate P. By the definition of blocking, we know that the program at every cycle should be in a state for which at least one B_i must be true and that the execution of S_i terminates. Let us call G a predicate stronger than (or at least equal to) P that satisfies

$$G \Rightarrow P \textbf{ and } \mathop{\textbf{OR}}_{i=1}^{n} (B_i \textbf{ and } wp(S_i, G))$$

This expression can be read as "any state satisfying G satisfies the invariant P, and at least one B_i is true together with the weakest precondition of the corresponding S_i for its termination in a state satisfying G." Note that the new predicate G is a strengthening of the original invariant P.

This expression can be rewritten in equation form as

$$G = G \textbf{ and } P \textbf{ and } \mathop{\textbf{OR}}_{i=1}^{n} (B_i \textbf{ and } wp(S_i, G))$$

Equations of this kind, which may be interpreted as recursive definitions of predicates, are called *fixed-point equations.* Their solution (when it exists) is found by an iterative procedure that appears to be amenable to mechanization. Van Lamsweerde and Sintzoff (1979) present equations defining the conditions for absence of deadlock, inevitability, and individual and global starvation. Their presentation, however, is beyond the scope of this book.

We now show briefly how the solution of the fixed-point equation above can be obtained. The right-hand side of the equation enjoys the property of continuity in the lattice of predicates ordered by the operation of implication. In less mathematical terms that statement means that there exists a chain of successive approximations starting from the weakest possible predicate T that converges to the desired solution. By indicating the predicates in this chain with G^k (for k = 0, 1, . . . , m), we have

$$G^0 = T$$

$$\vdots$$

$$G^m = G^{m-1} \textbf{ and } P \textbf{ and } \mathop{\textbf{OR}}_{i=1}^{n} (B_i \textbf{ and } wp(S_i, G^{m-1}))$$

The solution of the fixed-point equation corresponds to the G^k such that

$$G^k = G^{k-1}$$

There are two cases for the sequence defined above. In the first case the sequence of approximations is finite (and usually not too long). In this case the solution process can conceivably be mechanized. In the second case the sequence is infinite, and its limit is calculated by using mathematical induction. In principle, even this case can be mechanized, although it does not appear to be as straightforward as the first case.

The fixed-point equation written above defines a new (possibly stronger than P) invariant G, which must be maintained by the blocking-free program. If this equation is used to verify the absence of blocking, it is sufficient to execute a few iterations to find that G is identical to P to ensure freedom from blocking. However, if G is different from P, the program has to be redesigned. Fortunately, the equation can be easily transformed into a construction that directly supplies the strengthened guards B'_1 such that the resulting program is blocking-free. Similar constructions exist for the design of programs free of other undesirable global properties (see Van Lamsweerde and Sintzoff, 1979).

The above presentation discusses a method of deduction of a concurrent system design from its specifications, in principle equivalent in power to Dijkstra's calculus for sequential programs. Also the specifications are written in the language of the predicate calculus. No temporal operators are needed. However, the method implies the existence of shared data for the communications between processes. It is not clear how easily this method may be extended to a network of message-exchanging processes.

CONCLUDING REMARKS ABOUT CONCURRENCY

Concurrency will be used more and more frequently in the future in large software systems. However, it is unlikely that it will have any special impact on the majority of software specialists in the near future. The reason is that system manufacturers will supply the software needed to support the concurrent running of application systems. In other words, most of the software specialists involved in the creation of applications need not be aware of the features of concurrent systems. For this reason, at least in the near future, the problems treated in this chapter will be the concern of a relatively limited number of specialists.

Design for concurrency is a difficult problem

Correctness of design for concurrency is not easy to establish. Testing is even less helpful here than in sequential software because of the infinite possibilities of concurrent systems. Therefore a specialist in concurrent systems must be aware of the various correctness models studied by researchers. Unsupported intuition can be very deceiving, as the daily experience of developers of concurrent systems indicates.

On the other hand, we have seen that the necessary formalism and the complexity of the reasoning are more esoteric than that needed for sequential software and, therefore, are less accessible to software designers. However, the need for rigor and discipline is much more pressing in this area than in the more traditional developments. It is a task for the research community and the educational system to find ways to make the discipline of the design of concurrent systems more accessible to practitioners.

In this chapter we have shown two different approaches to the problem of correct design of concurrent systems. These are but two among several approaches. This multitude of approaches shows the considerable attention paid to this problem by the research community. It is not clear, however, that there is any conscious effort to transform these research approaches into a viable engineering discipline.

Concurrency and performance

Another issue has considerable impact on concurrent system design. One strong motivation for the use of concurrency is to obtain higher system performance. Thus a design method for correctness only, regardless of its usefulness, would not appeal to a designer as much as a method to predict concurrent system performance. An approach that integrates both correct and efficient design would be more appealing to the practitioner than the approaches we have just presented. Such an approach has not yet been established.

The interconnection between performance and correctness in concurrent systems is made manifest if we consider the effect on performance caused by the avoidance of some undesirable global phenomenon such as blocking. Usually, the avoidance of these phenomena imposes a process waiting time beyond the amount strictly needed for the accomplishment of the desired goal. This fact was hinted at by the construction we showed in the preceding section regarding the condition to avoid blocking. That construction creates additional restrictions on the synchronizing guards beyond the one needed to maintain a certain predicate invariant, i.e., to obtain the desired goal. These restrictions reduce the potential for concurrent execution, thus penalizing performance. So the designer may be faced with conflicting decisions: making the system blocking free and hence less efficient, or accepting the risk of blocking and, at its occurrence, using a recovery procedure. In this way the system may give better performance. However, the presence of a recovery mechanism affects performance also. The design decision about correctness thus depends on performance considerations.

HIGHLIGHTS

The need to design systems for concurrent operation is a consequence of both the application requirements and the desire to improve performance. There are two ways to organize systems made up of a set of sequential processes that may execute concurrently. One method allows the sharing of some global data, and the second method allows the exchange of messages. Concurrent systems present peculiar global phenomena, such as deadlock and starvation, that must be considered in the design phase.

The design of concurrent systems can be split into three levels: One contains all concurrency features, one deals with the individual process design, and one considers the implementation. A survey of a few techniques for concurrent system design was presented in this chapter. These techniques pointed out the intrinsic nondeterminism of concurrent systems. This feature, in turn, imposes the criteria of justice and fairness on the scheduler in order that the possibility of no progress for some process be avoided.

Two main categories of specification techniques were described. One type is based on temporal logic; it was illustrated by using the language of CSP for modeling the concurrent system. The second type transforms the concurrent system in a cyclic nondeterministic program represented in the language of guarded commands.

REFERENCES

Flon, L., and Suzuki, N. 1978. Consistent and complete proof rules for the total correctness of parallel programs. In *Proceedings of the 19th Symposium on the Foundation of Computer Science,* pp. 181–192.

Hoare, C. A. R. 1974. Monitors: An operating system structuring concept. *Communications of ACM* 17 (no. 10):549–557.

———. 1978. Communicating sequential processes. *Communications of ACM* 21 (no. 8):666–677.

———. 1981. A calculus of total correctness for communicating processes. *Science of Computer Programming* 1 (no. 1/2).

Manna, Z., and Pnueli, A. 1982. How to cook a temporal proof system for your pet language. Stanford University Report STAN–CS–82–954, Stanford, Calif.

Owicky, S., and Lamport, L. 1982. Proving liveness properties of concurrent programs. *ACM–TOPLAS* 4 (no. 3):455–495.

Pnueli, A. 1979. The temporal semantics of concurrent programs. *Lecture Notes in Computer Science* 70:1–20.

Van Lamsweerde, A., and Sintzoff, M. 1979. Formal derivation of strongly correct concurrent programs. *Acta Informatica* 12:1–31.

CHAPTER EIGHTEEN

Conclusion

NEED FOR A DESIGN PROCESS

G. Spencer-Brown said that we do not understand the beginning of anything until we have seen the end. We are now at the end of this book, but we are not at the end of the search for effective development methods for large software systems. Can we evaluate, then, what has been accomplished in this field?

Implementation-driven development is inefficient

To review, we remarked in the initial chapters of this book that large software systems are developed by a process centered around implementation methods and disciplines. Verification of design ideas is currently satisfied almost exclusively by actual testing of the product. These tests are not driven by any rationally determined procedure but only by the developer's experience and intuition. This process requires a large amount of the development effort to be spent in late phases of the process such as integration and system tests. The resulting product generally shows an unsatisfactory level of reliability, and the productivity of the process is low.

A design process must be formal to be effective

To establish a design-centered development process, we need a method that verifies design ideas at a much earlier stage. The system then must be represented in some precise form at design time so that design decisions can be discussed and evaluated on the basis of some mathematical theory. In this way the time-honored approach of other engineering development efforts could be introduced into software development. Better control of the process and of the quality of the product should be the result of this new approach.

In this concluding chapter we examine what we presented in earlier chapters to evaluate what has been accomplished. Also, all the difficulties and shortcomings are analyzed in the perspective of the preceding discussions.

WHAT HAS BEEN ACCOMPLISHED

Computer scientists have been able to attack the problem of designing programs and systems within the framework of a discipline analogous to the discipline used in other sciences. That is, we are able to talk about software entities as abstractions that can be studied and fully understood within the limits of the validity of those abstractions. This procedure allows us to give to the design phase of software systems the same role formal design definition has in all engineering development.

Another aspect of the research on software development is more akin to social sciences than to physical sciences. The result of the Belady-Lehman work about the exclusive dependence of the system development process on the architecture of the system has considerable importance for the economics of the software industry. The value of a particular system architecture is not to be seen only in terms of product advantages. It also can be seen in terms of the ability of the development process to produce economically the indispensable additions and enhancements that in most cases make the product successful.

Additional accomplishments of the computer science community are the results of the mathematical research about software, which help us to interpret the causes of observed features of software systems. The insight we gain by inventing realistic abstractions for software elements is instrumental in suggesting improved architectural arrangements as well as supporting design disciplines.

In this book we have described some of the concepts and methods that are part of these research accomplishments. We have also discussed techniques that are consequences of these concepts. For instance, Dijkstra's calculus permits us to design correct algorithms in a way that is not tedious for programmers. The concept of data abstraction allows us to extend calculus results in order to create programs of much larger size. Even though the research community is still working on some of the problems presented by the concept of abstract data types, an effective engineering discipline is emerging from the application of this concept.

Various formalisms can be created on the basis of abstract data to support an engineering discipline. Ultimately, the success of the practical application depends on the effectiveness of the chosen formalism. The formalism presented in this book owes its presence here, in part, to my bias, since I contributed to its creation. But in part it was chosen because of the existence of experimental applications that could be examined in detail.

Another important accomplishment is that the use of formalism in the design phase shows us how many logic difficulties are hidden by the current habit of informal design discussions. A formal approach makes these difficulties visible, and thus controllable, instead of allowing them to manifest themselves at unpredictable times and in surprising ways.

Overall, then, we have obtained a considerable improvement in both the understanding of the development process and the creation of methods for the design of the product. However, many software systems are still developed in an implementation-centered fashion. Thus the accomplishments we've outlined here either are not yet accepted by the development community or are insufficient to produce a serious impact on practical developments.

WHAT HAS NOT BEEN ACCOMPLISHED

In several areas the accomplishments of the research communities are short of being satisfactory. Let us examine some of these areas.

The first, and most important, area is *testing*. There is a great deal of literature about testing. Almost invariably, these works refer to the problem of test case selection for individual program testing. And they usually show that the difficulty of the selection of test cases is much greater than the difficulty of showing the correctness of the program through textual examination.

For some reason we are more easily convinced of the correctness of a program by tests (which we rationally know are unreliable) than by logical arguments (which we know, within the limits of the assumptions, are fully reliable). Logical arguments may end up in a tedious manipulation of symbols that is, by nature, error-prone. Unfortunately, the search for test cases is also a process of symbol manipulation, and it is as tedious and error-prone as the process of formal proof of a program and usually has limited applicability to practical cases. No known method of test case selection supplies a set of test cases that ensures correctness of a program.

So the difficult problem of test case selection has yet to be solved. The traditional approach in science, whenever a problem is too hard to solve by studying its intrinsic causes, is to use statistical methods. The random-sampling approach suggested by Duran and Wiorkowsky (1980), discussed in Chapters 1 and 8, and the scheme for testing developed by a data abstraction hierarchy, presented in Chapter 16, are but two proposals along these lines. And they may have considerable value in practice when they are associated with some rational form of design. However, a procedure for test case selection that at least increases the probability of correctness of the tested program would be very useful in practice. Also, it would be valuable to show that we cannot do any better in testing if this is the case.

Another area lacking adequate research results is the design for correctness in the presence of *location variables*. We indicated in Chapter 16 the potential for mistakes introduced by this feature of modern computers and programming languages. Even though the design formalism we have presented in this book limits and controls the use of location variables, it is impossible (and undesirable) to avoid them entirely. In fact, the use of the array data structure entails the use of location variables (the indices).

Some recent research on correctness of programs using these features does exist (Manna and Waldinger, 1981). However, the pervasiveness of the problems caused by the use of location variables is such that perhaps completely different computer architectures should be considered.

NEED FOR A NEW PARADIGM IN SOFTWARE DEVELOPMENT

We have discussed the high level of difficulty in introducing the design methods of formalism to current developers. We have also discussed the existence of system cultures that make it difficult to change the architecture of an existing software system. These factors indicate the existence of a well-established set of beliefs—a paradigm—that is a consequence of the developer's education. So the currently accepted paradigm among software developers will not be replaced by a new one centered around design methods unless an appropriate change is introduced in education. This opinion is supported by the emphasis on education of software developers and managers at IBM–FSD, as described by Mills et al. (1980).

Education emphasizes computer use instead of design of systems

The current emphasis in computer science education is on the use of a computer. The student learns how to program, how to use an operating system, how to debug a program, and even in some cases how to read core dumps. With few exceptions academic institutions educate students to use the computer as the sole tool for verifying design ideas. This situation is analogous to an emphasis in aeronautical engineering schools on teaching students how to fly an airplane instead of how to design it. But education in engineering is directed toward comprehension of principles for the design of the product, not the training for its use. And so it should be in computer science.

Perhaps the reason for the current emphasis on computer use is that programming (and by extension system design) appears to be such a simple activity. The only difficulty seems to be in mastering the use of a programming language. But we should be aware by now, after so many years of negative experiences and a declared state of crisis in the software industry, that programming is not that easy.

As long as the educational emphasis is on computer use, though, it is unlikely that a new paradigm based on a rational discipline for the development of software will be accepted by the software community. However, the economics of the process and the need for much more reliable products are already pressing for a change. Thus a rational discipline in software development may be on the horizon.

REFERENCES

Duran, J. W., and Wiorkowsky, J. J. 1980. Quantifying software validity by sampling. *IEEE Transactions on Reliability* R–29:142–144.

Manna, Z., and Waldinger, R. 1981. Problematic features of programming languages: A situational calculus approach. *Acta Informatica* 16:371–426.

Mills, H. D.; O'Neill, D.; Linger, R. C.; and Dyer, M. 1980. The management of software engineering. Parts I–IV: Principles of software engineering. *IBM Systems Journal* 19 (no. 4):415–420, 421–431, 432–450, 451–476.

Glossary

Abstraction: The description of a complex object or process by presenting only the features or properties necessary to illustrate specific aspects of particular concern.

Abstract data type: A data type whose data values are not defined by describing the representation but by specifying the available operations.

Abstract machine: An ideal machine designed in such a way that relatively short programs for the machine realize very complex functions.

Algorithm: The specification of a problem solution in a step-by-step manner. When this specification is expressed in a language usable by an automatic computer, the algorithm may be called a program.

Array: The association of zero or more elements of a certain type with an ordered sequence of integers called indices.

Availability: The percentage of the total time during which the system is working according to its specifications.

Axiom: A statement of a property that is accepted as an a priori truth in a logical system.

Command: A textual element in a program that corresponds to the invocation of a specific action in a real or abstract computing machine. A command can be regarded as an elementary step of an algorithm.

Computation The execution of a sequence of commands specified by a program.

Concurrent processing: The execution of a computational task in which some of the steps necessary to obtain the computation's goal are performed concurrently.

Construct: A textual framework in a programming language that permits the grouping of commands and data declarations to form, respectively, a control or a data structure.

Data expansion: A software design method that adds detail to abstract data types.

Data object: A named repository for values of a certain type.

Data representation: A software design method that defines the representation of a data type in terms of another one(s).

Data type: One or more repositories of values together with the operations that are allowed to transform these values.

Flow of control: The sequence of steps of an algorithm as specified by programming language constructs.

Formalism: A precise form of expressing appropriate real-world phenomena. In principle, the sentences of a formalism can be manipulated by an automatic computer to create new meaningful sentences or to check consistency with other sentences.

Function: In the context of a data type definition a function is one of the allowable operations that can transform the values of the data type.

Implementation: The realization of design ideas in a product. In the case of a software system it implies the creation of all the code, data, and documentation necessary for its use.

Instruction: A command for a real or an abstract machine.

Integration: The system development phase during which the various parts, which were developed separately, are put together to realize the required functionalities.

Invariant: A logic relation among program or system data objects whose truth value is not modified by the execution of a certain sequence of commands; e.g., the truth value of the loop invariant is not modified by the execution of the loop body.

Iteration: The repetition of a step, or a sequence of steps, in a computation with the purpose of obtaining a computation's goal.

Location variables: Data containing as a value a name (or an address) for another datum. Familiar examples are pointers, array indices, machine addresses, and base registers.

Logic: A discipline to bring precision to the analysis of ideas.

Loop body: The sequence of commands in a program that may be the subject of iteration.

Machine: A repository of data objects together with the ability to interpret control flow specifications (programs) and transform the stored data values by executing the data type functions specified in the programs.

Maintenance: The activity (in a software system) of modifying the software for the purpose of correcting errors and expanding its functionalities.

Message: A value of some data type that can be exchanged between concurrently executing processes. A message appears at an inlet of the receiving process after it has been put in an outlet of the sending process.

Module: Programs realizing a particular system function. In the commonly accepted interpretation of this term, a module is neither a data type nor a data type function.

Monitor: A set of data objects and the programs that can operate on them, which can be used by only one of the potential concurrent processes at the same time.

Nondeterminism: A property of a mechanism to produce, for the same cause, a set of different possible outcomes. These outcomes may be all equally acceptable.

Parameter: A piece of data made available to a procedure upon invocation, both for supplying the input and for receiving output of the invoked computation.

Predicate A function of the state space that can be evaluated only as true or false. Predicates are the subject of predicate calculus.

Process: Any entity in a concurrent execution containing all the necessary information to perform a fully sequential computation. A process execution may be delayed, but no more than one command within the process can be executed at the same time. A monitor (see definition) can be part of several processes.

Program: A specification or algorithm that is executable by a real or abstract computing machine.

Programming language: A formalism to specify the execution of computations on an appropriate machine.

Proof: The convincing demonstration that a thesis is consistent with axioms. This demonstration may use only acceptable rules of inferences. If the axioms, the thesis, and the rules of inference are expressible in a formal language, the proof in principle could be accomplished by computer. The validity of an automatic proof, however, would be restricted by its ability to be "convincing."

Quantifier: Operators that extend the evaluation of a predicate over a set of objects. There are two quantifiers: the universal **for all** and the existential **for some.**

Release: A new version of a software system that incorporates changes both for fixing known (noncritical) errors and for adding new capabilities to satisfy changed or extended requirements.

Reliability: The probability of a mechanism to perform according to its specifications.

Requirements: The user's view of the program or system behavior. Requirements are expressed in terms of the user's problem world.

Specifications: The description of what a program or a system is supposed to do. Specifications are expressed in terms of (real or abstract) machine entities.

State space: The set of all the possible combinations of values the data objects of a program or a system can assume.

System: A collection of data and programs that attempts to satisfy the user's requirements.

System culture: The set of beliefs and rules accepted, mostly in an uncritical manner, by the developers of a large system.

System state: A set of values for all the system data.

I N D E X